Context, Plurality, and Truth

Missional Church, Public Theology, World Christianity

Stephen Bevans, Paul S. Chung, Veli-Matti Kärkkäinen, and Craig L. Nessan, Series Editors

IN THE MIDST OF globalization there is crisis as well as opportunity. A model of God's mission is of special significance for ecclesiology and public theology when explored in diverse perspectives and frameworks in the postcolonial context of World Christianity. In the face of the new, complex global civilization characterized by the Second Axial Age, the theology of mission, missional ecclesiology, and public ethics endeavor to provide a larger framework for missiology. It does so in interaction with our social, multicultural, political, economic, and intercivilizational situation. These fields create ways to refurbish mission as constructive theology in critical and creative engagement with cultural anthropology, world religions, prophetic theology, postcolonial hermeneutics, and contextual theologies of World Christianity. Such endeavors play a critical role in generating theological, missional, social-ethical alternatives to the reality of Empire—a reality characterized by civilizational conflict, and by the complex system of a colonized lifeworld that is embedded within practices of greed, dominion, and ecological devastation. This series—Missional Church, Public Theology, World Christianity—invites scholars to promote alternative church practices for life-enhancing culture and for evangelization as telling the truth in the public sphere, especially in solidarity with those on the margins and in ecological stewardship for the lifeworld.

Context, Plurality, and Truth
Theology in World Christianities

Mika Vähäkangas

PICKWICK Publications · Eugene, Oregon

CONTEXT, PLURALITY, AND TRUTH
Theology in World Christianities

Missional Church, Public Theology, World Christianity 9

Copyright © 2020 Mika Vähäkangas. All rights reserved. Except for brief quotations in critical publications or reviews, no part of this book may be reproduced in any manner without prior written permission from the publisher. Write: Permissions, Wipf and Stock Publishers, 199 W. 8th Ave., Suite 3, Eugene, OR 97401.

Pickwick Publications
An Imprint of Wipf and Stock Publishers
199 W. 8th Ave., Suite 3
Eugene, OR 97401

www.wipfandstock.com

PAPERBACK ISBN: 978-1-5326-8264-3
HARDCOVER ISBN: 978-1-5326-8265-0
EBOOK ISBN: 978-1-5326-8266-7

Cataloguing-in-Publication data:

Names: Vähäkangas, Mika, author.

Title: Context, plurality, and truth : theology in world christianities / by Mika Vähäkangas.

Description: Eugene, OR : Pickwick Publications, 2020 | Missional Church, Public Theology, World Christianity 9 | Includes bibliographical references and index(es).

Identifiers: ISBN 978-1-5326-8264-3 (paperback) | ISBN 978-1-5326-8265-0 (hardcover) | ISBN 978-1-5326-8266-7 (ebook)

Subjects: LCSH: Theology—Methodology. | Globalization—Religious aspects—Christianity.

Classification: BR118 .V23 2020 (print) | BR118 .V23 (ebook)

Manufactured in the U.S.A.   FEBRUARY 4, 2020

An earlier shorter version of chapters 4 and 5 has previously been published as "Modelling Contextualization in Theology", *Swedish Missiological Themes* 98/3 (2010) 279–306.

To Theo Jørgensen (1935–2018)

Contents

Preface | ix

1 Introduction | 1

2 Globalizing World as the Context of Theology Today | 9
Christianity at the Roots of Today's Globalization | 9
Three Dimensions of Today's Globalization | 14
    Economic Globalization and Its Social and Ecological Consequences | 14
    Information Age | 20
    Cultural Globalization | 25
Consequences of Global Changes for Christianity and Christian Theology | 29

3 On the Need of Renewal of Theology in the Pluralistic World | 39
Theology as a Eurocentric Confessional Enterprise | 39
The Theologian's Bubble of Reality Holds No More | 44
Mission Studies and Contextual Theology as the Broadening of Horizons | 47
World Christianity as the Renewal of Mission Studies | 50
Theological Pluralism à la World Christianity | 54
Even Secular Societies Need Open-minded Theology | 58

4 On Contextuality in Theology | 64
Theology and Positionality | 64
Truth, Context, and Hermeneutics | 68
    The Truth and Truths: Contextual Theology between Modernism and Postmodernism | 69
    On the Nature and Role of Tradition in Today's Theology | 75
Ways of Constructing Contextual Theologies | 80
    Types of Western Missionary Approaches towards Non-Western Cultures | 82
    Classifying Contextual Theologies | 84

5 A Model of the Contextual Process | 90
   The Hermeneutical Circle | 91
   The Gospel and the Worldviews | 95
   The Dynamics of the Socio-Cultural Context | 104
   Theological Method | 110
   A Closer Look at the Hermeneutical Circle | 112
   Narrative and Reference to the Truth | 116

6 On the Inevitably Syncretistic Nature of Christian Theology | 119
   Religion Is Naturally Syncretistic | 119
   From Imperial Religion to Heretical Imperative | 121
   Christian Religious Authority Is More Splintered Than Ever | 127
   No Clear Boundaries for Christianity | 129
   Translatability Makes Christianity Global and Diffuse | 132
   The Pilgrim Church, Tradition, and Flexibility | 137
   Balancing between Normativity and Neutrality | 141
   Incarnation as the Doctrinal Basis for Christian Syncretism | 143
   Incarnation as the Basis of Contextuality and the Syncretistic Nature of
      Christianity | 146

7 Four Levels of Theology: Do Special Revelation
   and Pluralism Fit Together? | 159
   Theology Informed by Pluralism or Pluralistic Theology? | 162
   Four Levels of Theology | 169
   Four Levels of Theology and the Encountering of Pluralism | 178
   Facing the Critique against Essentialism | 181

8 Concluding Remarks | 185

Bibliography | 189
Index | 203

Preface

THIS BOOK IS A product of a long process, one of those projects that gets sidelined when everything else, supposedly more urgent, pushes onto the center stage. This also means that I have been involved in several communities during the process and there are very many people that I would ideally like to thank. I sincerely apologize for not including everyone who deserves it.

Lutheran Theological College Makumira, later Makumira University College of Tumaini University, has had an indelible impact on my theological thinking. Although all of this text was written after my time in Makumira, first as a student and then as a teacher, I feel a sense of indebtedness towards the Makumira community—teachers, students, supporting staff, families, and the workforce in homes. Another major background influence for this text is Prof. Charles Nyamiti from Catholic University of Eastern Africa. Those familiar with his texts will trace his influence even where there are no references, especially in relation to the Trinitarian doctrine. Alongside this book project, I have been in contact with the Kimbanguist Church, eventually studying their theology. The warmly welcoming Kimbanguist community has been a useful reminder of the great variation of faith and praxis based on the Bible. While this book does not deal with Kimbanguist theology, my Kimbanguist friends have been a constant reminder for me not to essentialize the portrait of Christianity excessively. Other projects alongside this book have all involved anthropologists and I am thankful for them for helping me to relativize the theological gaze on faith communities while strengthening my identity as a theologian. Here, I thank especially doc. Dr. Päivi Hasu, University of Jyväskylä and Prof. Karen Lauterbach, Centre for African Studies in Copenhagen.

The text of this book began to evolve after returning to Finland and encountering another theological world and life reality. I want to express my gratitude to my alma mater, University of Helsinki faculty of theology, especially department of systematic theology and now latest the Helsinki Collegium for Advanced Studies. For the last decade, my main point of reference, though, has been Lund University Centre for Theology and Religious Studies. This community has been inspiring and supportive, and I express my thanks for having been able to be part of it. Especially the research seminar community of Global Christianity and Interreligious Relations has been very important to me.

My stays in South Africa have been partly periods of concentrating on this text, and without them this book would still be half-finished. I want to thank the faculty of theology in Stellenbosch, especially Prof. Henry Mbaya, a good friend and colleague, and Desmond Tutu Centre of the University of the Western Cape. Additionally, I thank Durham University for welcoming me there to finalize the manuscript.

I have received constructive criticism for parts or the whole of the text from a couple of colleagues and am truly thankful for that: Docent Dr. Pauli Annala from University of Helsinki, Dr. Jonas Adelin Jørgensen from Copenhagen University, Dr. Elina Hankela from University of Johannesburg, Prof. Steve Bevans from Catholic Theological Union and Ms. Pauliina Vähäkangas from Yonsei University. All of them could contribute with views and ideas that complement my lacking competence, the last of those, my daughter, updating the old man with the wisdom of the following generation. Ms. Irinja Vähäkangas from University of Cape Town, another daughter, has contributed with language editing and sharp remarks on the contents, too. Prof. Auli Vähäkangas, University of Helsinki, has been a critical and supportive companion throughout the process, with whom I have been able to dialogue on the issues in this book. Ms. Eliisa Vähäkangas, my natural sciences-oriented daughter, has reminded me constantly about the vastness of what can and would need to be known and has thereby kept me a little humbler. I am thankful for all these colleagues and the four wonderful women of my life.

This book is dedicated to late Prof. Theo(dor) Jørgensen, a colleague and mentor from Copenhagen University. Although he never was my teacher, he left a lasting impression. I feel that every meeting with him was special. He had the gift of listening—and of arguing—with a great dose of humor and wit, never superficial, always intellectually and existentially challenging. He combined deep commitment with great intellectual and personal openness. Typical of him, when staying briefly at Makumira, he would join the upbeat youth choir—definitely as the most senior youth!

In Helsinki, 15th February 2019

1

Introduction

TODAY'S WORLD IS OFTEN considered to be more pluralistic than ever and this pluralism goes hand in hand with globalization. In the studies on World/Global Christianity as well as in intercultural theology it is commonplace to point out the post-Christendom context of theologizing. However, as Kwame Bediako points out in his doctoral dissertation, this situation is not new to Christian theology, but it is rather a matter of returning to the situation akin to that of the patristic times.[1]

Although it has often become commonplace to refer to western Christendom as a monolithic system, that view can be contested. Even at times of the greatest outward pressures towards uniformity in western Europe there existed a varied flora of folk religiosity in the form of Christian and pre-Christian practices and piety, as well as dissenting theological views. One also tends to overlook the linguistic and cultural diversity as well as the strong Jewish presence until the Holocaust/Shoah. Thus, religious and cultural plurality has been present, albeit glossed over in favor of the nationalistic and established churches' interests.

Today's situation differs from the past, mostly because cultural and religious plurality is usually recognized, often tolerated and sometimes even celebrated. The new development is thus not diversity but a developing sense of pluralism. What is different from the past is that due to technological advancement and the record-high levels of international migration, cultural changes, and exchanges have become quicker than ever. The difference is, thus, quantitative rather than qualitative. This intensification of diversity as well as rise of cultural and religious pluralism has invited reactions, as well. Especially the recent upsurge of populist nationalist politics that has in some countries entered in courtship with churches regarded national

---

1. Bediako, *Theology and Identity*.

has led to a renewed fabrication of myths on national monolithic cultural, religious, and linguistic unity.

Western hegemonic nationalistic cultures and establishment churches attached to them have undergone drastic changes. Cultural imperialism and colonialism belonged to the instruments of power, and now both of them are largely condemned as ethical failures. From being the yardsticks of civilization and true faith, the colonialists' cultures and religions have become suspects of cultural imperialism and less than philanthropic approaches.[2] Therefore, former colonial powers and churches attached to them tend to suffer from a colonial hangover.

In a hangover, there are two common ways of reaction. First, one rejects the lessons of the previous night, as well as one's present state, and continues drinking. This is the situation the western powers perpetuate by perhaps paying lip service to global equality but in practice continuing to impose their economic and political agendas—sometimes extending to crude military interventions. Among the churches, there are actors that are not willing to see anything fundamentally wrong with the western missionary movement of the colonial era and, thereby, continue as if nothing has changed. The task of making the other into one's image persists and the normative approaches of the past remain the rule for this strain of Christians and churches.

Another common reaction following a hangover is distancing—this will never happen again! One convinces themselves that a single act of willpower will galvanize a fundamental change and one will never end up in this pitiful state. Yet, the tendency to sin remains, and humans are masters in self-deception. The argument goes: if the former misguided missionary movement was mistaken in imposing its revivalist and anti-scientific conversion on the local populations, this can never happen again with the much more advanced and open-minded establishment churches. How could it, now that this open-minded faith is so much superior to the narrow-mindedness of the bygone eras? Of course, the new responsibility, the enlightened (wo)man's burden, is to convert these converts of the previous backward Christian paradigm into the present superior paradigm.

This new paradigm is no longer called conversion or faith but, rather, takes on new shibboleths like development, human rights, civil society etc.[3] In this, the enlightened Christians can happily join hands with secular actors (who fiercely reject colonialism and all the cultural imperialistic imposition attached to it) once again for the benefit of the misguided native. The

---

2. Césaire, *Discours sur le colonialisme*, 3–5.
3. Grosfoguel, "Decolonizing Post-Colonial Studies," 25, 28.

bad old colonial mission has renewed its skin in this move, and carries on its global feast under a number of new names, just as its bedfellow colonialism does. This neo-colonial paradigm is so much superior to the former that only a few are prepared to acknowledge that it is, in an Indian idiom, "same, same but different." In spite of the spiritual and economic decline in the former western establishment churches, they still have the financial assets and intellectual resources to exercise power over their southern counterparts. Therefore, *"plus ça change, rien ça change"*—"the more it changes, the more it remains the same." Surprisingly often, the old colonial paradigm reappears in theology (and development thinking) in a seemingly benign guise of progress and development.

In this study, the aim is to map out the terrain for theology in the pluralistic and globalized age. In this age, on one hand, especially the academia has the tendency of rejecting religion and, thereby, theology. On the other hand, if theology and religion are tolerated, they easily procure a place in the construction of historical national consciousness.[4] This book is, thus, a proposal for a prolegomenon for theology that attempts to learn from colonial lessons by not denying the problematic nature of the western Christian claim of spiritual, cultural and intellectual supremacy. In other words, the aim is to answer to the following question: How to make theological sense of religious plurality both within and outside Christianity? The starting point is attempting to find a solution that is not exclusive in the sense of one claiming to represent the Truth, the whole Truth and nothing but the Truth. This modernist position in the field of contrasting truth claims does not appear intellectually convincing. The only Truth propagated by the national and scientific white male elites has tended to favor these very same elites far too much for being able to convince the others about its universal, neutral and objective nature. Another easy way out of the present crisis of truth claims would be to adopt a position of complete relativism that denies any possibility of our concepts referring to any truths in a more than very subjective and non-foundational manner.[5] No matter how enchanting such an

---

4. However, there is also the opposite development of increasing interest in religion especially in social sciences and history, and there this interest usually exceeds the instrumentalist nationalist use of religion.

5. Relativism can mean different things. Cultural relativism in the positivist manner builds on differentiating between facts and values. While facts would be provable and therefore not relative, there would be no way of judging values (Appiah, *Cosmopolitanism*, 13–31). Epistemological relativism that considers everything as social construction would see everything relative, even the so-called facts. In religion, the dividing line between facts and values is not quite as easy to uphold as a positivist would wish. Therefore, in this study, I use the term relativism to denote a position considering everything relative without distinguishing between facts and values.

approach may seem, I would rather see a person planning a nuclear power plant (if one must be constructed) specialized in engineering and nuclear physics rather than Tarot-cards or horoscopes. Even if the correspondence between our concepts and the truth is less direct and clear than some positivists would wish, disregarding any correspondence at all does not seem to be the most viable option either.

The attempt here is to formulate proposals for theology that would provide solutions to the challenge of religious and cultural pluralism in such a manner that one leaves as many openings to different theological traditions as possible. The attempt is, thus, not at all to make a complete systematic theological presentation but, rather, to discuss a number of questions that could provide some keys to the issues around truth and plurality. This solution aims for a degree of ecumenical openness, even though it will be clear to the reader that there are certain traditions from which I tend to draw more than from others—from Africa and Europe more than the rest of the world, and from Catholic and conciliar Protestant theological traditions more than others. My position is that of a North European Protestant who has spent considerable time in Africa and it is only from that position that I can argue anything. At any rate, the attempt is to argue in an ecumenical manner in such a way that, inasmuch as possible, denominational differences would not become the first stumbling blocks in the discussion. Some of the argumentative moves in this study are almost self-evident today, whereas others will most probably not become too widely accepted. Yet, I hope that even the proposals that will lead one out of her comfort zone and lead to their rejection, will yield fruitful cognitive dissonance and discussions.[6]

This study belongs to the field of systematic theology even though the topics taken up would often be placed under Mission Studies, World/Global Christianity, intercultural theology or any of the other neologisms replacing Mission Studies today. Placing the questions of theological, religious and cultural pluralism under Mission Studies or the like is one western ethnocentric method of marginalizing these questions, turning one's gaze inwards and towards the past, which Christians of the West are so proficient at. However, I claim that the questions of contextuality and religious plurality within and outside Christianity must belong to the very core set of questions within systematic theology. As an outcome of secularization and the declining importance of churches and theology in western societies, systematic theology has increasingly turned into a historical discipline or into

---

6. Thus, I attempt basically to address the question of plurality and universality in Christianity, a question that is elegantly presented in Wild-Wood, "Afterword," 332–35.

denominationally limited in-group thinking. Gone are the days in which, for example, the great Lund theologians (e.g., Aulén, Nygren, and Bring) in Sweden could openly and confidently construct their thoughts with the notion that they may have relevance beyond the immediate ecclesiastic-denominational context. Much of this confidence was built on the premises of common humanity, which often was and remains a code-word for cultural imperialism. Consequently, this bygone approach should remain bygone. The aim of this study is to outline such markedly Christian and, therefore, confessionally limited principles, which, in spite of their confessional nature, would simultaneously open avenues for an open theological approach in the pluralistic world.

The argumentation comes, therefore, from a specific position: I am a theologian of a Lutheran background with some studies at a Catholic university. For most of my working career I have worked on African theologies, living half of the time on the continent and currently being multi-located in Europe. There is a certain minority or outsider position involved: coming from Europe in Africa, one is an outsider. In Europe, as a Finn, one is a cultural and linguistic outsider. This is all the more so for the one who has additionally absorbed influences from Africa. Within theology, this background easily leads one to being pigeonholed in the neat square box of Mission Studies or its contemporary equivalents, all the more so when one combines intercultural and interreligious interests with empirical approaches. However, my claim is that if academic theology is to survive as a discipline within secular universities, it must learn from decolonial debates and discussions on encountering the religious other placed under Mission Studies. This is because relating to the other is the Achilles's heel of both western theology and Enlightenment modernity, due to their universalising tendencies.

An alert reader will readily see that the trends and frameworks behind this study draw from a theological position often described as inclusivistic. Additionally, western late-modern ethos as well as post- and decolonial approaches in the majority world are the cultural preconditions transposed with the baggage of my background. Resulting from this, plurality is seen as something positive and life-enhancing rather than threatening. In spite of the specific position the argumentation emanates from, attempts have been made to keep the specificities of positionality from forming unnecessary obstacles to the credibility and acceptability of the argumentation. I strive to argue in a manner that would allow also readers not necessarily sharing my starting point to take my proposals into serious consideration. Therefore, there is no attempt to construct a theological system or a water-tight theory but simply to propose ways to approach religious plurality without losing Christian identity while remaining open to the pluralist challenges.

I will not deal with theological or ethical content issues like soteriology, Christology or climate change more than is necessary for elaborating my points about the nature and role of theology in today's world. This means that very many topics that are important for the content of Christian theology and ethics are not dealt with at all or only in a very limited manner, due to the fact that my intention is not to propose another full theological system but rather to provide tools for theological elaboration today.

In this study, pluralism is used to refer to the social and religious reality of many religions and truth-claims and not an epistemological position. Yet, the way the concept of pluralism is used here is that it is more than diversity. A society can be for example religiously diverse by the very fact that there are several religions. Yet these religions might not interact too much in which case there is no pluralism. However, in the (rather common) case of mutual exchange, cooperation and overlapping of religions the condition is pluralist, as well. Thus, religious (and cultural) pluralism is a starting-point rather than the result of this study. Orthodoxy is used here to refer to the correct or right faith, rather than as a designation of a specific group of Christian traditions. In the case that the term Orthodox is referred to in the sense of a denominational marker, it will be referred to as Eastern Orthodoxy. A working definition to Christianity, until its boundaries are discussed in a more detailed manner in chapter five, accounts for all religious groups that base their faith and life on the Christ-narrative of the New Testament.

Modernity and the Enlightenment are seen here as siblings. Modernity is a cultural, technological, economic and social result of the Enlightenment as a historical process and as an ideological position. Modernization and Enlightenment are processes that are deeply entangled with each other as well as with globalization in its several dimensions and forms. All these, in turn, are deeply related to the intellectual, political and economic histories of the western countries.[7]

Coming from Europe and being a product of academia which is ethnocentric also I am inevitably a product of Enlightenment. My questions, arguments and plausibility patterns are all related to the Enlightenment legacy, also when rejecting it. One dimension of Enlightenment legacy, stemming ultimately from the Judeo-Christian narratives of Genesis, is the idea of universal humanity, and consequently equality of humankind. This ideal, perceived as universal, is the foundational doctrine of liberal democracy

---

7. See Robins, "Interrupting Identities," 61–64.

and human rights thinking. This is the air that I have been breathing all my life. The theological ideas proposed in this book stem from this root but at the same time, they ultimately lead to the deconstruction of the Enlightenment liberal project. This means that the outcome is bound to be internally incoherent to a certain extent, and a work in progress.[8]

Theology, unless otherwise mentioned, refers to Christian theology. Theology is used here in two senses: the primary sense is the intellectual enterprise that attempts to express the faith-content of Christianity in verbal form as clearly as possible, with a (varying) degree of critical and self-critical thought. This can be called constructive theology. In the secondary sense, theology is referred to as a study of the aforementioned, an analysis of constructive theology or theology in the primary sense. This logocentric use of the term theology is not meant to be exhaustive and thereby I do not want to suggest that theology could not be expressed in other forms, as well. However, the addition of, for example, visual arts and music in this already rather complicated discussion would have complicated the discussion methodologically and contentwise to an extent not at all manageable for me.

Tradition refers to any religious or cultural *commune bonum* of a group that is handed over from generation to generation. This tradition contains therefore not only the logocentric exercises but also music, visual arts, rituals and unexpressed ways of Christian life.

This study begins with a sketch of the pluralistic global age that is not intended to be a full-fledged analysis but an indication of which dimensions of globalization and pluralism and their interchange affect religion and theology in my view. The following chapter, three, expresses what kind of renewal is needed in academic theology on the basis of the altered global context.

The chapters that follow propose ways of tackling fundamental questions related to the global pluralistic age. First, in chapter four, there is discussion on the meaning of contextuality for theology and chapter five outlines a proposal of how to perceive the contextual hermeneutical process that is the basis of constructive theologizing.

Once the importance and meaning of context for theology is established, the study proceeds to exploring the consequences of the inevitably syncretistic nature of all religion for Christian theology. All contexts and all religions are namely syncretistic, in the sense that they are mixtures of earlier and contemporary religions. Empirical studies of religion are rather clear about that, and yet Christian theologies often tend to overlook this. The argument of this chapter is that syncretism is not only something that

---

8. See Wynter, "'Genital Mutilation' or 'Symbolic Birth'?"

Christian theology needs to acknowledge. Rather, Christian theology must embrace the idea of the syncretistic nature of Christianity and thereby theology itself. In doing so, Christian theology is not only honest to itself but also true to its doctrinal contents.

The last chapter before the concluding remarks faces the challenge of acknowledging religious pluralism as a social fact and syncretism as a theological starting-point. Will this lead to a formless mishmash of religious ideas with no space for truth claims? Here, I propose a way of perceiving revelation in a manner that would simultaneously cater for taking the phenomenon of social and religious pluralism as well as Christianity's inevitably syncretistic nature seriously, while still being able to stake truth claims.

2

Globalizing World as the Context of Theology Today

IN THIS CHAPTER, I map out the dimensions of globalization that are of importance for the position and nature of academic theology. First, I will briefly discuss the connection between Christianity and globalization and proceed thereafter to deal with globalization from three perspectives: economy, information technology and culture. The chapter ends with an analysis on how these three dimensions of globalization directly and indirectly affect Christian academic theology.

Christianity at the Roots of Today's Globalization

Technological advancement has been incredibly rapid during the last half a century. I was born in a world with practically no computers and with black and white television as the epitome of everyday technology—even that not possessed by many. I was very interested in the world from early on and, therefore, had pen-pals all over the world with whom I exchanged letters. Sometimes it would take half a year for an answer to arrive across the Iron Curtain—the Polish communist government was probably short of French-speaking censors to read our letters.

The fact that my childhood and youth sound like the Stone Age in the ears of my (now adult) children creates a perspectival failure that suggests that globalization is a very recent phenomenon. In spite of globalizing processes speeding up during the latest decades, the phenomenon itself is much older. The basic structures of recent global economy were constructed during the colonial era in the Atlantic triangular trade of slaves from Africa to America, cotton from America to Europe and industrial goods (and colonial violence) from Europe to Africa. A similar triangular trade existed in Asia in the late nineteenth and the early twentieth century with opium being transported from British-controlled India to China, tea and porcelain from China to Britain and industrial goods (as well as colonial violence) to India. In both examples, Europe was the producer of the industrial commodities, while some colonially controlled areas were producers of raw materials and others of semi-processed or labor-intensive goods. In all of the cases, Europe coerced the other territories into this circle of trade either by brute force (e.g., Opium wars against China) or by utilizing the local divisions, conflicts and inequalities (e.g., acquisition of slaves from Africa). The oppression by brute force and economic structures was completed with ideological and mental oppression whereby the cultures and minds of the colonized were denigrated and derogated.[1] Today, the structure remains similar even though the USA, Japan and South Korea have progressed to the highest level of the colonial ladder, becoming producers of high-end products, and China is making its way up and becoming the main contestant for world hegemony once the American era is over. Thus, the roots of the present economic and political world-order can be traced back at least more than half a millennium when European colonialism was in the making.[2]

The intellectual and mental foundations of globalization are of even older pedigree. I would claim that Christianity is an inherent intellectual and mental factor behind the emergence of globalization.[3] However, Christianity is not the first religion with global views. Judaism, for example, precedes it with some very clear global content wherein God, who revealed herself[4] to Abraham, Isaac and Jacob, was seen to have a special relation with their offspring. Yet, she was still often regarded in the Hebrew Scriptures as the God

---

1. Césaire, *Discours sur le colonialisme*, 12.

2. Here, as in the following description, I rely quite much on world-systems theory. Wallerstein, "West, Capitalism, and the Modern World-System." However, while Wallerstein tends to emphasize geography and certain countries as core, semi-periphery or periphery, while recognizing the differences between countries and groups of countries, I would emphasize the role of social-economic classes more in line with Marxist social analysis. Additionally, I tend to emphasize the role of religion and culture in general more than usual in world-systems theory.

3. See Rupprecht, "Orthodox Internationalism," 212–13. On the intermingling of economy, politics, culture, religion, etc. in coloniality, see Grosfoguel, "Decolonizing Post-Colonial Studies," 6–14.

4. Coming from a linguistic background, like most of the humanity, not distinguishing she and he, I feel very reluctant being forced to choose between those pronouns. To mark this unease, I will consistently choose she in cases when a gender-unspecific noun would be needed. This does not mean that I would consider God female rather than male, or humanity female rather than male but that I object the gender segregation imposed on one writing in an Indo-European language. To my relief, Swedish has recently introduced a gender-inclusive noun, "hen," borrowed from Finnish ("hän").

of the whole world. Micah's eschatological vision in Chapter 4 is an even more radical globalizing image where the Mount of Zion is not only the center of the whole world, but also gathers the peoples of the whole world, a view that can be described as centripetal. However, there are some notable exceptions to the centripetal vision, in favor of a more outwardly-geared approach, as evidenced in the book of Jonah where he is sent to preach to the people of Nineveh outside of Israel.

The Jesus-movement and its consequent Christianity inherited the global views of the Jewish mother-religion but in a radicalized form. No longer could one expect peoples to come to the Mount of Zion; rather, Christians were expected to actively spread the message and attract disciples from both near and far. Jonah's mission to Nineveh turned this new religious context into a global vision,[5] an ambitious project appearing for, probably, the first time in world history. The goal was built on the Jewish faith in a global creator but was coupled with an activist agenda in which followers of the gradually established new faith were expected to actively engage with others.[6]

A great deal of attention has been paid to Christian expansion within the Roman Empire, and it may be that understandings of the ends of the earth were often limited to the known *oikoumene* of the time. However, the new faith expanded well beyond the limits of the world known to the Romans, to today's Ethiopia and the whole of Nile valley, and east all the way to India and the western parts of China, to mention a few major directions. Thus, one may conclude that there was a border-crossing tendency in early Christianity that facilitated its spread into new cultures and geographical areas. This is unmistakably a globalizing force even if it had not yet reached true global coverage.

In medieval and reformation Europe, according to Peter Beyer, the relative independence of the church paved the way for the development of subsystems in society that facilitated functional differentiation which formed a basis for the modernization process. Modernization, in turn, was the precondition for globalization as we now know it.[7] While Catholic Europe did not yet undergo the functional differentiation, Spanish and Portuguese colonial conquests especially in America launched the gradual

---

5. See, e.g., Bevans and Schroeder, *Constants in Context*, 10–11. On the relation of an expansive Christian agenda to globalization see Hanciles, *Beyond Christendom*, 16–17.

6. Simon Coleman aptly describes the active and all-permeating nature of the global dimension in the lives of (conservative Evangelical) Christians. Coleman, *Globalisation of Charismatic Christianity*, 5–6.

7. Beyer, *Religions in Global Society*, 66–70, 122–41.

development of international law, on one hand, and to human rights on the other hand. Iberian exploitation of the indigenous population was so merciless that it led to a theological-juridical reaction led by Dominican Bartolomé las Casas.[8] Ivan Strenski argues, taking Francisco de Vitoria and Hugo Grotius, both hailed as fathers of international law, as examples of theologians influential in the emergence of economic globalization, that Christian theology provided legitimacy to globalizing ambitions in this field. He further notes that even today's economic globalization makes use of Christian theological thought for its legitimation. Indeed, it may be argued that economic globalization is not a natural process but, rather, that it has been facilitated by the global horizons of Christianity.[9] I would go even further and maintain that Christianity itself was already a form of religious globalization and, therefore, it could serve as an impetus in other spheres such as the economic and political. In turn, the later economic, political and cultural processes connected to globalization have fed into the Christian processes of globalization, considerably accelerating their speed.[10] Meanwhile, Christianity has had its own ideals concerning the human global community that have been in interchange with the global visions of other expansive projects.[11] Additionally, one needs to be cognizant of the fact that globalization of Christianity contains a strong element of local adaptation rendering it actually glocalization.[12]

Globalization is far from a simple phenomenon with a history of unilinear development. Firstly, while its economic impact tends to be an overwhelming focus of discussion, globalization also incorporates political, religious, cultural, social, and technological aspects which tend to intertwine and overlap, often making it difficult to differentiate between the various dimensions of a specific globalizing process. Secondly, as alluded to above, globalization should not be seen as a single process but, rather, a conglomeration of different processes, often pulling in different directions. What makes them all merit the label "globalization" is simply that they have

---

8. See Irvin and Sundquist, *Modern Christianity*, 20–24.

9. Strenski, "The Religion in Globalization." See also Stackhouse, "Social Graces," 47–54. On USA and its globalizing policies as an example of the Protestant mindset: Kurth, "Religion and Globalization."

10. Coleman, *Globalisation of Charismatic Christianity*, 5.

11. Christian visions can mostly be classified under Robertson's category "Global Gemeinschaft 2" although, the theological visions of, for example Apartheid or different fundamentalisms, were/are of the "Global Gemeinschaft" type. Robertson, *Globalization*, 78–79. On fundamentalist visions, see Beyer, *Religions in Global Society*, 28–30.

12. For this in relation to Pentecostal/charismatic Christianity see Robbins, "The Globalization of Pentecostal and Charismatic Christianity."

global dimensions: that is, they transcend a regional and national scope. Thus, the construction of oppressive late capitalist economic systems, often by coercion,[13] across the globe is globalization just like #metoo movement[14] attempting to end harassment against women. They are very different phenomena but both transcend national and continental borders. Thirdly, globalization takes on different forms.

To sum up: here, the empirical dimension of globalization is taken to mean, on one hand, the "penetration of bounded political, cultural, and geographic entities by ideological, material, and virtual products originating elsewhere."[15] On the other hand, these bounded entities may accommodate themselves to different influences and take new forms that, in turn, may begin to penetrate other contexts.[16] Furthermore, the logic or meaning of globalization is taken here to be "the compression of the world and the intensification of consciousness of the world as a whole."[17] The role of the western missionary movement in the intensification of consciousness of the world as a whole was enormous in the nineteenth and the early twentieth century. For example in Finland, the mission magazine was the most widely spread printed media of its time and its pages were full of stories from China and other places then considered exotic, but especially Northern Namibia (Ovambo) which was the biggest Finnish missionary field. Missionaries' stories were thus pivotal in creating a sense of a unified world among the readership. Together, the visible processes involved as well as global ideologies and ideas form a multidimensional and layered web of phenomena that can be classified as "globalization."[18] Rather than a simple concept, globalization is thus an umbrella term for entangled or intertwined phenomena and developments that make our world shrink.

---

13. See, for example, Klein, *Shock Doctrine*; Wallerstein, "West, Capitalism, and the Modern World-System," 571–72.

14. See Bateson, "#Metoo is Complex."

15. Tétreault, "Contending Fundamentalisms," 18. Tétreault's definition builds on Peterson, *Critical Rewriting of Global Political Economy*. This definition comes close to that of the Yale theologian Max L. Stackhouse ("Social Graces," 42). It is somewhat broader than what Ivan Strenski suggested ("Religion in Globalization," 631–32). Jehu Hanciles and Robert J. Schreiter list several dimensions of globalization that are meaningful for the study of religion and globalization. Hanciles, *Beyond Christendom*, 15; Schreiter, *New Catholicity*.

16. See, e.g., Robertson, "Glocalization," 29–31.

17. Robertson, *Globalization*, 8.

18. On the variations in globalizations see Pieterse, "Globalization as Hybridization," 45–46.

Three Dimensions of Today's Globalization

As stated above, globalization has numerous intertwining dimensions but for my purposes here, I will concentrate on just three dimensions which I consider to be of specific importance for my topic, namely economic, information technological and cultural globalizations. These three dimensions are not easy to separate or even differentiate: for example, social media is about information technology but at the same time they are a big business and a major cultural phenomenon.

Economic Globalization and Its Social and Ecological Consequences

Economic globalization has gone hand in hand with the expansion of the monetary economy, intensification of global economic links and increasing commodification of goods, services and even human relations. While monetary economies existed in areas like China, the Arab world or parts of India prior to European colonial expansion, colonialists or Christian missionaries were often the ones to introduce money, wage labor and taxes or collects. The monetary economy was, indeed, a vital ingredient of the colonization process. Especially after the abolition of slavery, money was the means of engaging the colonized into the global capitalist system. For example, the British colonial administration introduced the hut tax not so much to collect funds, but to speed up the process of monetarization and force even the reluctant traditionalists into participating in the monetary economy.[19]

European colonialism, after the initial plundering tirades, like Spanish Cortez's in what was to become Latin America, was based on two kinds of logic. One was that of settler colonialism where the colonized area was populated by the colonialists after having been depopulated through ethnic cleansing, genocide or diseases. In some cases the colonial argumentation built on the concept of *terra nullius*—a country not belonging to anyone. The decimated population was thus wiped away from history or the remnants of the diminished aboriginal population (like the Khoi-San in Southern Africa or the Aborigines in Australia) pushed to ecologically harsh environments were supposed to have always preferred to live in the harsh surroundings rather than the more hospitable ones occupied by the settlers.[20] In this case, the new settler population was already culturally and economically equipped to serve as cogs in the global capitalist wheels.

19. Thus, Potkanski, "Sonjo Community," 202–3.
20. See Budden, "Necessity of Second Peoples' Theology in Australia," 62–64.

The other logic was that of seeing the local population as a resource to be exploited. In its early crude form this meant the enslavement of the locals, sometimes even freighting them across the oceans—e.g., from Africa to the Americas.[21] Slavery as a system was clumsy and ineffective because the transfer of labor was capital-intensive involving buying and selling of the labor unit—the slave. At the same time, it did not tend to produce laborers with high levels of motivation or ambition leading to a low level of productivity per worker. No wonder that this form of labor was mostly limited to large scale agriculture where the other main means of production—land—was immobile and even the transfer of production of one crop to another often required years of work. Thus, the productive process was slow to change, to begin with. The slavery-type of labor exploitation could also take place under euphemisms as "indentured labor" or other kinds of inequitable contracts. In more flexible types of production, slavery is a liability. An industry which is affected by economic cycles rotating between boom and bust is not well served by slavery because the quick increase or decrease of labor is impossible. This renders the slave workforce unadaptable to the whims of the capitalist mode of production.

Therefore, the most widespread and durable means of exploitation is that of wage labor. It became the norm within the global labor market and functioned both in the colonies and the "motherland." The benefit of paid labor is that it can provide the workers incentives to work longer and more intensively, as well as improve one's skills, as all of these would lead to increased income. The benefit of this system is also that it appears to be ethically superior over slavery. After all, the workers are involved in the labor at their free will, and the pay is defined through a negotiation between the employer and the worker. If one of them is not happy with the contract, it may be discontinued. Subsequently, this system is naturalized as ethically neutral, basing on the "invisible hand"[22] of supply and demand which is often considered as almost a law of nature. This ethical neutrality of capitalism

---

21. One needs to remember that while European-led globalization and slave trade were rife on the West Coast of Africa, a similar economic-political Arab expansion had gone on for centuries on the East coast, with slave trade as one of its strong economic components. Eventually this Arab-led international web of political and economic relations had to give way to and adapt to being a vehicle of European colonialism.

22. Adam Smith is usually regarded as the father of the invisible hand theory in economics. However, the term goes back to Shakespeare (Wight, "Treatment of Smith's Invisible Hand," 342) whose idea of an invisible hand was less predestined and psychologically more nuanced than many twentieth century theories which tend to see it producing more predictable results and being void of ethical dimensions. For Smith, an invisible hand was a matter of human instincts and there, human ethical nature played a great role. See Wight, "Treatment of Smith's Invisible Hand."

is almost uncontested, especially after the fall of communism. This is rather astonishing considering that much of the capitalist advancement has been carried out with the help of IMF and World Bank economic coercion, sometimes coupled with USA-backed military coups (Latin America in the 1970s and the 1980s) or a war (e.g., Iraq). What makes the neutral image of forces of capitalism even more astonishing is that the so-called free market often is far from free and the reins of economy are shifted in the hands of the rich and politically connected in manners that include felonious acts.[23] Communism was formulated, after all, as a reaction against the global capitalism but turned into an oppressive system with Soviet Union's imperialist exploitative tendencies vis-à-vis its satellite countries.

Colonialism could be seen as one necessary step in the formation of global capitalism. Necessary because despite the capitalist credo of freedom, many cultures would have proved much more resistant against capitalism without the, often not so gentle, push of colonialism. Colonialism was also needed to solve internal European problems: population explosion and limited markets. In industrializing European countries, the population was increasing exponentially, which proved to be good news to the industrial capitalists, because the supply of labor remained above the demand, facilitating extremely low pay to the unskilled workers. However, too much of an excess in population leads to starvation and restlessness. So, spreading out the population into colonies came to be regarded as a viable solution. At the same time, these colonies served as pools of raw materials and markets for industrial goods.

The colonial global capitalist system produced a cornucopia of wealth for the capitalists, at the same time as it generated misery on several continents among those who did not have scarce means of production to offer to the global market—capital, skills or valuable raw materials (which were and are, often exploited by those with means of violence at their disposal). The world was then divided up between the few capitalists, those who struggle to make it upwards on the economic ladder, and the vast group of paupers. The global owning class is relatively small, and while the majority of the owning class resides in the industrialized countries, there are members of this class virtually everywhere. In the lower segments of the global owning class, industrialized countries' real estate holders and pension scheme owners form the greatest group without realizing it. Owning your house in rural Africa does not make you rich on global scale, but owning your house in a country with a high average level of income and high real estate prices does

---

23. See Klein, *Shock Doctrine*.

because that house, if turned into other type of capital, gives you a considerable financial base.

For most of the history of capitalism, capital has had a comparative advantage over labor.[24] Only in politically manipulated situations have the workers had the ability to improve their lot considerably. Today, this is the case in the European Union, for example, which advocates the global capitalist principles of free movement, but only to an extent. Global free movement of capital is almost complete, and the free movement of goods is not considerably restricted. There is almost free movement of labor within the Union, but not globally. The aspirant laborers travelling to Europe drown in the Mediterranean, are blocked into camps or forcefully returned to their countries of origin. All the while the EU birth rate remains minimal and the demand for labor already surpasses the supply in areas of economic growth, providing the workers the opportunity to demand higher pay. The EU and wealthy nation states with their restrictions on immigration limit the global capitalist chances of unlimited labor exploitation. However, they simultaneously provide it an impetus to increase productivity per worker through automatization, among other measures. Thus, nation states both benefit from and cause harm to neoliberal[25] global capitalism.

Global capitalism has led to an incredible expansion of economic activity and intensification of the exploitation of natural resources. The result has been a tremendous increase of resources at the disposal of humankind, leading to a situation of increasing total wealth. This mostly benefits the superrich, but on the global scale has also contributed to the gradual diminishing of extreme poverty, as well.[26] There are greater resources than ever for science and technology, and never have so many diseases been curable. Never have so many people been able to read and write. Never has there been as great a production of food and other commodities. And, never have

---

24. Piketty, *Capital in the Twenty-First Century*.

25. Neoliberal refers here to the principles of Milton Friedman. Friedman, *Capitalism and Freedom*.

26. The decrease of global poverty depends largely on China's development which has led to large numbers of poor attaining a higher standard of living—albeit for a high cost in environmental degradation and hard-handed governmental interference in citizens' lives in the form of imposed birth control and systems of controlling internal migration. Despite the country being nominally communist, there is a very strong element of competitive market economy which is, however, strongly controlled by the state. The result has been phenomenal growth of both the economy and economic inequality. Even elsewhere, poverty has reduced although statistical analysis shows that economic growth and poverty reduction correlate more strongly in affluent than underdeveloped countries due to structural factors perpetuating inequality in the latter. Fosu, "Growth, Inequality, and Poverty Reduction."

there been as many people to share these commodities as today. That said, tomorrow there will be many more. Combined with the population growth, there have never been as many people as affluent as today, and masses as vast willing to attain those levels of affluence. So, regardless of the limitations of natural resources, this increase in produced resources is a mixed blessing. Taking into consideration the natural resources, the picture looks more sinister.[27]

The intensification of the exploitation of natural resources has led to the increased commodification of these resources—even of the earth's commons like water or air. The idea of buying natural water in a bottle was unthinkable in my childhood in Finland, where tap water was potable (but not always tasty). Today the quality of tap water is much better than in my childhood, and yet water is bought in bottles more than ever. Conceptually, water has been transformed from a common into a commodity. This change has had serious effects in places where water infrastructure is privatized. While, previously, municipalities and other public actors would have required funds from the consumers to maintain the infrastructure, privatization has led to the selling and buying of water. The scarcer water is and the more one lets the market mechanism steer the distribution of water, the more blatant the inequality becomes. In the Western Cape, South Africa, townships and informal settlements with huge populations are suffering from a chronic scarcity of water and middle class is told to take measures to conserve water. All the while, it still is running from the taps as the wine farms and the rich with their own water supplies continue as usual, watering their precious crops and lush lawns and having their dams and swimming pools supplied.[28] In the Near East, the water situation is explosive, and some have attributed political unrest like the Arab Spring and the consequent protracted conflicts like the Syrian civil war, partly to the water shortage.[29] Water may ideally be an earth's common, but because it can be possessed and traded through storage and channeling, it has come to be used as a means of power and control since the introduction of irrigation-based agriculture—actually in some areas already several millennia ago.[30]

A similar development is occurring with air, through CO_2 compensation mechanisms. While the idea of making the polluter pay is laudable, the side effect of this is that by paying, the polluter purchases the legal and

---

27. For the relations between population, affluence, technology and worldview see Conradie, *Redeeming Sin?*

28. See Janssen, "'Day Zero.'"

29. E.g., MacKenzie, "Arab Spring Runs Dry."

30. See Wittfogel, *Oriental Despotism*; Vähäkangas, *Between Ghambageu and Jesus*, 29–33.

ethical right to pollute to a certain extent. As a result, air, which has genuinely been a common due to the impossibility of storing or channeling it,[31] is transformed into a commodity as well.

In addition to the commodification of the earth's commons, increased economic activity has led to a scarcity of resources, as in the case of fresh water above. The same applies to certain minerals but, most of all, the biosphere where the wild fish stocks are collapsing, forests are being razed and wild animals are disappearing. One can no longer live as a hunter-gatherer in most of the areas where it was once the way of life and fishing is becoming a dying profession in many countries. Global capitalism is proving to be efficient in exhausting the resources of the biosphere and inflicting, oftentimes irreparable, damage to the biotopes.

Industrialization, the early love child of matured global capitalism, has led, with a very high level of probability, to global climate change. This, in turn, renders vast areas of land uninhabitable, like Sahel, North Africa and Near East and Central Asia. The greatest streams of asylum-seekers and prospective migrants to Europe tend to come from these areas. Traditional ways of living, often depending on subsistence farming or keeping cattle, are becoming unviable through climate change. These types of economies have been among the least integrated into the global monetary economy, which means that people coming from such backgrounds are also the least experienced on how to negotiate their lives in such a system. Consequently, this situation is making them doubly vulnerable as they are not free to simply move elsewhere to carry on their traditional ways of life, and in entering the global capitalist system they begin from a position of considerable disadvantage. Not adding insult to injury, but turning the injury fatal, the very countries which launched global capitalism have contributed the most to climate change so far and benefited the most from the global economic system. Yet they continue to deny these people the access to their countries. However, in fact, many of the people knocking on the gates of Europe are not these subsistent farmers and herdsmen but the skilled and mostly urban middle-class, which possesses the mental and cultural resources to navigate the capitalist system—this is what they have been doing before their situation turned untenable.[32]

---

31. Of course, the British tendency in industrial communities to have a rich West End and a poor East End is related to pollution and flows of air. In Britain, winds mostly blow from (south)west to (north)east. Thus, foul-smelling pollution mostly travelled from the factories towards the poorer areas.

32. See Nieminen et al., *Ulkomaista syntyperää olevien työ ja hyvinvointi*, 34; *Working Together*, 128–30; Phillimore and Goodson, "Problem or Opportunity?" 1727.

Moreover, in these kinds of catastrophes, someone is always benefiting, and often it is the political, military and economic powers that be. This is one of the sources of the perpetuation of some conflicts. For example, in Eastern Congo, the decades-long conflict is fanned by the competition of possession of mines that produce strategic minerals for our mobile phones and satellites. Different armed gangs (called rebel groups) and governmental troops from neighboring countries and the Congo itself struggle to keep these sources of income, which are hardly accounted for, for themselves.[33] In this kind of situations, disorder serves as a political instrument to safeguard the interests of the elites.[34]

The present world order produces a deeply divided world where some countries are havens of stability and well-being, others are trying to manage in the middle and in several countries and regions in the bottom the rule of law exists only in name, if at all. In terms of individuals and families, there is a similar threefold division where the owning class concentrated in the wealthy countries is doing well, the large global middle class is struggling its way up, and the global paupers are barely making the ends meet.

Information Age

Yet, the story of economic diversification and division of the world in spite of the globally integrated economy is not the complete story. We live in an information age where data travels, at best, at the speed of light from one side of the globe to the other. Never before have we had as many possibilities of gaining information on almost everything around the world, often in real time. This development in the transfer of information has been a long-time coming. That said, it has accelerated exponentially from the times of conveying messages by messengers on foot or horseback, drums, smoke or fire or, eventually, complicated flag codes as in the early colonial Cape Town in the seventeenth century when one wanted to ensure that the arriving ship and the colony were in the same (Dutch) hands.[35] The introduction of electronic means of communication like the telegraph, the radio and eventually television sped up communication, but it was only with computer technology and the internet that instant communication became multidirectional, as anyone with the skills to build websites could begin to share information to larger audiences. Recently, the internet has developed into a bundle

33. Stearns, "Causality and Conflict."
34. Chabal and Daloz, *Africa Works*.
35. The Castle of Good Hope museum exhibition has an enlightening explanation on the information security measures of flag coding in the Cape Colony.

consisting of websites, apps and social media where information, personal contacts and businesses intermingle. Christians, especially missionaries and other mission-minded people have been eager users and developers of each new form of communication, including the printing press, the radio, the portable film projector, the television and the internet.[36] Recently, especially radical jihadist Muslims have made the internet an essential component of their strategy, thereby becoming perhaps the most internet-based form of religion.[37]

Especially the introduction of social media has levelled the ground in the dissemination and production of information. Now anyone with an internet connection and a mobile phone in a Syrian city under siege can share film, pictures, sound and text with the rest of the world, just like a victim of police brutality in the USA. Ordinary people can ignite revolutions via social media like in the case of the Tunisian Arab Spring. Information has undergone democratization at a scale that was previously unthinkable.

This development has several consequences. The amount of information available for an average internet user in form of text, pictures and films is endless. In addition to the information available on websites, there is also the social media which serves as channels for sharing information both among peers as well as from the top down, like Twitter which is used by many political leaders and influencers. Social media contains readily available information as well as potentially available information, which is accessible only by joining a group or being accepted as a friend. Today's people are drowning in the flow of messages of all kinds: news and entertainment from traditional media, personal and public messages on social media and, naturally, more or less welcomed advertisements.

Another consequence of the democratization of the production of information is that now anyone can produce news at a very low cost—if you already own a computer and a mobile phone with a camera, the cost is basically that of electricity and internet connection (for which a middle-class citizen of an affluent country would usually pay, at any rate). This has led to the emergence of "independent media" produced by people who do not trust or tolerate traditional media and do not have the economic resources to launch traditional media of their liking. Traditional commercial and even state-owned media have expanded into the internet and adapted to its conditions. This has brought them technologically closer to "independent media" which means that the distinction between the two types of media has

---

36. See, e.g., Søgaard, *Media in Church and Mission*. As early as then, he recognized the potential of computers for Christian mission.

37. E.g., Fisher, "Swarmcast."

been blurred. Thus, we should rather visualize a continuum between two ideal types rather than strict two-option taxonomy.[38] What distinguishes "independent media" from traditional media is that "independent media" is openly anti-establishment and often advocates radical political or social goals, whatever they may be. Traditional media, for its part, tends to stay mainstream due to its commercial interests.[39] In some cases, the strong emphasis on advocacy leads "independent media" to ignore voices that differ from its agenda. In many countries traditional media attempts to uphold the air of objectivity and balance between various opinions while in some others, like the USA they often have given up the former ideals and become serfs of major political players. Before the technological democratization of the dissemination of information, only totalitarian state propaganda could openly function much like "independent media" propagating a very narrow view on reality, whereas today it is difficult to draw the line between "independent media" and state-run propaganda posing as such.[40] Some "independent media" eventually grow into commercial media and sometimes commercial media turn into presenting one-sided narrow views, either partially or completely on the basis of populist financial calculation or political pressure.

When anyone can post "news" on the internet, it is no wonder that it is full of facts and "alternative facts."[41] In principle, the verification of facts and "alternative facts" is easier than ever by comparing the almost boundless amount of available information. However, when we are bombarded with such massive amounts of messages, verification of everything becomes impossible due to lack of time. Therefore, verification becomes a selective process based on the interest and biases of the individual. What complicates the matter is that oftentimes a core event has taken place and can be verified, but the interpretations provided happen out of context and turn the provided message into disinformation serving the message creator's goals. An additional advantage for those producing disinformation is that we,

---

38. Rauch, "Are There Still Alternatives?" 756–62.

39. Rauch, "Are There Still Alternatives?" 762–63.

40. For example, state-funded internet trolls may produce content that looks like citizens' journalism while it is a government scheme. Also in the past, the border between totalitarian state propaganda and free press was at times extremely porous like in Apartheid South Africa. See Matisonn, *God, Spies and Lies*, for a detailed and insightful, albeit rather subjective analysis of South African media history.

41. The present political climate in the USA as well as Europe has led to an increased discussion on truth, "post-truth," etc. as if politically motivated disinformation was a new phenomenon. However, we experience a certain crisis of the concept of truth in public debates which makes this discussion more topical than before. See Poole, "Lies, Damned Lies and Alternative Facts."

the consumers, generally want to be cheated in the sense that we gravitate towards believing in whatever news is pleasant for us or conforms to our previous beliefs.

Virtual reality has become a site of contest between governments, interest groups, individuals, paid and unpaid trolls, hackers and even criminals. In this very nasty virtual world there are people and groups deliberately willing to insult you and make you angry, to cheat you out of your money or pressurize you into accepting their views. In order for social media not to suffocate in the tsunami of malevolent or unpleasant messages, algorithms are delivering us from this evil. Social media and search engines, with the help of algorithms, learn what you prefer to see, and the threatening flood of information turns into a pleasant stream of desirable information. The downside of this is that you no longer see what people of very different backgrounds or opinions think and you are isolated into a virtual bubble or echo-chamber of your political, religious etc. tribe. This spills over into the physical reality when social media contacts, naturally with help of algorithms, recommend you bars, restaurants, clubs, movie theatres, gyms, cultural events, etc. The outcome is an algorithm-Apartheid that we willingly keep up, partly not noticing the phenomenon and partly by actively engaging into the game by excluding some unsuitable people from our social media networks. The insular virtual and social reality bites only occasionally, for example when there are surprising political developments like Brexit or the electoral victory of Trump. In urban liberal educated circles neither was considered a real possibility due to the deep insularity of our social realities. In spite of the well-educated liberal urban myth of inclusivity, we shield ourselves from the other—both in the virtual and the physical world. Encounters with the truly other are always a perplexing, oftentimes disturbing and even bewildering experience. The very otherness of the other challenges our certainties and threatens our identity as a part of a group.[42]

42. Here, Paul Ricoeur's distinction between *ipse* and *idem* identities is useful. See Ricoeur, *Soi-même comme un autre*, 140. Group identities, on which we largely build our self-image, are *idem* identities whereas the identity which makes me exactly who I am, distinguishable from anyone else, is the *ipse* identity. From *ipse* perspective, any encounter is an encounter with the other but from *idem* perspective, I encounter the other only when encountering someone not belonging to my group. Even here, in the human encounters, there usually is a dimension of gender, cultural, social, religious, vocational etc., difference making the encounter partially an encounter with the other. However, the commonalities can cover the otherness existing in the other dimensions and often it is only in clashes or irritation, or even amusement over our differences that the otherness of the other reveals itself to us. However, when the commonalities hardly extend beyond common humanity, otherness cannot be glossed over by the existing points of contact.

Thus, while one would have expected the democratization of the flow of information to lead to an increasingly united world with a common vision, it has rather led to a tribalized (social) media existence where the new tribes may be global, interracial and so forth. However, this simply creates the illusion of a unified world that actually does not exist. Additionally, while the internet is technically the same across the world it is, with the bundle of attached social media, divided linguistically. English virtual reality is huge, but it is not the only one. Spanish and French virtual realities are substantial, as well, with less contact with the English one than the much smaller Nordic, Swahili or Afrikaans virtual realities that are deeply connected to the English one. This is due to the small size of these languages as mediums in the internet and the relatively high level of English proficiency in these linguistic groups. When you include a difference in alphabet—like Arabic, Korean or Japanese—the connectedness to the English virtual reality further decreases. When this is coupled with the bundle of social media being incompatible with the English one, like Chinese Weibo or Russian V-kontakte, the points of contact become even scarcer. This incompatibility and separation of internet and social media is promoted, in these two cases, by the respective governments in public-private cooperation that involves major companies like Baidu and Yandex.[43] Therefore, the division of virtual reality is not only a result of linguistic and cultural divides, but also political ones. Thus, even our global social tribes are not quite as global as we tend to imagine, because they are further limited by language and differences in social media.

Therefore, the power of social media in uniting the world is very limited but instead it has a huge potential for uniting bigots globally. People with extremely violent ideas are not usually in majority except in particular historical circumstances. However, through social media, the peculiar chivalry and Christian crusade-inspired Norwegian terrorist Anders B. Breivik could find other deranged bigots.[44] Likewise, ISIS could summon notable numbers of frustrated young hotheads in Iraq and Syria despite such extreme ideas being very marginal in Islam in general.[45] Social media has become the echo-chamber of global bigotries that feed into each other. European fascism carrying out violence in the name of Christian culture is an excellent springboard for violent jihadism that turns conservative Islam into its spitting-image. And, the more violent jihadism there is to manure

---

43. See Budnitsky and Jia, "Branding Internet Sovereignty."
44. See Syse, "Breivik," 394–97 on Breivik's ideology.
45. See, e.g., Awam, "Cyber-Extremism."

European ethnic chauvinism, the more colorful does the flower of fascism blossom.

Cultural Globalization

Another major consequence of the information age is cultural globalization—which, however, is not only a product of the increased flow of information even if entangled with it in multifarious ways. In addition to the information age, also migration, religions, and global capitalism play their roles in cultural globalization.

The global flows of information described in the previous section lead to rapid and visible cultural changes. Memes spread like wildfire in the social media, and books, films and songs are launched globally. However, these quick changes usually affect the very surface levels of culture, while the deeper values and basic ways of being and knowing are far slower through the changes based on flow of information.

Much of Christian mission since the very beginning has depended on the dissemination of information—the proclamation of the Good News. It has often involved the movement of people, but inasmuch as Apostle Paul has been the model, the missionaries' sojourns in their fields have been transitory.[46] However, in many cases one realized that, in the long run, more profound cultural changes demand a longer involvement. Even in such cases, the number of missionaries usually remained very marginal in relation to the local population. This made these changes a matter of information flow rather than the flow of people. Especially Islam shares this kind of missionary approach with Christianity, although Buddhism as well as (Neo)Hinduism have adopted similar expansionary tactics. On one hand, these global religions play a globalizing role by creating global religious communities and, on the other hand, by adapting to the international religious market. In the case of Buddhism, Mindfulness has become one of the major international products to further Buddhist values and ideas,[47] whereas Yoga serves as a similar vessel for Hinduism. However, such products can only convey a limited set of values and practices because in their commodified form, they are secularized. As such, however, they can serve as stepping-stones to these religions. In Christianity, global capitalist commodification has taken a different route as capitalist ideals and self-help techniques are baptized into theology in some forms of what is called the Prosperity Gospel.[48]

46. See, e.g., Donovan, *Missionary Letters*.
47. Hornborg, "Mindfulness."
48. However, one must realize that the Prosperity Gospel is not a unified

Let us take two very different examples of information-based cultural change. Joel Robbins has studied a very isolated Papuan ethnic group Urapmin's Christianization. The Urapmin chose to become Pentecostal Christians by their own initiative, with no missionaries from outside involved. Young Urapmin men emigrating from and immigrating back to the community due to work or schooling brought Christianity with them to the community from the 1960s onwards. In spite of this new religion being exclusivist, some old rituals, like offerings of pigs to spirits, have persevered.[49] They are such that address Urapmin basic cosmological needs which the newly introduced Christian religion could not change. This is obviously not a case of subversive anti-colonial action from the part of the Urapmin. Rather, cultural deep structures persevere. This means that even in a case where Christianity does not show external marks of adaptation, like Urapmin Pentecostalism that does not drastically differ from the international trends, the way in which the same catalogue of rituals, texts or ideas are perceived is different.

The Finnish society has undergone a thorough process of modernization over the course of the last century, transforming from an utterly poor agricultural country into one of the wealthiest nations with top-level technology. The visible cultural changes are striking. My grandparents could still have died of hunger, and my parents' generation was still subjected to suffering from hunger during and following the war years 1939–1945, whereas for my children, that is just distant history. The role of the churches in the society has diminished drastically and marriage has become a ritual usually following the birth of the first child. The nation is growing increasingly tolerant towards sexual minorities, albeit among the last in western Europe.[50] Yet, the basic Finnish values of independence, a sense of responsibility, perseverance ("sisu"), diligence and tolerance,[51] remain very much in continuation with the past. At least I can see a strong Lutheran fingerprint in them. Even if Lutheran faith may be disappearing, the Lutheran ethic is going strong. There has been relatively limited immigration to Finland, due to rather late urbanization and industrialization, meaning that the countryside could provide the needed work force. Moreover, the very isolated

---

phenomenon. (Vähäkangas, "Prosperity Gospel"; Lauterbach, "Fakery and Wealth"; Haynes, "Pentecostalism and the Morality of Money"; Robbins, "World Christianity") In some forms, especially American, the ideal of a good life responds on an individual level to the ideals of global capitalism. Ritual activity, like repetitive prayers, corresponds closely to secular capitalist self-help literature regarding how to motivate and equip oneself to succeed in the competitive capitalist job market.

49. Robbins, *Becoming Sinners*.
50. See A. Vähäkangas, "Conformity and Resistance."
51. World Values Survey, *WV5_Results, Finland, technical record*.

linguistic reality of the nation has made it more difficult to migrate to than the rest of Europe. This isolation has lately been amplified by very restrictive immigration and draconian asylum policies. Thus, new ideas have rather been travelling as flows of information than with people. However, cultural changes on the surface level gradually affect the deep level of values, as well.

Migration is as a natural a state for human beings as rootedness, or in Kwame Anthony Appiah's words, "the urge to migrate is not less 'natural' than the urge to settle."[52] Whenever we feel that our surroundings are conducive for good life, we tend to grow roots in a place. When there is hope to thrive better elsewhere, migration becomes an opportunity. In addition to this, human curiosity and some people's tendency for seeking adventure have also contributed to migration. There have also been streams of forced migration such as slave trade or ethnic cleansing. Today, the volume of migration surpasses that of the earlier ages. This is because the sheer size of the human population has exploded, partly facilitated by migration, and because transporting both humans and information has become easier, faster and relatively cheaper.

When ideas travel with people, also deeper cultural structures travel. An example would be the Afro-American religions like Voudoun, Candomblé and Santeria which are based on West African religious heritage, and came across the Atlantic with the slaves. Centuries of oppression and material, as well as cultural marginalization, could not demolish these traditions and the cultural values implicit in them. On the surface, they could turn into a Catholic cult of saints, but the African heritage was preserved underneath.[53] Also in cases of the amalgamation of different peoples, voluntary or imposed, deep cultural elements or rituals remain even of the recessive culture. An example could be how Jews, often victimized by forced proselytization by Christians in Europe, could retain some of their heritage and sometimes even import dimensions of it into the dominant culture. It can be maintained that during the golden age of Spanish mysticism, suppressed Jewish spirituality found ways of expression within Catholicism, for example in the works of Therese of Avila.[54]

Above, there have already been references to global capitalism as a shaper of culture. It is obvious that on the surface level, global capitalism has made its inroads in almost every corner of the world. Almost all over,

52. Appiah, *Cosmopolitanism*, xvi.

53. For recent studies on the interchange between Afro-Brazilian religions and Catholic rituals see, e.g., Oliveira, "Orixás"; Roca, "Catholic Saints, African Gods."

54. See Carrión, "Scent of a Mystic Woman," 133–34. See also Maroney, *Religious Syncretism*, 26–43 on the context of interchange between Judaism and Christianity in Spain.

you can eat a more or less tasteless meat patty stuck in a white wheat bun, and complete the fare with strips of potato deep fried in fat and a fizzy drink overloaded with sugar and chemical substances. From the perspective of the environment, nutrition and gastronomy, the triumph of this junk food is a complete mystery, considering that in many countries more wholesome options could be cheaper. From the point of view of capitalist logic and its myth-spinning abilities, this is a beautiful example of how the construction of a marketable public image, the creation of customer fantasies about affluence and freedom and clockwork logistics can turn rubbish into valuables. Global capitalism "adds value" to such cultural phenomena that can be turned into marketable commodities that people can be convinced to pay for them. Most visible are the material dimensions of culture such as various consumer items. However, immaterial goods like computer programs, mobile phone games, music, films and other entertainment are occupying an all the more central role as the computerization of our cultures progresses. The internet of things leads gradually to the situation where the material and immaterial dimensions of commodification get intertwined.

Technology is the dimension of science that is put in direct service of global capitalism. Through it, science takes the shape of commodities, which, in turn, change our lifestyles and, subsequently, our cultures and values. During the earlier stages of technological advancement accelerated by global capitalism, means of transport represented the front on which the culture-changing technological advancements progressed the most. Trains, cars and, eventually, airplanes reshaped cities, agriculture, and working life and boosted the emergence of the capitalist ideal human being. In the core of the capitalist ideal of a human stands the concept of freedom, interpreted as the freedom to choose (between commodities which, in turn reflect the choice of lifestyle).[55] In many ways, in the age when means of transport represented the epitome of technological advancement, the iconic commodity was the car, which represented mobility and, therefore, freedom. Later, information technology occupied an ever-increasing role in the transformation of cultures and values. In this age, freedom is about freedom to express oneself, through both material commodities and the virtual world of social media. Today's iconic commodity is the smartphone, through which one becomes globally virtually mobile and through which much of the social and economic life of the globally-networking generations takes place. The cultural change galvanized by the mobile phone is even greater than that of the car. While the car facilitated one's transport from a place to another to shop, meet friends, attend church service etc., all this can happen in and

---

55. Friedman, *Capitalism and Freedom*, 1–6.

through the mobile phone. It has become an omnipresent attachment of the human hand, an ever-present window in the virtual world that is becoming more real than the material world.

The omnipresence of information technology is a relatively new technological development, and companies are only gradually exploring the possibilities it provides for the global market. Cultural changes are slower, and we probably have seen but the very beginning of the cultural transformation processes stemming from this.

Consequences of Global Changes for Christianity and Christian Theology

The developments outlined above have profound effects on religions in general, Christianity in particular, and eventually on theology as well. The increased division of the world, coupled with the incredible flow of information, albeit within the algorithmically separated bubbles, has facilitated the creation of global alternative realities. These bubbles function as greenhouses of global religious bigotries, so that they can grow shielded from the cold winds of otherness. In these cocoons of religious extremism, global reach is celebrated because it gives the impression of greatness and inclusivity—no matter how exclusivist and minor the movement is. These bigoted global communities need not be violent but they are still harmful, in the sense that they instil feelings of religious superiority and intolerance.

The rise of new Constantinian-type Christendom projects was still inconceivable some years ago when the rise of World Christianity was supposed to lead to a post-Constantinian period, where Christianity would be freer from politics and governmental meddling. The fact that Christianity was no longer predominantly the religion of the presently secularizing western countries was supposed to lead to a new era.[56] It looked as if the state- and national-churches as well as church-endorsed fascisms, especially in Europe and Latin America, had discredited themselves as oppressive structures to the extent that they would not become viable options again. Just like the daydreams about the end of history in political sciences,[57] this vision of the end of religious-political syndicates of power was supposed to belong only to the past. The rise of global bigotries, however, raises anxieties and fears prompting people to resort to backward looking identity politics

---

56. Hanciles, *Beyond Christendom*.

57. Fukuyama, *End of History*. By the "end of history" Fukuyama means a state in which the best form of governance has gained global hegemony and the ideological conflicts are over.

where certain strands of Christian thinking find asylum from modern secularization and the powers of pluralism.

Religiously motivated violence is only stone's throw away from religious superiority and intolerance. It is the fruit of seeds sown by such attitudes. Religiously motivated violence is a problem of all major religions, even though militant Islamism has gained most notoriety in the western media. Hindu extremists persecute religious minorities in India, Buddhist nationalists carry out ethnic cleansing and genocide of Muslim Rohingya in Myanmar and Christian anti-balaka gangs in Central African Republic have definitely not only been on the defense against the Muslims.

The way religiously motivated violence is reported plays into the hands of the extremists when they are taken as representatives of their religion without critical examination. During the Utöya and Oslo terrorist attacks in Norway 2011, I was in Turkey and followed the news mainly through Muslim majority countries' media. Breivik was presented as an extremist Christian. That felt completely false to me—this is not what Christianity is all about. Yet, Breivik was clear about his "Christian" motivation for the atrocities he carried out. This was a healthy experience for me because that is exactly how the western media deals with Islamist violence and would probably be how an average Muslim feels about the western coverage.

In this vicious circle, interreligious relations grow tense and religious people need to repeat like parrots to each other, as well as non-religious people, that the atrocities committed in the names of their religions do not really represent what these religious are all about. Yet, the extremist message gets the media attention because a murder makes a better headline than an encyclical or a fatwa.[58] Subsequently, one wonders why religious leaders and people do not distance themselves more clearly from these atrocities. How often and how vehemently should Christian leaders in Europe repeat that they do not condone the European neo-fascist and nationalist terrorist attacks against asylum seekers, Muslim immigrants or Jews? At what point would such repetition just become an advertisement of the extremist nationalist propaganda? When rejecting an idea you usually repeat it and provide it more coverage in the public square. The same questions apply to European Muslims and Muslim leaders in relation to violent Islamism.

---

58. Note: a fatwa is a statement of a Muslim religious authority on any issue at stake and, thus, the way in which Muslim communities relate their traditions to changing circumstances. See Agrama, "Ethics, Tradition, Authority." Many in the West believe that the word means a religious order to assassinate someone because the western media has mostly used the word in relation to its plentiful reporting on violent Islamism. Responsible Muslim scholars do not issue fatwas prompting violence.

In this climate, the tenser the relations between religions grow, the more dangerous it gets for religious minorities, who are often in a position where self-defense is difficult or impossible. It is the persecution of religious minorities, be it Christians in the Middle East, or Muslims by Christians in the Balkans wars, which provides material for the bigots' propaganda for many years to come.

Islam has become the threatening enemy of the West. While some time ago it looked like the increasingly secularizing Europe was about to turn her back to Christianity for good, the situation looks somewhat different now. When nationalists in Europe, propelled by increased number of asylum seekers in 2015, consider Muslims to be enemies and Islam a threat to European lifestyles, Christianity makes a comeback to the political and public agendas. Christianity has become a hobby-horse of xenophobic Europeans to ride against the tide of immigration. Through this, Christianity is defined first and foremost as that which is not Islam. Liberal secularism cannot achieve that because within that paradigm, religion is a private matter which leaves the door open for the progress of foreign religions in terms of social impact.[59]

Purely political and ethnic nationalism seems to appear a little hollow and shallow and, thus, one draws from the European religious history—in Greece, the Nazi movement Golden Dawn flirts with Greek pre-Christian religions while simultaneously attempting to domesticate Christianity for its political ends, much like Nazis in the Third Reich.[60] However, Eastern Orthodoxy and Greek national sentiments, especially against Islam and Turkey/the Ottoman Empire, have been hand in glove. Thus, it is no wonder that Greek nationalist ethos finds its avenues also and primarily through Eastern Orthodox Christianity. In other European countries, attempts at creating and riding the wave of European religions other than Christianity have been even less prominent. This situation has led to a split in many churches: on one side you have the nation-minded traditionalists and, on the other, internationally-minded Christians emphasizing the ethical imperative of the Christian faith over the preservation of national Christian identities. Alongside these two groups, there is a number of people who consider religion irrelevant in their lives, also when encountering Islam.

From perspective of the western churches, both the nationalist and the ethical approaches are ways of attempting to communicate the Christian message to that third group of the religiously disinterested. Therefore,

---

59. The recent Pew research confirms that Christian identity and negative views on Islam correlate quite strongly in western Europe. "Being Christian in Western Europe," 50–51, 61–80.

60. Fotiou, "'We are the Indians of Greece,'" 230–31.

nationalism can be a way of attracting people by playing on their national sentiment and emphasizing how the faith of the forefathers is a part and parcel of the national identity. Likewise, the ethical emphasis seeks to underline the importance of the Christian faith as a motivation to ethical action and, thereby, attract people who share the Christian ethical ideals but have difficulty with the dogmatic content. The outcome of the meeting-point of these Christian perspectives emphasizing ethics of inclusion and political liberalism is a number of, more or less ad-hoc, platforms and campaigns of cooperation when the need arises, like when the number of asylum seekers soared and governments had difficulties catering for them. At any rate, until now, there seems to be no major political constellation growing out of this cooperation. Liberal politics and the Christian faith both strictly and neatly comply with the Enlightenment model of relegating religion to the realm of the individual and the private, rather than the political and the public. Open-minded Christianity is, thus, a lightweight in politics.

The case is quite different with Christianity mounting the bandwagon of nationalistic identity politics. Because Christianity is included in the ideological package of many of these nationalisms, nationalism is becoming the channel through which Christianity is openly played out in the political arena. This means, at the same time, that much of the public understanding of the Christian faith is formulated by the nationalists because politics gains much more space in the media than religion. It is clear that (sometimes very dubious) political actors are using Christianity for their specific ends. At the same time, it is apparent that there are ecclesiastic groups that operationalize the political tide to gain control of the churches and further their vision of a Christian nation. The models for these churchmen are the glorified, and partly fictitious, past settings of national churches. In such narrations, one tends to turn a blind eye to what dimensions of Christian faith one needed to compromise in order to keep a good standing with the political and economic powers that be.

In the Eastern Orthodox world, such visions build on the concept of "symphony" between the church and the state in true Byzantine spirit that has proved incredibly resilient. Just think of Russia where, after over seven decades of aggressive anti-Christian Soviet Communist rule, in a couple of years symphony was formed between the emerging Russian national state and the Patriarchate of Moscow.[61] However, a closer look reveals that the Soviet religious policy was not altogether different from the Byzantine. Ideologically, of course, there was never any space for Christian faith in the communist state. However, because the church existed at any rate, it

---

61. Miroshnikova, "Evolution of the Byzantine Legacy."

needed to be controlled and contained in the sly Soviet manner, infiltrating communist moles in the church and assuring that the church leadership would not be independent from the stately manipulations. So, there was a communist type of symphony in which the church was a junior partner and the state the senior one, with the goal of gradually strangling the church.[62] Today's Russia builds openly on Russian national identity, unlike the Soviet Union which based itself on seemingly internationalist communism. However, Russian nationalism was never absent from the Soviet Union.[63] In the making of the new Russian Empire, nationalism has replaced communism and Eastern Orthodoxy dialectical materialism. The former KGB spy, Vladimir Putin, whose organization formerly persecuted Christians, has declared himself a true Russian Orthodox Christian and formed a strong alliance with the Moscow Patriarchate. While the Russian Orthodox Church is not a monolith behind the Putinist regime, this neo-Byzantine system has fortified the positions of the nationalist theologians in the church and Russian Orthodoxy in the ideological map of Russian politics.

In the Catholic sphere, there are attempts at re-establishing old religious-political systems. However, in many cases, the memory of oppression is too recent to render such attempts any major glow. Such is the situation in Spain, where Franco's fascist repressive regime is still too fresh in mind to allow for a new try. Also in Latin America, the unholy trinity of military juntas, the capital and the so-called conservative wing of the Catholic Church is rather recent history, and yet Bolsonaro's presidential campaign flirting with nostalgy for military dictatorship was successful. In Poland, the latest era of terror was communist while the Roman Catholic Church served as a channel of liberation. Therefore, the ruling PIS-party has formed an alliance with conservative Roman Catholicism, resulting in an overarching give-and-take relationship between ecclesiastical conservatives lobbying their agendas, especially on sexual morals and family issues while the government can rely on the conservative Roman Catholic support. Like in Russia, the national sentiment and religious identity forms a whole that serves the purposes of the political and religious powers that be.

On the Protestant side, isolationist nationalists are appealing to Christianity, especially in its Lutheran form, in the Nordic region. However, due to the higher level of secularization the alliance between politics and religion is less robust than in the examples above. Yet, there is a clear nostalgia for the imagined monolithic cultural-religious context of the past. It

---

62. Rupprecht, "Orthodox Internationalism," 219–23.

63. This is clearly depicted in the Soviet national anthem where the "enormous Russia" was referred to as the root or mother of the Soviet Union.

is imagined because in these nationalist daydreams one tends to ignore the existence of ethnic and religious minorities who often suffered under, more or less hard-handed, homogenization efforts by the national states. This can be exemplified by Finnish speakers in Sweden or Sami and Romani speakers in every country they inhabit.

Surprisingly, Hungary is a country where political nationalism and Protestantism interact most potently. This is surprising in the sense that the Catholic Church is the largest Christian community in the country.[64] However, some of the leading FIDESZ politicians are very active Reformed Christians. They obviously cannot appeal to the Hungarian national identity as Reformed but, rather, as Christian as opposed to Muslim. Here, on the contact-zone of centuries of encounters between the Muslim Ottoman and the Catholic Habsburg Empires, religious confrontations play the strings of deep sentiments. While FIDESZ is radically nationalistic, Hungary also has a properly Nazi-minded Jobbik-party which yielded 20% of the votes in 2014 and is staunchly anti-Semite. Here, the ugly face of European nationalism, that often gets concealed behind euphemisms like "immigration critical," is laid bare. Naturally, it is not the case that all European nationalists are racist although there appears to be a high degree of correlation.

The Evangelical Lutheran Church in Hungary serves as a case in which the church leadership is at least partly critical towards the government while the membership is divided about immigration politics between the humane and the governmental draconian approach. The Lutheran church was one of the first in Hungary to react on the needs of the asylum seekers and still is one of their strongest supporters in spite of the negative attitude of the government and the general public.[65] The Hungarian churches receive plenty of financial support from the government but there is the fear that the churches speaking up against the government policies (e.g., on immigration) may be financially punished.[66]

Attempts at constructing Christian states in the line of the Charismatic-Pentecostal tradition are rarer and for an example, one needs to turn their gaze beyond Europe. The then Zambian president, Frederick Chiluba declared his country Christian in 1991. His populist religious-political program stemmed from his Charismatic-Pentecostal background and built on individual and national spiritual renewal that would automatically yield

---

64. Barrett et al., *World Christian Encyclopedia*, 353.

65. See Neuberger, "Hungarian Lutheran Church Opens Its Doors to Refugees."

66. *Hungary 2017 International Religious Freedom Report*, 12–13. Indeed, the reformed church, which is closest to the government, received a lion's share of the additional December 2017 budget in spite of the Roman Catholic Church representing the majority of Christians in Hungary. (p. 12)

blessings to the nation. Eventually, Pentecostals have strongly entered into the Zambian political arena.[67] Even Ugandan President Yoweri Museveni has recently begun to make use of Charismatic-Pentecostal rhetoric for his political goals.[68] Thus, even Pentecostal traditions, that have often been perceived to be politically passive, do not prove immune against the attempts at creating new Christendoms. While Evangelical, Charismatic, conservative and Fundamentalist Christian influences in American politics is tangible in the USA, it is discrete from the Christendom-model as there the alliance between religion and politics builds on civil religion[69] that is vaguely Christian, but can easily cover other monotheistic religions—especially Judaism.

Early secularization prompted Christian theology to take the Enlightenment seriously, basically producing two kinds of responses: reaction in the form of Fundamentalism[70] and later Evangelicalism,[71] or accommodation in the form of Liberal Theology. In this new political climate, nationalism has become a way for certain theologians to avoid encountering the Enlightenment, in a somewhat romantic manner. When theology turns into an ideological dimension of nationalism, it becomes a tool of political mythmaking and does not need to argue for its religious credibility, because its credibility now hinges on the political ideological package. While Fundamentalism, in its isolating tendencies from the rest of the society, does not need to appeal to the wider public it engages with the Enlightenment in a very profound manner—the Enlightenment is its raison d'être. It is engulfed in a constant debate, especially between the opposing views of creationism and the evolution theory. When becoming a religious-ideological dimension of a political program, theology no longer needs to engage itself critically with the surrounding culture. Its fate is now dependent on the political

---

67. Kaunda, "From Fools for Christ to Fools for Politicians."
68. Alava and Ssentongo, "Religious (de)Politicisation," 681.
69. See Bellah, "Civil Religion in America."
70. I use the term "Fundamentalism" in its original theological sense, referring to the American (and to a lesser extent British) Christian theological movement that begun in the early twentieth century as a reaction against Liberal Theology and Enlightenment ideas. Later, in colloquial use and even in social sciences, the term has been applied to any kind of reactionary religious movement. While there are common denominators between the movements placed under this tag, the problem of applying Fundamentalism as an umbrella term is that one easily glosses over the theological differences between religions and misses the specific nature of each religious movement's reaction against Enlightenment.
71. According to Klas Lundström, while the doctrinal contents of Fundamentalism and Evangelicalism are practically the same, the difference lies in their relation to the surrounding society. Fundamentalists attempt to isolate themselves from the rest of the society whereas Evangelicals tend to be more open, missionary minded vis-à-vis the larger society. Lundström, *Gospel and Culture*, 181–89.

credibility of the nationalist ideology it has become a part of. This leads to an anti-intellectualization of theology, which is a blow to critical theology in the sense that one section of theological sphere has intellectually castrated itself.

Another dimension of the global processes of change influencing religions is the increasing cultural pluralism that also produces religious pluralism. The result is not only that there are more religions coexisting in our societies but also that these religions interpenetrate in the lives of individuals and groups, producing religiously hybrid multiple identities as noted above. This pluralization has several implications for Christianity and theology.

First, it serves as a strong factor fuelling secularization on political, social and individual levels. When several religions exist within the same sphere, it is no longer easy to argue that one's religion is the only correct one. After all, for most people, religion is something one is born into and is often taken as a self-evident part of one's identity. When and if the person begins to question and investigate religious issues, things become less self-evident and in the critical spirit of the Enlightenment, the cultural plausibility structures strongly suggest that either no religion is correct or all of them are on par in their truth-claims.

The former state- and national-churches in Europe erode much in the manner of Kilimanjaro glacier, the disappearance of which I have had the questionable privilege to follow. The glacier first got thinner and thinner, until it eventually shrank rapidly to the point of disappearance. Formal church membership usually survives the loss of active church membership for some time and cultural Christian identity often survives for some time after the disappearance of formal membership. Thus, while active participation in the Church of England is minimal and the official membership is rather low, at about one tenth of the population[72], the Church of England still enjoys a special place in the expression of the English national and cultural identity. The ties of the English(wo)men to that church have grown very thin and it is shrinking in size. Similar developments are on the way, especially in many West European countries.

Secularization theorists assumed that the rest of the world would follow the secularizing tendencies of western Europe, but this did not happen. The next stage of the discussion was to question the "exceptionality of Europe" in comparison to the rest of the world[73] while some theological and

---

72. See, e.g., Faith Survey, https://faithsurvey.co.uk/uk-christianity.html. One should note, though, that the membership in the CoE is not a clear-cut issue. Therefore, the membership figures can justifiably be set at different levels.

73. Davie, "Is Europe an Exceptional Case?"

religious circles rejoiced the failure of those theorists. Global Christianity studies were often written in rather triumphalist tones, pointing out that the losses in West Europe were abundantly compensated for by "Christianity's phenomenal growth" in the rest of the world.[74] However, even though the West European development has not, and probably will not, be repeated in the rest of the world, the pious Christian dreams on the new global Christian era seem unlikely as well. It appears that there are limits to Christian triumphs in different contexts. The often exalted South Korean Christianity is no longer growing and at least the most audacious among Korean Protestants already dare to talk about the diminishing numbers in church pews.[75] So, Christian progress outside the western countries cannot be taken for granted.

Secondly, while Christian membership has its ups and downs depending on the context, the Christian messages can experience a fate independent of Christian membership. Chinese "cultural Christians" are a well-known and widely discussed phenomenon. They are Chinese people who are not religiously Christian, nor do they wish to be despite respecting Christian values.[76] In some way, there is a similar development in western Europe where many people subscribe to neighborly love, the necessity of forgiveness, the equality of all humans (as images of God), and many other teachings that Christian churches have been propagating for centuries (alongside many such teachings that served the oppressive status quo). After all, the United Nations' Universal Declaration of Human Rights could be seen as an attempt to codify a specific set of Christian values into a universally-applicable catalogue of norms, although the origins of the very idea of universal human rights remains contested.[77] In that sense, the declaration may be less universal than it claims to be. These gospel values are sometimes expressed even more strongly outside churches than inside. This is so because of the new Christendom projects that usually venerate authoritarianism and national community, at the cost of freedom and an individual as well as global Christian fellowship. It means that the direction of mission in Europe needs to change, in some cases, so that the world would need to evangelize the

---

74. See Frederiks, "Whither Theology in World Christianity?"

75. This is based on my observations and church host presentations on visits to Korean megachurches during IAMS 2016 assembly, and eventually confirmed in later discussions with Korean theologians.

76. For an interesting historical analysis of one of the roots of cultural Christianity in liberal theological American mission see Hu, "Spreading the Intellectual Gospel."

77. Glendon, "Source of Human Rights." On the contested roots of modern human rights see Pacc, "Socio-Cultural and Socio-Religious Origins of Human Rights."

churches rather than the churches evangelizing the world. The result could be that the churches become Christian again.[78]

The tension between emphasis on gospel values and Christian identities vis-à-vis the world is perceptible in Christianities of other regions, as well. Western ecclesiastical factions, often described as conservatives and liberals on the basis of their approach to the Bible, tend to interpret this tension in their own terms. However, Christians emphasizing gospel values over exclusive Christian identity need not be liberal at all in their views about the Bible and critical biblical interpretation. Likewise, western conservative conclusions about the majority world Christianity landing neatly in their ecclesiastical political laager may be misleading. The fact that, for example, an African church abhors homosexuality does not automatically lead to that church endorsing the rest of what belongs to the conservative Christian agenda in the West. In relation to the political powers that be, that African church may be either quietist or attuned to liberation theology. Or, in terms of Christian responsibility of the creation, African Evangelicalism has given birth to Farming in God's Way in Zimbabwe,[79] an Evangelical ecologically conscious approach to small-scale farming that challenges the pie-in-the-sky-when-you-die type approach to environmental and other "worldly" matters that has been contaminating much of American Evangelicalism recently. American Evangelical climate denialism and short-sighted alliance with conservative nationalist and even racist political populism is not necessarily shared by Evangelical constituencies elsewhere. That anti-intellectual hypocritical politicking about climate change and the environment in general is yet another round of western Christian pursuit of self-interest at the cost of the majority world, resembling the spiritually sounding support for slavery, racial segregation, cut-throat capitalism etc.

The pluralization of the religious reality as well as the pluralization of Christianity through its globalization have profoundly changed the landscape in which theology is constructed. While many would say that the time for theology is over, one could rather maintain that theology is needed now more than ever.

---

78. WCC Uppsala General Assembly Message points out that the assembly met "first of all to listen [to the world developments]" (*Uppsala Report*, 5). The themes (racism, the world economic system, arms race, diversity and minority issues etc.) that the Report deals with, and the manner in which they are approached, witnesses to the fact that the assembly had been listening to the world and also receiving methods and ideas on how to approach these themes.

79. Farming in God's Way, "Overview," http://www.farming-gods-way.org/overview.htm.

3

On the Need of Renewal of Theology in the Pluralistic World

As argued above, academic theology has largely contextualized itself in the Enlightenment rationalism especially in the West. Even if this move is perhaps intellectually satisfactory to many an academic theologian in the West, it is too little too late for many academic peers in other disciplines. Simultaneously, Enlightenment rationalism is too bitter a pill for many of the churches to swallow, as well as for many theologians of the majority world. While many attempts have been made to form a new truce between the Enlightenment, and especially Evangelicalism, in the extensive faith and science debate, it seems that new approaches are needed. On one hand, Enlightenment universalism is increasingly challenged, and so is the often so Eurocentric view on theology that is its conversation partner.

Theology as a Eurocentric Confessional Enterprise

At a seminar in Finland a couple of decades ago, a student was pondering on which good theologian's thought she should write her dissertation on. She was not certain but wished to work on someone who was not German. The professor thought aloud: "Are there good theologians other than Germans?" Be that a joke or a Freudian slip of tongue, such remark was one that was very well in line with the spirit of the day. Traditional theology as an academic discipline could be justly be described as a Eurocentric confessional enterprise and this was the case with practically no exceptions until World War II. Even today in much of Europe, the situation is not much different. The notion of Eurocentrism here refers to cultures of European background, thus extending, for example, to North America covering the mainstream culture of European origin. But why call it Eurocentric?

First, it was, and largely still is, Eurocentric simply because of the hegemony of European cultures in academic knowledge-production and institutions.[1] Although at the time theology was formulated as an academic discipline in the Medieval Ages, there were traditions of extremely high intellectual quality in some other larger cultural areas, like India, China and the Islamic world, it was the western European intellectual tradition that served as the basis of today's global academia. One needs to note in this conjunction, that theology was one of the three original faculties in most of the medieval universities, alongside philosophy and medicine. Thus, academic theology and the western university system grew hand in hand. Theology is in the historical core of the creation of western hegemony of white male bourgeois knowledge.[2] Campus culture is surprisingly similar globally even today, in terms of the form and content of teaching as well as the institutions constructing campus life. This is partly due to the western roots of academic traditions and partly, of course, due to the global mobility of academics. Just like medieval universities helped the ruling elite to bring intellectuals from the margins into the fold of the centres of power, so does even today's academia. Thus, the questions of method and academic procedures are a part of the western package that even academic theology belongs to. English language, the paramount colonial language, functions as the modern Latin that almost all credible academics need to know.

Second, as a highly historically-conscious discipline, theology builds predominantly on western intellectual and ecclesial history. The Latin Church is the centerpiece, and the Greek Church Fathers and some other Orthodox traditions are often also included. Eastern Orthodox academic voices are rather marginalized in the global theological dialogue even today, as are voices from the majority world. Oriental Orthodox traditions are virtually ignored, even in church history, despite them representing one of the mainstream Christian cultures until the end of the first millennium.[3]

Third, the contents of theological debate that are the most visible, and published by most of the large publishing houses, mirror the questions and challenges of the western world. For example, even though the science and

---

1. See Wallerstein, "West, Capitalism, and the Modern World-System," 562.

2. See Grosfoguel, "Decolonializing Post-Colonial Studies" on the production of this knowledge.

3. There are exceptions, though, like MOPAI-project led by Prof. Samuel Rubenson which has produced an electronic library of early Christian sources in Arabic, Armenian, Georgian, Greek, Latin, Slavonic and Syriac (Monastica, http://monastica.ht.lu.se/). On the early medieval World Christianity see Jenkins, *Lost History of Christianity*. Oriental Orthodox traditions are the non-Chalcedonian ones like Coptic, Ethiopian (Tehwado), Syriac etc.

faith debate exists in the majority world, it is much more central in the industrialized countries. Whichever ethical debate happens to be on top of the agenda in the western churches, reserves the most visible place in the West-dominated international theology. For example, the responsibility of a Christian under a corrupt regime or questions about religious persecution are seldom internationally heard in academic theology despite these being essential in the lives of multitudes of Christians in the majority world. Likewise, one of the contextual theologies' pet topics about the relationship between gospel and culture is almost a non-existing question in the West, in spite of the fact that many of the ecclesiastic cultures of the West have been estranged from everyday cultures, thereby rendering this discussion of great relevance in the West as well. However, as this question has traditionally been consider a part of Mission Studies, formerly denoting the study of Christian expansion in the non-western world, one tends to overlook the question and the results achieved so far.[4]

Fourth, those who are internationally renowned to be important theologians, that is worthwhile being researched and studied, tend to be twentieth century German- and lately also English-speaking men.[5] This has partly to do with the question of theological agenda. As long as theology is dominated by men of limited cultural (and social) background, one tends to attach importance to people who have a similar agenda. Additionally, one generally tends to favor not only the ones who think alike but also who are alike.

The result is that there is theology in general and additionally, there are specific theologies like feminist, Black, African, Asian, Mujerista, Minjung etc. The implication, mostly not openly pronounced, is that theology without epithets is real or somewhat universal, whereas theologies with labels are second-rate endeavors that may be of interest to the real academic theology by providing it material to develop further. However, as pointed out above, this theology without epithets could well be labelled as Eurocentric (or later even Anglocentric), male and bourgeois.

However, it would be unfair to label all western theologians as insensitive to the global realities of Christianity. Some of the European theologians considered among the greatest did react to the drastic changes in the state, nature and role of Christianity in the world. Karl Barth, towards the end of

---

4. An interesting exception to this is Broggi, *Diversity in the Structure of Christian Reasoning*.

5. A case in point would be the widely distributed *Modern Theologians* where only white males have reached heights that allow them a place in the chapter headings. The book has evolved into an increasingly plural collection by the way of extension in each new edition—adding chapters beyond the standard in theology.

his career, could be interpreted to pass the baton to theologians from the majority world.[6] Karl Rahner's work on the role of non-Christian religions in salvation addressed a question utterly central in the majority world.[7] Jürgen Moltmann was involved in an intensifying global theological dialogue which profoundly influenced his theological agenda.[8] In spite of the elevated status of these men in western theology, this openness has not expanded significantly especially in Europe. One of the reasons in Europe may be the precarious situation of theology in the European academy.[9] In such a situation, in order to secure the survival of the discipline at the university, one easily resorts to emphasizing the historical importance of theology and Christianity to western cultural roots and history, thereby, limiting the discipline often both culturally and denominationally. However, this efficiently blocks the way to renewal and regained relevance. Thus, the attempted goal is not achieved and irrelevant theology is pruned out from the branch of humanities at an increasing number of universities. However, this choice of means of survival is well in line with the equivalent ecclesiastic-political trend that attaches the hopes of European Christianity's survival to its role in the national identities in Europe. Even if many academic theologians promoting theology as a historical discipline probably do not realize it, this move plays into the hands of Christian nationalists by emphasizing the role of Christianity as a national identity-bearer.

This paralyzing limitedness in western theology stems basically from the European recent genealogy of ideas. Modern ideas, with an emphasis on rationality and science, challenged the older theologically geared grounds thinking. In the past, majority Christian views formulated the ideological hegemony, in cooperation with the political power. At least since the French Great Revolution, this was seriously challenged and an individual's freedom of conscience was emphasized. The basic assumption of this emphasis was faith in human rationality. If humans just gained freedom and would be enlightened to objective scientific truths, they would obviously choose them.

Since then, one of the main tasks of academic theology has been to relate to modern thought. At times, the choice has been a frontal attack

---

6. Matheny, *Contextual Theology*, 59–60.

7. Rahner, *Anonymous Christianity*; Rahner, *Observations on the Problem of Anonymous Christians*.

8. For example, in 1972 he refers to a couple of Latin American liberation theologians, and two Japanese thinkers (Moltmann, *Der gekreuzigte Gott*) whereas in 1997 Latin American liberation theologians are already one major discussion partner (Moltmann, *Gott im Projekt der modernen Welt*).

9. See, e.g., Moltmann, *Gott im Projekt der modernen Welt*, 219.

against modernity, and at times, contextualization in the modern world.[10] In both, unsurprisingly, there has been a common denominator in that religion is seen still to have a meaningful role in the modern world, and that religion is approached confessionally. Confessionality, in this case, means that religion is approached from within and argumentation is related to a specific faith community's argumentation even if it might not be in line with it. In theology, whenever it is constructive and not only an analysis of someone's constructive approach, one stakes religious truth claims which makes it confessional, regardless of the contents of those truth claims, or whether the confession is ecclesiastic or the theologian's private confession.

This confessionality has placed theology at loggerheads with modernist science. In spite of religion and science at time reaching a truce, whereby science was granted sovereignty in the increasing area of empirically provable facts and religion in the shrinking gaps in between them, scientists have sometimes proposed their metaphysical convictions as scientific truths. In this case, rationalistic (or sometimes also mystical-religious), conclusions based on the empirical are applied to the non-empirical gaps as well.[11]

As the ideological hegemony was transposed from Christian faith to empirical sciences following the Enlightenment, and religion retreated into the disprovable gaps, religion increasingly became a matter of private conviction. As a result, universal truth claims would begin to appear preposterous, considering that at the same time Europe was growing increasingly plural in terms of religion, especially after World War II. Yet, theology continued being confessional—for to approach religion confessionally is what defines theology. This resulted in theology turning into an anomaly in academia. From a modernist point of view, it lacks scientific rigor and, therefore has no place in academia. Whereas, from a late modern perspective the obvious lack of pluralism makes it naïve and limited, as theology is generally still an exclusively Christian exercise in Europe.

Is the only way forward to do away with theology and replace it with religious studies that have embraced the modernist project?[12]

---

10. The frontal attack approach was most visible in the Protestant Fundamentalism (see Bendroth, "Fundamentalist Imagination"), whereas liberal theology represented an attempt to contextualize Christianity into the European and American academic male sphere (on liberal theology see Buckley, "Revisionists and Liberals").

11. An example of the first, namely, rationalistic conclusions on existential questions by a natural scientist is Richard Dawkins (*God Delusion*) and of mystical-religious Fritjof Capra (*Tao of Physics*).

12. It must be noted that not all religious studies would fit in this category as experiential turn has contributed to the blurring of boundaries between the two disciplines. See, for example, Ferrer and Sherman, "Introduction."

The Theologian's Bubble of Reality Holds No More

In spite of the apparent juxtaposition between modernist rationalism and Christian theology, these two were also engaged in a loop of mutual assertion in two ways. First, both partners strongly propagated (their version) of the Truth. Secondly, they both mostly operated within the national projects.

Varying temporally, locally and denominationally, there has been palpable tension or even conflict between "scientific" worldviews[13] and Christian theologies. In the case of communist regimes, it was a matter of a mortal conflict, whereas in the western block the theme "faith and science" was played out in multiple variations. Within the modern framework, in spite of the occasional conflict, the idea of one undivided reality was the common ground for modern science and theology.[14] The point was rather to convince the other about the veracity of one's conception of reality. In much of modern western academic theology, there has been an attempt to construct systems where modern science and the Christian faith could be reconciled.

The other common denominator was the national projects. Although both science and Christianity hold universalizing ideals, they mostly conformed to the project of the construction of national states. In Christian churches, this became most clearly visible in Protestant and Eastern Orthodox circles, where the dominant churches in their respective regions developed into national or even state churches like in the Northern and Eastern Europe. Despite its decidedly universal character, even Catholicism became a vessel for nationalist, and sometimes even fascist, endeavors like in Franco's Spain or Salazar's Portugal or in Latin America. Similarly, science was also harnessed to serve the national interest, and in times of conflict Christians and scientists alike seldom provided much opposition to the hollow nationalist war-frenzy.

Resulting from the competing capitalist and communist economic systems and nationalisms, despite the modern ideal of the one undivided truth, the world became a battleground of competing truths. However, these national truths often gained a hegemonic position in nationalist states so that the justification and existence of the nation and the national state

---

13. Worldview is used in this book to mean a person's cosmology that covers both the basic understanding of material and possible spiritual realities. Additionally, epistemology or theory of knowledge belong to worldview. The human being's position and role in and relation to the cosmos plays a central role in worldview.

14. Lesslie Newbigin's (*Gospel in a Pluralist Society*) concern for maintaining trust in science under the onslaught of postmodern critique is quite telling, especially when he considers that it is Christian theologians' responsibility to do so.

went uninterrogated. In most cases, the national narrative was built on homogeneity: ethnic, linguistic, cultural, religious, among other forms of unity. The result was that the national plausibility pattern reigned supreme in one country, whereas across the border there was a completely different plausibility pattern.[15] What was true in the Soviet Union was a blatant lie in neighboring Norway—in history, economics, politics, religion, culture. Each nation clung to its own universal truth. These truths could stand on their clay feet because the connections between the nations were limited and, thereby, the incompatibility of outside perspectives could be dismissed as curiosities.

All through the twentieth century, there were growing voices challenging the modern concept of truth. These voices, opting for the polyvalence of truth and the deconstruction of essentializing and reifying tendencies of social realities like nation or gender, came to be labeled for example postmodern or late modern, depending on the emphasis and degree of critique against modernism.[16] This critique often took the form of judgment against the grand narratives, both in terms of content and use. Several historical developments contributed to the development of pluralism in the western societies which was the precondition of postmodernism.

Globalization was intensifying through colonialism, Christian mission and trade in the earlier part of the century. Later, heightening industrialization led to labor-based immigration to the western industrialized countries, creating notable cultural-religious minorities. Eventually, tourism increased the movement between different parts of the world. Intensified means of communication, especially the internet, have made the world shrink like never before. An affluent person with the right passport and sufficient funds can communicate with any part of the world at any time and usually travel there within a day. Western societies began to turn pluralistic not only through immigration but also from within, with political, cultural and religious alternative movements, which often borrowed some of their inspiration from outside of the West. The quintessential white man started to see his hegemonic position crumble.

While western societies are increasingly pluralized through the introduction of new minorities, there has also been a counter-trend of visibility and vociferousness among longstanding minorities, including ethnic, religious and sexual. Thus, the turn from monolithic to pluralistic societies is partly true and partly a fabrication, as there never were any completely

---

15. On plausibility patterns see Berger and Luckmann, *Social Construction of Reality*, 110–21.

16. See Cahoone, "Introduction," 1–2.

unified nation states. After all, according to Benedict Anderson, nation states are imagined communities where the unity builds on the shared image.[17] This does not, however, render these communities less real. Rather, the ground on which these communities are built is not an objective but subjective reality. Academic Christian theologies with their universal claims were a part of this game. They thrived in national states' bubbles of reality where there was only one nation, one religion and one reality (even though whether it was religious or "scientific" was often a matter of contention). By their very existence, these universalizing theologies provided support for patriarchy, nationalism and confessionalism. Within their limited bubbles, these theologies could be universal, relevant and credible as the correct interpretations of the Christian Truth.

In the pluralistic western societies, marked by an intensified experience of global unity, any universalizing claims are met with deep suspicion. Even the nationalist populist desire to seal off the rest of the world beyond the national boundaries and restore national unity is an acknowledgement of this pluralism. If all immigrants left, and all ethnically national people would think alike, one could relive the mythical golden era—or so the argument goes. However, as demonstrated, the monolithic paradise lost does not exist even for the nationalist populist.

In grass-roots theology, Christian churches can, if they so will, continue marketing their doctrines as the universal Truth very much in the same manner as any café can claim to have the "world's best coffee." Academic theology, however, has the responsibility to be critical and to attempt to formulate argumentation in a manner that communicates across religious divides. This is so for two reasons, one stemming from the nature of theology and the other from the nature of academic reasoning. Theology is the result of mission in the sense of it emanating in the situation of encountering the other.[18] Either one needed to explain the meaning and content of one's Christian faith to people of other persuasions or one needed to clarify the content of faith vis-à-vis those one attempted to label as heretics. In both cases it was a matter of convincing the other—and oneself, as well. Academic argumentation, in spite of occasional sectarianism in schools of thought, is in principle an exercise of open discussion where the most convincing argument wins. Academic theology cannot be an exception to this.

---

17. Anderson, *Imagined Communities*.

18. Kähler, *Schriften*, 89, 189–90. See also Bevans and Schroeder, *Constants in Context*, 11; Bosch, *Transforming Mission*, 16. Kähler (*Schriften*, 89) emphasizes that especially "Heidenmission" (mission to the gentiles) is the parent of theology thereby placing special emphasis on the encounter with the other.

Even if a theologian would not subscribe to a relativistic worldview, due to philosophical and/or theological reasons, the plurality of worldviews is an issue that one is required to address not only as a topic to be dealt with but as the context in which theology is constructed. This plurality needs to be a part of the package from the very beginning. Traditional western academic theology is generally ill equipped for this task due to its long term engagement with modernism. Methods, approaches and theories in mainstream western theology have often been bypassing the pluralization process of our societies.

Both from the perspective of credibility as well as of ethics, western Christian theology needs to be thoroughly renewed. It has no space in western academia if it only concentrates on defending the existing positions by arguing for the historical relevance of theology. In that case, theology can be transferred to departments of history to aid analyses of western intellectual history. Academic theology only as Christian theology has no place in western academia in the long run when the level of religious participation in the former national and state churches is declining, and has not even been replenished by growing churches established by immigrants. Ethically, explicit or implicit Eurocentric universal claims tally all too well with the colonial project. The expulsion of such theology from the academia is, therefore, even a righteous endeavor.

Mission Studies and Contextual Theology as the Broadening of Horizons

Mission Studies has represented the broadening of horizons in theology, insofar as through it, non-western cultures and religions were gradually introduced to the theological agenda, resulting in contextual theologies where the interaction between faith and culture or social reality was brought to the forefront.

Expressed in a pointed and generalized way, Mission Studies during colonialism used to be a rather colonial study of a rather colonial Christian enterprise. The reality, of course, was that there were a multitude of approaches to colonial atrocities, colonialism itself, Eurocentric paternalism as well as local religions and cultures.[19] At any rate, one cannot overlook the fact that the high tide of the western mission was contemporary to western colonialism, and these two were interwoven in many ways.

Apart from the similarities and points of conjunction, there was an inherent difference between mission and colonialism in terms of their logic.

19. See Vähäkangas, "Can the Study of Mission Become Postcolonial?"

In colonialism, the mother country was in the center in all perceivable manners: administration, hierarchy, resources, economic structures etc. In mission, it was the (expected) convert who was in the center. The goal of the western mission at the time was to convert individuals or peoples, or to establish churches. In each variation, the goal is inherently bound to the local people. This was the case even in the most paternalistic and Eurocentric mission enterprises, where local cultures were completely despised and the goal was to transform the converts into Europeans, albeit with strange physical appearances. Colonial logic, however, does not rule out a genocide and colonization of the country with settlers, unlike Christian missions that aimed to Christianize (and alongside it, usually civilize or westernize) the local population.

The relative proximity to the locals resulted in many missionaries turning into skillful ethnographers and eventually studying theological questions related to the local Christians' spheres of life.[20] Consequently, missionaries and missions were generally eager to support the creation of local contextual theologies, albeit often within the parameters of one's denominational preferences. Thus, the role of the context of theology was profoundly acknowledged in many missionary circles from early on. In this manner, what should have become a concern for all theology—western theology and ecclesial practices often quickly losing contact to people's everyday realities—became predominantly the hobby of mission scholars. Even in cases when there were serious attempts towards contextualization, like, e.g., Rudolf Bultmann's demythologization (*Entmythologisierung*), the similarities between the western and non-western projects were often overlooked along with opportunities for mutual enrichment.[21] A partial reason for the lack of communication may be that while missionary circles tended to be on the conservative side, western contextual theologies (which never called themselves contextual but were very conscious of adapting to modernity) often had a radical or liberal edge.

Gradually, contextual theologies of the majority world would stand on their own feet as majority world Christianity grew academically stronger. This was first the case on a larger scale with Latin American liberation theologies starting in the 1960s. The significance of contextual theologies to theology has been their role in reminding western academic theologians

---

20. In Tanzania, Bruno Gutmann (1876–1966; Jaeschke, *Bruno Gutmann*) would serve as a paradigmatic pioneer-era example whereas Raimo Harjula is a later missionary example of a champion of African theology and study of African traditions. See Harjula, *God and the Sun in Meru Thought*; Harjula, "Towards a Theologia Africana."

21. E.g., Bultmann, *Jesus Christus und die Mythologie*.

that, as all theology is crafted in context, there can be no universal theology.[22] Additionally, contextual theologies have diversified theological enterprises so that even if the paradigmatic middle-aged Euro-American white man remains the dominant type, there is recognition of the existence of other theologies and theologians as well. Contextual theologies have also reminded academic theology of its mutual dependency with faith communities while western academic theology, especially of the more liberal strand, has not always been strong in that. Without faith communities' interest in academic theology, there is little value in it outside the limited academic theological circles, and, as described above, theology is an endangered species in the academia. Thus, there would hardly be students of theology without communal rooting, thereby risking the future of the discipline. This interest in academic theology stems from relevance in two senses. On one hand, academic theology should deal with issues that are relevant for faith communities and use their life and thought as a starting point. On the other hand, academic theology must provide added value, in the sense of challenging the faith communities' traditional approaches. Finally, contextual theologies have explored ways to also interact with academic disciplines other than philosophy, most notably sociology, political studies and cultural/social anthropology.[23]

Meanwhile, Mission Studies increasingly paid attention to local initiatives in majority world Christianity, which meant relative marginalization of western missionaries who had been the main focus of especially earlier mission historical research.[24] Mission Studies have maintained a close link with contextual theologies. However, they tend to be more empirically oriented than many contextual theologies. Previously, mission theology held the place of pride in Mission Studies, but now various empirical approaches seem to have become the mainstream.[25] While mission as an object of study has roused interest outside theology, for instance, among general historians due to the abundant data on intercultural encounters available in mission archives, what flies under the flag of Mission Studies or missiology has remained almost entirely a theological enterprise. This means that the discipline has remained theological, making one of the major tasks of

22. Bergmann, *Gud i funktion*, 13–30.

23. See Frostin, *Liberation Theology*, 9–10.

24. In this sense, it is telling that the history of the International Association for Mission Studies was titled *Witness for World Christianity* (Anderson et al.).

25. This was clearly visible in the International Association for Mission Studies general assembly in Seoul in 2016 where there were about 130 papers, and the purely theoretical-theological approach was a small minority in comparison to different empirically-based papers.

Mission Studies within academic theology that of serving as a reminder of Christianity's global character and the plurality of religions.

World Christianity as the Renewal of Mission Studies

Mission Studies as a moniker for the discipline has often become a liability in western secular academia, although in many majority world and confessional contexts it still enjoys relative popularity.[26] In the West, mission is branded colonial, intrusive to people of other faiths and narrow-minded.[27] Redefinitions of the term mission have not made the situation any better because there does not exist a commonly agreed upon decolonial definition of the term that has gained recognition beyond the discipline. In this junction, decoloniality would not only denote the end of overt colonial structures but also conscious attempts to break free from the inherited colonial patterns of thought that still largely direct the relations between the West and the former colonies.

That said, there have been various attempts to replace the title Mission Studies. Suggestions have included new names emphasizing the theological nature of the discipline, like Intercultural Theology or Interreligious Theology. In other cases, the title simply refers to the object of study, like World or Global Christianity or Christianity in the Non-Western World. Although these names do not reveal any allegiance to an older academic tradition, it is clear that the most significant numbers of the people involved in these studies come from a theological background. This means that the boundary between Mission Studies and the study of World Christianity is porous, as many scholars would feel familiar with both. However, the relationship that does require further clarification is between theology and World Christianity.

It goes almost without saying that World Christianity does not share the old school theological Eurocentrism. Rather, it can be seen as a critique of a theology that got stuck to western Christendom and missed what was possibly the greatest and fastest religious transformation in history: Christianity's demographic shift of gravity to the majority world.

Contextual theologies were an early reaction to theological Eurocentrism. There, in addition to paying attention to contexts and opening up to disciplines beyond philosophy, as indicated above, another major issue was the question of interlocutors. In these new theologies, the prime interlocutor was no longer the privileged academic but often, rather, the oppressed

---

26. See Bevans, "Migration and Mission," 179.
27. See Matheny, *Contextual Theology*, 3.

with whom and by whom these theologies were constructed, at least ideally.[28] In World Christianity, the question of context is central and openness, especially to empirical realities, allows many disciplines to contribute. However, the question about for whom, with whom and by whom World Christianity is done is not quite as articulated as in many contextual theologies. By virtue of World Christianity being more pronouncedly academic and definitely less ecclesiastic than many contextual theologies, it tends either to overlook the question of interlocutors or it implies a general decolonially minded academic audience. As no production of knowledge is innocent, this difference is notable. This difference may stem from the fact that this new discipline still needs to establish itself in the western academia.

Yet, another difference between contextual theologies and World Christianity lies in their methodology. Contextual theologies, in spite of their critiques of Eurocentric theology, generally still participate in the project of traditional theology, namely, making sense of the Christian faith. This sense-making is, in the case of contextual theologies, largely a logocentric exercise where written texts are made to relate to each other. The contextual theologies' insistence on lived realities seldom translates into major methodological modifications. References to lived realities often remain on an anecdotal level or are based on the author's life experience. World Christianity definitely differs here as, in many cases, the analysis of Christian faith in a context builds on robust empirical data. This data is often collected ethnographically or in other qualitative ways. This turn to empirical data is the next logical step in the work of dismantling the hierarchical and centralized ideas of faith communities and theology, started by contextual theologies. In contextual theologies, the consciously theologizing subject becomes central, resulting with the academic theologians gaining a pivotal position, despite attempts of the opposite. When Christianity is studied empirically a possibility opens up of listening to the, often oral, grass-roots theologies. However, this is not a sufficient precondition for decolonializing theology if the western epistemological ground remains unchanged.[29]

Does this mean that World Christianity should be the name for religious studies that concentrate on the study of Christianities (also) beyond the western cultural sphere? Do the researchers of World Christianity approach their topic from outside, as if uninvolved? Were it so, the launching of World Christianity would be for religious studies what Anthropology of Christianity is for anthropology. Traditionally, anthropology studied cultures foreign to the researcher and the western academic community.

---

28. Frostin, *Liberation Theology*, 6–11.
29. See Grosfoguel, "Decolonizing Post-Colonial Studies."

However, when anthropologists of religion could no longer ignore the rise of Christianity in many of their fields they began to address it, first in exotic places but then also back home.[30] Is there a difference between Anthropology of Christianity and World Christianity other than that World Christianity is not bound to the anthropological academic traditions?

Traditionally, an anthropologist is a specialist in crossing boundaries of culture.[31] She lands in an exotic culture, learns the language, customs and other cultural features, and makes an analysis of that with the help of anthropological theories (that her study ideally contributes to). She comes from outside but through her fieldwork becomes a marginal insider and, thus, a broker between the western academic and the local world. When returning home, she re-enters the western academic culture and interprets the object of study to the rest of that community. The boundaries between insiders and outsiders have been blurred in many ways when anthropology has been applied to western contexts and some of anthropologists do not come from the western cultural sphere. Yet, the described case still is the paradigmatic one even if criticized and rejected in some strands of anthropology. A scholar in World Christianity can work in the same manner of old-school anthropology, but that is not and has never been the standard approach because of the relative novelty of the discipline.

What makes it difficult for a researcher of World Christianity to wholly embrace the paradigmatic anthropological approach described above is that, inasmuch as World Christianity is a theological discipline, it profoundly shares the world that it is studying. World Christianity does not only cover faith communities of the majority world, but also of the West leading to the conclusion that in the theological endeavor of meaning-making, the researcher and the researched are facing the same task. It is, therefore, not so neat to make clear divisions between the field and academia back home. Late modern approaches in anthropology have also crossed the border between the researcher and the research object as the other and thus share a similar ethos with World Christianity. Considering the foundational criticism against theological Eurocentrism inherent in World Christianity, it would appear erroneous to simply bypass the world Christians' critique and replace the theological Eurocentrism with secular one. Therefore, it seems right to exercise World Christianity as a theological discipline, in the sense of entering into the theological debates of Christianity all around the world and remaining within that discourse also when analyzing the data.

---

30. Bialecki et al., "Anthropology of Christianity."
31. Michael Jackson's book title *At Home in the World* describes this ideal well.

Therefore, inasmuch as World Christianity can be seen as an offshoot of theology, the relationship between the researcher and the researched is very complex. Unlike anthropology, theology is a practice-related discipline, rather like law or medicine. Medicine is researched and practiced in hospitals and clinics, and law is being applied and pondered in courts. Likewise, theology grows and lives in faith communities where it is applied and practiced, and in the case of World Christianity, also researched. In medicine, there is generally one normative paradigm that is usually regarded as objective by the practitioners.[32] Theology, therefore, comes closer to law. Law is based on values, and there is no universally accepted approach to law. Yet, even if a lawyer represented a different school of thought, she can participate in the legal discussion and can analyze legal systems and theories other than her own. If she comes to a normative judgment of a legal theory, she has no Archimedean point to stand upon. Likewise, a theologian may be or may not be a member of the faith community she is studying. However, irrespective of her own convictions, she is a member of the community of theologians in search for transcendental meaning, and in this sense a stakeholder in the process of the faith community, irrespective of her own faith commitments.

If the researcher of World Christianity is a Christian theologian, as often is the case, the relationship between the researcher and the researched can get very complex, no matter how unproblematic the fieldwork might feel like. Beyond the usual issues surrounding power relations, also questions related to various fault-lines within Christianity or within a denomination or a church must be taken into account.[33] When there is a shared faith commitment on both sides, the researcher can simultaneously be a cultural outsider (eventually hopefully becoming a marginal insider) and an insider as a member of the same imagined community. However, if the variation between the researcher's confessional background and the studied community becomes extensive, there may be some doubt about belonging to the same imagined community, or it may be denied by one of the partners. Yet, there are bound to be many familiar elements in the studied community. In such a case, the studied could be seen as quasi-others.[34]

The World Christianity approach to the study of religion should be thoroughly post-colonial. This means that it may not take a western

---

32. This would not be case in pluralistic medicine, e.g., in China where the government fosters both school medicine and Chinese traditional medicine. Also, in some African countries, the state cooperates with traditional medicine practitioners.

33. On the complicated relations between the researcher and the researched when both are stakeholders in the same community see Vähäkangas, "Om mig, den andre."

34. See Vähäkangas, "How to Respect the Religious Quasi-Other?"

normative position, be it theological or secular. The faith of the studied communities has to be taken seriously and in case the researcher ventures into normative judgment, it needs to be system immanent. System immanence means that the phenomenon is assessed according to its own premises. For example, if a church claims to be proclaiming the prosperity gospel, one needs to figure out how one understands the term prosperity gospel in the church and compare it to the proclamation of that church to see whether this is the case.[35] Thus, the researcher's cultural and religious background does not become normative. That said, its influence on the research process is inevitable and needs to be assessed self-critically.

Theological Pluralism à la World Christianity

The renewal required of theology in western academia can model itself on World Christianity. What works for World Christianity, works *mutatis mutandis* in theology. The resulting theology (as a discipline) needs to be religiously, culturally and methodologically pluralistic.[36]

Academic theology as a discipline can no longer only be Christian because in today's pluralist societies there is no reason for academia to favor only one religion. After all, it is in the nature of openness of academic discourse that it welcomes plurality of voices. Muffling of differing voices is not in line with the community that is committed to searching the truth, no matter whether it is unattainable or not. While Christian traditions historically play a central role in the construction of European (and American) identities, one cannot overlook the Jewish and Muslim contributions of the past and present.[37] Today, the reality is far more plural, and academic theology needs not only to cover these three monotheistic religions from the Near East, but also any other major religions in each location.

The first step in encountering the challenge of religious pluralism is to acknowledge the syncretistic nature of all religions.[38] For some, this sounds like truism while many theologians still stick to the notions of pure religion. In the study of World Christianity, the interaction between Christianity and other religions is sometimes the central question and in most of the other

---

35. E.g., Vähäkangas, "Prosperity Gospel."

36. Thus also Phan, "Doing Theology in World Christianities."

37. This insight is extensively expressed in the Nordic joint Master's program Religious Roots of Europe, where the contributions of all the three monotheistic religions to European identity and culture are studied (https://www.lunduniversity.lu.se/lubas/i-uoh-lu-HARRE).

38. Vähäkangas, "Theo-logical Positions vis-à-vis Syncretism."

cases it simply cannot be overlooked. Thus, it constitutes an important dimension of the analysis. When much of such research is done on majority world Christianity, there is a danger of western theologians viewing majority world Christians as syncretistic while overlooking the syncretistic elements in their own theologies and churches. This hints to the tendency of Europeans to see majority world Christians first as specimen of ethnicities and only secondarily as Christians. Conversely, one often lumps Europeanness with Christianity in spite of the fact that we are speaking of the world's most secularized continent. When syncretistic elements mature enough, like in Europe, they tend to turn into pure orthodoxy. Moreover, a syncretistic attitude towards secular Enlightenment is often not considered to be such, as the counterpart is not seen to be a religion. Thus, what is done in the study of world Christianity needs to become a standard approach in theology.

Additionally, in world Christianity one can seldom bypass the question of interreligious relations. Christian life takes place in a world of religions and ideologies, and both Christian practice and theological thought need to be consciously placed in this context. Majority world Christianity, even in cases when it is now a majority in a given area, has usually only recently been a minority religion. Thus, encounters with the religious other are in its DNA, whereas in the West, the tradition of these encounters has often been forgotten and results in a European Christianity's Chihuahua-syndrome—a big dog's soul in a small body. Likewise, many former national or state churches have not become accustomed to a situation in which they represent the minority of the population and yet relate to other churches and religions as if they still were in the majority.

This interreligious encounter must be made the very core of theological exercise. Therefore, Christian theology must become a strand among others, incorporating Muslim, Jewish, Buddhist etc. theologies and theologians in faculties and departments.[39] This would inevitably lead to projects

---

39. E.g., in Münster there is Catholic, Protestant and Islamic theology, and in Free University of Amsterdam Protestant and Islamic theology. This approach comes close to the second of the three alternatives for theology described by Moltmann (*Gott im Projekt der modernen Welt*, 220–21). On Islamic theology in northern European universities, see Leirvik, "Islamic University Theology." What need to be noted from the outset is that different religions' approaches to critical examination and exposition of one's faith varies and one cannot expect that what might be called as Muslim, Jewish or Buddhist theology in the faculties of theology would be wholly equivalent to Christian theology. This is down to the differences between religions and the fact that these theologies do not share the same history of participation in western academia. Such an inclusion presupposes willingness to learn and adapt from both the old Christian academic theology and the other religions' theological traditions introduced into western academia.

of comparative theologies and interreligious theologies,[40] depending on the positions of the academic staff. What needs to be emphasized here is that the requirement of theology as a discipline to pluralize does not necessarily mean that all resulting theologies would be pluralistic. A pluralistic discipline is truly pluralistic when it allows for multiple voices. However, in general, a pluralistic context of theology can be expected to lead to an increasing number of pluralistic theologies.[41]

There are several ways of dealing with the challenge of religious and ideological pluralism in a situation in which a hegemonic position is not attainable for an academic theology, not even in a limited sense of a national-confessional reality bubble. One would be to give up any metaphysical truth claims and simply concentrate on the analysis of existing theologies and religious phenomena. However, in that case, theology would lose its central task of posing the fundamental human existential questions and turn into religious or historical studies. Another possibility is to resort to absolute or temporary relativism. In absolute relativism, one claims that no credible judgments are possible between, say, religious movements. In temporary relativism the judgment is postponed to the possible eschaton.[42] However, I do not need to wait until the eschaton to judge that the bloodthirsty ISIS which sets up violent regimes is ethically less acceptable than Engaged Buddhism which is a kind of Buddhist liberation theology,[43] for example. It means that I have a certain set of values and truths against which I assess religious ideas and practices, even if I might shy away from expressing them in less obvious cases. In order for these values and truths to serve a pluralist theology, they need to be formulated in an ecumenical and interreligious theological dialogue and be open to modifications, and even rejection, when encountering valid and convincing arguments. This is open confessionality, in contrast to closed confessionality where the outcome of theologizing is

---

40. Comparative theologies could be seen as theologies where different faith traditions are involved in the theological argumentation in a comparative manner, whereas, in interreligious theology the resulting theology consciously takes influences and contexts from several religions. However, they can be defined in various ways. See, e.g., Clooney, *Comparative Theology*; Knitter, "Comparative Theology." See also Tracy, "Theology: Comparative Theology"; Leirvik, "Islamic University Theology," 133.

41. The concept of pluralism is tricky in theologies of religions because there does not exist a consensus on what pluralism might mean. Thus, Gavin D'Costa (*Meeting of Religions and the Trinity*) analyzes that theologians who perceive themselves as pluralists are actually not.

42. Hick, *Faith and Knowledge*, 178.

43. Engaged Buddhism could be described as Buddhist liberation theology in the sense that it engages strongly in issues of social justice. See Queen and King, *Engaged Buddhism*.

known already at the outset. Closed confessional theology would be theology within a certain denominational and school of theology mold no matter what happens. Possible truth claims in a pluralistic theological project must be based on a theory of knowledge that allows for not only truth claims but also modesty and flexibility.

In World Christianity, one tends to celebrate cultural pluralism. This is very much in line with the Zeitgeist of globalization. Western academic Christian theology is still relatively monocultural, as outlined above. Theology can no longer afford to externalize the task of cultural plurality to contextual theologies, Mission Studies or World Christianity. Rather, the multiplicity of voices in terms of cultures and subcultures need to be recognized throughout. All theology is contextual, in the sense of it being constructed in a time and a place, and failure to recognize this does not make it universal. Once one has recognized the cultural boundedness of one's work, there is an opportunity to ponder how to best communicate across the disciplinary, cultural, linguistic, religious etc. borders.

Methodological pluralism is probably one of the fields where there is the most willingness to change within theology. World Christianity is not the only model pupil in the class; there are also other theologians who are open and innovative in terms of seeking new partner disciplines, methods and theories. This openness is generally a prerequisite for innovative approaches in any humanities. After the hegemonic era of grand narratives, religions can no longer be approached solely as ideas, ideals, doctrines or principles. Lived religion cannot be bypassed in theological studies any longer. These methodologically progressive researchers have already largely moved on to incorporating lived realities into their agenda, and the rest of theology is to follow. While the death notice of grand narratives was definitely premature, the world of ideas must today be related to tangible and social realities also in the study of religion and theology.

Academic theology, as a Eurocentric discipline, needs to be renewed if it is to retain its academic and ethical credibility. This renewal needs to also account for its self-understanding, so that theology is no longer a Christian enterprise in dialogue with western modernity but, rather, an interreligious process in which religions and (post)modernities are in interaction with each other. Instead of earlier closed national-confessional bubbles, theology needs to exercise open confessionalism where truth claims do not lead to exclusion but, rather, encourage the inclusion of dialogue partners. This renewal also needs to cover methodologies by opening up towards lived religion, without losing sight of the role of the contents of faith and religious ideals.

World Christianity, as an academic discipline, can serve as a resource in this renewal because it can be seen as a result of a similar process of decolonization in Mission Studies. In this process, Mission Studies and World Christianity have had to engage in a global balancing act between western secular academia and Christian faith communities (that sometimes run universities or theological seminaries of their own) all over the world. If this discipline were expelled from academia, that would be a loss for both academia and the discipline. The discipline can provide academia with vistas on the most populous religion around the globe that other, less involved, disciplines would miss. The rest of academia serves as a constant source of methodological and theoretical contributions, as well as constructive criticism. Losing connection and credibility among the faith communities, on the other hand, would have strong adverse effects on the social impact of the discipline and, thereby, indirectly on the credibility of the discipline. World Christianity can, and should, function as a critical partner in dialogue with faith communities. Likewise, theology needs to find itself a new post-colonial and academically credible role that does not lose relevance in the eyes of the faith communities.

Even Secular Societies Need Open-minded Theology

The Enlightenment idea of the moral and practical supremacy of the secular state over a confessional state has become almost a universal credo of politics in many countries that are strongly religiously plural.[44] Alongside the practical-ethical triumph of the secular model of governance in democracies, a number of modern myths have become almost hegemonic. Four of these modern myths relate to secularization and the secular state: the existence of religion as a distinct category, individuality of religion, disappearance of religion with the scientific progress, and secular objectivity. These four myths render secular society immune against religion, in the sense that it can behave and exist as if religions did not exist. Let us begin by examining the four myths and their impact on state-religion relations. After that, we will relate the discussion to the role of academic theology in a secular society.

Religion is a slippery and contested concept and even the scholars of religion cannot come to an agreement on how to define it. Considering the

---

44. However, for example Lebanon that houses three major religious groups (Christians, Shia and Sunni Muslims) as well as a number of minor religious traditions has a confessional political system where the top political positions are distributed according to religious belonging. Nassar, "Sectarian Political Cultures."

difficulties in its definition, Enlightenment thought has devoted surprisingly much time relating to it. In a way, one can claim that Enlightenment constructed religion as its other. Before the Enlightenment, the word religion meant Christianity for Christians, *din* was Islam for Muslims, and so forth. However, there was no general category of religion. For Enlightenment thinkers, religion became a useful general category in which to lump all the irrational and superstitious elements of cultures. What is noteworthy is that useful and clever elements of, for example, Christian faith, such as acceptable dimensions of ethics and metaphysics, were placed under the category of philosophy. In France, even today, much of the most interesting theology is constructed under the banner of philosophy, while theology is often relegated to a relatively narrowly ecclesiastic-confessional exercise in the closed sense.[45] Enlightenment needs religion as its counterpart, for this task it is important to imagine religion as a distinct category. In other words, modernity needs to essentialize religion in order to argue for its raison d'être and viability.[46]

What is problematic with the idea of religion as an entity separate from the rest of culture is that nobody seems to be able to point out where the borderline between religion and culture runs. This is because culture and religion cannot actually be separated. Most African languages did not even have a word for religion before the advent of Islam or Christianity. In today's Tanzania it is not at all uncommon for a person to maintain that she has no religion. You should not mistake that person for an atheist, though. Not having a religion simply means that one is not Christian or Muslim, but that one only follows the culture of one's ethnic group. This culture invariably contains belief in God, spirits or the likes, and rituals that an outsider would label religious. From the point of view of the person concerned, they are integral parts of her culture, inseparable as a distinct unit called religion.

In the secularized post-Enlightenment Europe, it is supposedly possible to make such distinctions, if not separations. This naïve faith in distinctions occasionally yields hilarious results. In Sweden, there has been wide discussion on the acceptability of school year closing ceremonies in churches. Some have maintained that it works against the principle of secularity of the state, whereas, some others point out that it is just a question of Swedish tradition and culture. As a result of this debate, the Swedish National Agency for Education has formulated a detailed, but not particularly clear, policy on schools' visits to churches, mosques, synagogues, and

---

45. Examples of interesting philosophers who were/are simultaneously notable theologians are René Girard and Paul Ricoeur.

46. On religion as a modern western concept see Asad, *Formations of the Secular*; Fitzgerald, *Religion and the Secular*.

other places of worship. This document outlines that there may not be any "confessional" elements in such visits like prayers, sermons or blessings. However, a popular hymn from the Church of Sweden hymnal may be sung because it is tradition.[47] Thus, the fact that the hymn traditionally belongs to the end of year festivities at schools makes it non-confessional? Even in post-Christian Europe it is impossible to draw definite lines of demarcation between secular and religious, within cultures. Therefore, as cultural beings, humans are also religious beings. This interwovenness of religion and the rest of culture means that the secular state-ideal is just an ideal because you cannot separate politics and religion or state administration and religion. Denial of the religious dimensions of the nation leads to blindness that is not useful for equality between religious groups, but opens the gates for majority religion's covert influence, a governmental crypto-confessionalism.

However, although religion as a distinct phenomenon is a modern invention, it is difficult to avoid this category. Therefore, even in this study, I will continue using the term, albeit with the cognizance of the nature of this concept as a modern invention. Likewise, as I will argue below, there is actually no such thing as a secular state. Rather, it is an ideal. Yet, for the sake of brevity, I will use the term "secular state" for states that claim to be secular.

The second popular modern myth on religion is that religion belongs to the sphere of the personal and individual. This is one of the foundational principles of the Enlightenment ideal of a secular state. However, it is naïve to envision that the separation between the (majority) church and the state would lead to a situation where an individual leaves her religion in the bedroom and/or kitchen when going to work or getting involved in politics or social life. Firstly, as argued above, religions are an integral, and even indistinguishable, part of culture. Therefore, it is difficult to think what exactly should be left behind when entering the wider society. Secondly, a sharp separation between the personal or individual and political or social is a misconception of human nature. While striving for a distinction between an institution and a private person[48] is a requirement of running a modern bureaucracy, the person who occupies the office cannot be ignored. That said, there is a difference in how various persons carry out their official duties, depending not only their abilities but also their values and ethics. Additionally, as critical scholarship, for example feminist scholarship, has pointed out: the personal and the individual are deeply political—home and family, irrespective of its size and form, is a foundational political and social

---

47. Skolverket, "Skol- och förskolverksamhet i kyrkan," 5.

48. On Weber's views on "Amt"—office—as the central dimension of functioning bureaucracy see Krems, "'Bürokratie' bei Max Weber."

unit. In democracies this observation is easily overlooked. However, in totalitarian systems, where political activity is suppressed, politics is largely played out in the domain where religion is supposed to retreat to in order not to be mixed up with politics. Thirdly, religions are a fundamentally communal phenomenon. They thrive as communities and an important, often the most important, element of religious life is communal worship. Thus, to imagine away the communal dimension of religion is to misconceive the phenomenon. No matter whether we want it or not, religion is not only an individual matter but, as long as it exists, it will have its repercussions on the society at large.

The third popular modern myth is the secularization theory, or the disappearance of religion. As outlined above, the secularization theory has been largely dismissed as a universal theory. There is even talk of the "return of religion."[49] However, rather than religion returning, it is a matter of modern secularism softening up due to increasing pluralism, so that religion is noticed again. While the death of religion is an exaggeration, its forms, modes and roles in society are in a constant flux.

Fourthly, and finally, secular modernism has a strong tendency of presenting itself as the scientifically objective position. One could maintain that this is the cornerstone of modern credo.[50] As I will discuss in the next chapter, this scientific objectivism has been challenged from within science as well as from outside, for example, from philosophy. One way of attempting to save modern objectivism is to make a distinction between facts and values. Facts would then belong to the sphere of objective knowledge and values rendered dependent on personal convictions, including religious ones. While one could imagine how certain mechanical readings of measurements in natural sciences might not be affected by values, the planning of research procedures even in the natural sciences can hardly be value-free. Does one accept, avoid or completely reject the use of animals in testing? How big risks in order to reach certain gains in human pharmacological testing one is prepared to take? What is worthwhile researching? All these are primarily questions of values, not of facts, yet they can become essential issues in defining the results at the end of the scientific research process.

Scientific objectivism is a philosophical choice and a position based on an individual value judgment. You can only believe in objectivism if you want to.

The four modern myths above cannot serve as the basis of producing a purely secular state out of which religion has been sanitized. Religion

---

49. See McClure, "Post-Secular Culture."
50. Grosfoguel, "Decolonizing Post-Colonial Studies," 5–7.

cannot be defined and limited either as a distinct dimension of culture or as a distinct dimension of private life.[51] It does not disappear, nor does it automatically represent a flawed and superstitious subjectivist view on reality as opposed to modern scientific objectivity. Therefore, the phenomenon of religion is, and will be, a part of social, political, and economic life even of modern secular societies.

Due to the ideological opposition between modern secularism as an ideology and religions, forms of religion claiming epistemological hegemony or unwilling to adapt to pluralist realities lock horns with modern secular states. In such situations, religion can be a very disruptive social force. Secular states often lack the means, skills and even interest to encounter religious plurality and non-conformist (vis-à-vis modernism) forms of religion—until it is too late and a conflict erupts. The conflictual relations between some Muslim communities, or forms of Islam, and western secular states are a sad story of mutual incapability of communication. Considering that western secular states have much larger resources than the, mostly immigrant and often marginalized, Muslim communities, this must be preliminarily counted as a failure of the secular states. On both sides, there is a lack of abilities and means for successful and meaningful communication—the worlds have been too far from each other and secular religion-blindness has greatly contributed to this, when all forms of Islam have been interpreted through the individualistic modern paradigm.

Religious studies can contribute to an increased understanding of religions on the side of the state by raising the consciousness and level of knowledge on religions. On the side of religious communities, religious studies can increase the level of knowledge of other religions and of one's own religion to an extent. As such, religious studies can contribute to the general level of knowledge and facilitate dialogue.

However, when there are dysfunctional or disruptive theologies in the religious communities, religious studies cannot challenge them from inside the way theology does because religious studies does not participate in the discourse of the religion. Religious studies are supposed to merely describe and analyze them or when they take a critical stance on the studied religion that is not done system immanently, using the argumentation and logic of the religion. Religious renewal, innovation and adaptation to new contexts come thus rather from theology than from religious studies. All religious communities theologize; make sense of their faith and relate it to the context. However, theologies in religious communities tend not to be critical

---

51. See, e.g., Hiebert, "Critical Contextualization," 288.

in relation to the community's self-certainties, nor are there often many resources or external challenges available.

It is here that academic theology reveals its usefulness for the secular state. One does not usually realize why the former mainline churches have much fewer difficulties in encountering modernity than most of the other forms of religion. This is due to the fact that they have been utilizing the resources of academic theology for hundreds of years, resulting in a continuous flow of robust challenges from the universities. In Roman Catholic theology, one sometimes refers to academic theology as a quasi-Magisterium, in the sense that one of its tasks is to critically contribute to the teaching of the church. In academia, theologians were provided spaces that are safe from direct use of ecclesiastic power. Thus, there was the possibility of the emergence of historical critical studies of the Bible. Without theology being studied in universities, this would probably not have taken place, or if it had, there would have been a considerable delay. The results of historical critical Biblical studies have been thorough and have arguably provided former mainline churches major tools to relate to modernity in various ways. The wishes of the emergence of European Islam, that are sometimes heard, remain pious desires in case there are no safe spaces of creating daring and critical theologies. This would not have happened within Christianity without academia and is not likely happen in Islam, either. The difference between the two is that Christian theology had the possibility of developing when theology was still a priority in the universities whereas secularism is now hampering the development of Islamic theology in Europe.

Theological academia, if it grows to be appropriately multi-religious, can serve as a space to create a common language and visions, allowing for the possibility of participating in common language games. This would not necessarily mean that the result would be interreligious theology in the sense of one theology serving several religions nor that religious communities would adopt this common language. However, university-trained theologians would be able to communicate with each other and, beyond theology, towards the rest of the society thereby functioning as brokers between religious communities and the rest of the society.

The resulting academic theology, if true to its calling and if it is to be of use for the larger society, needs to take the present context seriously. In the following chapter, the concept of contextuality will be discussed in more detail.

4

On Contextuality in Theology[1]

As has been argued above, any theology is inevitably bound to its context. The World Christianity approach to theology is an acknowledgement of contextuality that situates contextuality in the globalizing and multireligious world. However, early contextual theology suffered sometimes of isolationist cultural romanticism which downplayed the profound manners in which cultures interact and blend.

A proper understanding of theology requires an adequate picture of the interchange between context and theology. Therefore, the three following chapters will be dedicated to that topic. In this chapter, the treatment of the topic begins with general discussion regarding the relationship between religious truth and its context-boundedness, on one hand, and its roots in Christian traditions, on the other. Thereafter, there will be an exposition of earlier proposals on how to see and classify the contextual process. The following chapter will then contain my proposal on the contextual process in theology.

Theology and Positionality

Any academic enterprise, theology included, even in our late modern world, needs to be primarily interested in finding the truth or truths no matter how the concept of truth is interpreted. This may sound as a truism for some but that it is so only for some tells us about the present intellectual climate. Theology should always be constructed in a fruitful (and sometimes painful) tension between the uncompromising spirit of pursuing the truth at

---

1. An earlier version of chapters 4 and 5 has previously been published as "Modelling Contextualization in Theology" in *Swedish Missiological Themes*. I thank SMT for the permission to publish this expanded version.

all costs and one's identity. Or in other words, theology happens in tension between neutrality and commitment.[2] In any constructive theology, the theologian, or the constructor, is in the focus no matter whether she wants it or not. Even when a theologian intends to remain purely in an analytical role and avoids taking any constructive role, the choice of the topic and the method of analysis inevitably bring the researcher into focus. Theologizing is an enterprise in which the subject cannot be separated from the object. One cannot have God as the direct object of study and, therefore, the object is revelation in one form or another. In any case, revelation is a matter of human reception and eventually of human interpretation of that which is judged to be divine revelation by the theologian in question. Because human agency, in the form of the thinker, cannot be separated from the theological process, theology becomes a nodal point of different dimensions of the theologian's individual and collective identity. Any theology inevitably reflects the theologians' background but is not reduced to that due to the human ability to transcend oneself, or to reach for new horizons. This is a result of the power of human imagination or intellectual freedom.[3]

Therefore, Christian theology is never only Christian but it involves many other dimensions of identity as well. Thus, no one can ever be only a Christian; there are always several other identities, as well. They can be related to ethnicity, nationality, race,[4] social class, gender, sexual orientation, occupation, educational background, membership in different social entities, and so on. In theological processes, these identities appear either as concealed or open realities. They are concealed in the case when the theologian does not openly ponder the influence of her personality on the process, and open to the extent the identities are reflected upon. Typically, the denominational identities tend to be openly expressed in theology because they are often unavoidably visible when a theologian builds on a specific theological tradition. Many other types of identities are more commonly concealed, unless they represent the other—one that is not a European/American white petit bourgeois heterosexual male of a relatively advanced age. Other identifications tend to be rendered explicitly visible as they are specifically labelled. Thus, there is theology and feminist theology, theology and African theology, theology and LBGTI theology and many more.

2. McGrath, *Christian Theology*, 171–3.
3. Rahner, *Foundations of Christian Faith*, 31–35.
4. Writing this in Stellenbosch, South Africa, one cannot avoid remarking the role of racial identities, a phenomenon often discreetly overlooked and denied. The history of racism cannot be deleted from the consciousness of humanity, not even in societies where one has the luxury to decide not to perceive the various ways in which racial prejudices still function in our communities.

As long as the theologian conforms to the norm and does not work on a theological construction that challenges the normative views of the human agent behind and within the theological process, it is traditionally viewed as a matter of real theology. The one diverging from the hegemonic norm needs to label her theology to denote the difference. This leads to several results. First, the author's identity is affirmed by this marker of identity. However, at the same time, this label affirms the marginality of the person and their theology. In the following, I will be often referring to examples from Africa because that is the context in which I have mostly taught, researched and constructed theology. In the case of African Christian theology, one makes a strong claim of two dimensions of identity at the same time, just the way one does with any given theology with a denominator. Thus, an African Christian theologian is an African and a Christian at the same time. There may be differing opinions as to which of these intertwining and intersecting identities is more basic or dominant, or how the two are equal. However, both dimensions need to be present for contextually relevant Christian theology in Africa. In all circumstances, there is a need to satisfy the demands of both dimensions of one's identity.[5]

However, this is not necessarily a starting point which would definitely need to dim the zeal to search for the truth. In contemporary thought many tend to forgo the idea of perfect objectivity. Following this line of thought, in research it is important to clearly express the theoretical premises and intersections of identity which can be shown to shape the work. Likewise, it is important for the researcher to be as clear as possible about the dimensions of one's identity that affect one's thinking. In this sense it is more objective, for instance, to be openly African and Christian than to try to hide behind a mask of objectivity, and yet be led by these dimensions of one's identity. Of course, at the same time there are many other dimensions of identity, which mold the work of a theologian. Thus, there are always dimensions of us, which remain more or less hidden to our casual discussion partner. These dimensions only reveal themselves to those who get to know us better, as academics and as persons. Finally, our mind conceals some dimensions of our psyche even from ourselves. This means that a human being, and her thought, ultimately remain mysteries even to the person herself. In this

---

5. This kind of a tension between cultural identity and Christian identity is actually a healthy one. In some countries where Christianity has intertwined with the local culture for a long time, Christians have difficulties in realizing the radical subversive dimension of the gospel. In that situation the gospel has become culture to the extent that the salt has lost its taste. The outcome may be a complete lack of criticism in direction of the society, and Christianity may become one of the excuses of oppressive structures or atrocities, as has often been the case in the history of Europe.

sense, there cannot be final truths in the field of humanities and even less so in constructive enterprises such as theology or philosophy.

However, this hidden side of the human mind and the impossibility of reaching final, absolute conclusions cannot serve as an excuse for intentionally biased or poorly reasoned ideas. The complex character of reality is no license for intellectual laxity or the lack of honesty. This means that despite considering myself a Christian, I need to address the tricky issues in my conviction that I would address in those of another person. Also, regardless of being molded by a certain culture, I still need to approach my culture critically and abstain from biased judgments against other cultures. Thus, in this kind of a rigorous intellectual endeavor nothing is true just because it is Christian (in the way I conceive Christianity) or because it is, for instance, African (in the way one perceives Africanness). Conversely, nothing can be dismissed simply on the grounds that it is African and, thus, perhaps not compatible with traditional western notions of Christianity or truth. Nothing short of these key principles betrays the quest for truth.

Yet, Christian theological academic thought is always caught in a tension between the notion of universal tradition and the need of relevance in one's context. In some cases, the solutions to this tension grow somewhat naturally. Or, at least, so gradually that this tension is not obvious, as was the case in many European contexts before modernization and secularization. In some other cases, like in modern Europe or in Africa, the forms of Christian life and the general context are so different that the tension between contextual relevance and the Christian traditions, often assumed to represent universal truths, becomes striking. In Europe, societal and cultural changes have been so quick and thorough that the religious tradition, which used to be a central element of social life, morality and identity, has now become marginal or even irrelevant to most of the population. Still, some dimensions of Christianity persist, either as relics of the past or thoroughly transformed. In Africa, Christianity has spread so rapidly, and in such a strange cultural format propagated by western missionaries, that the tension between the new religion and the life worlds of the people is inevitable. This has led to the formation of African Instituted Churches, as contextually relevant options, alongside churches established by missionaries. In these, the aforementioned cultural tensions continue to be a major topic in theology.

The rapid expansion of Christianity is largely indebted to African indigenous ways of contextualizing the gospel. One could maintain that even if theological thought has always been contextual, in the sense of trying to meet the intellectual needs of its socio-cultural context, in Africa only the modern western missionary movement has necessitated a conscious effort of understanding the role of context in theology. Christianity spread so quickly in its western garb that there was no time for organic growth of local theological solutions in the churches established by missionaries. Contextualization lagged behind the expansion. This delay was also partly due to European hostility towards foreign cultures that tended to eliminate the possibilities of local theological solutions from the outset. As a result, a need has been felt for trying to figure out how to relate the universal missionary religion to diverse socio-cultural contexts. In Europe, most churches are clinging to past glories and trying to preserve any bits and pieces of their social role that they can thereby attempting to relate to the dimensions of European life worlds that have remained the most unchanged. In this way, the churches have been paving the way of their transformation into representatives of past traditions. Thus, they are becoming an instrument of perplexed Europeans to anchor themselves to their historical and cultural identities. It is not by chance that many of the European populist political movements use Christianity, often in a denominationally specific manner, as a way of defining national identities in a way that excludes the immigrants as discussed before.

Thus, African and European ways of gaining and maintaining relevance are fundamentally different. In Africa, one attempts to reach a higher social and existential relevance of Christianity through exercising active theological imagination. In contrast, in European populist movements Christianity is useful due to its minute contemporary relevance. It can be used to exclude those who do not share the cultural past in which the church had a greater relevance. Therefore, one may conclude that the African (as well as any other contextual theological) approach is a more viable way forward than the European approach building on historical identities. This is because in the historical identity-negotiation in the European populist style Christianity is made into a servant of an ideology foreign to the Gospel accounts. The Gospels give very little support for nationalist ideas and ideologies. Additionally, such servitude robs theology of its critical role and if that is missing, one may question the usefulness of having a serf of a political ideology in the academia. Thus, the following introduces some of the discourses on the role of contextuality in theology.

Truth, Context and Hermeneutics

As it has been made clear, a theologian, just like a philosopher, has no way of escaping the concept of truth and the problems involved in it. In this part of the chapter, I intend, on one hand, to lay open the starting point and philosophical-theological prerequisites of my thinking in order for the reader to better understand why contextuality in theology is described and analyzed in this work in the way it is.

That said, admittedly, having been actively involved in dialogue with African Christian theology for a long time, practically ever since I began to study theology, has changed me and challenged my western assumptions and theological convictions. However, that is partly what is supposed to take place in genuine dialogue. Therefore, one cannot consider me a less European theologian because of that.

The aim of this part of this chapter is to serve as a theoretical exploration of the philosophical and theological prerequisites of contextuality, a kind of prolegomena for contextual theology. What needs to be emphasized at the outset is that contextuality in theology cannot be considered only a preoccupation of majority world theologians or missiologists. Rather, it should be a basic dimension in the way we understand theology today or, for that matter, in any human effort to make meaning of anything. The way one understands contextuality or constructs a theory of contextuality has repercussions on how one perceives method in theology, as well.

The Truth and Truths: Contextual Theology between Modernism and Postmodernism

The western cultural sphere[6] has approached the cultures of other spheres (and sometimes also cultures on the fringes of it) in various ways over the last few centuries, often with varying degrees of intolerance. As the West has dominated the global political and cultural stage during the last centuries, first in the form of colonialism and later in the form of neo-colonialism, we shall first have a look at the developments in the western intellectual climate affecting the idea of contextuality. Secondly, under the cultural, political and economic pressures laid by the West, majority world thinking has needed to respond and react to the challenges from outside, which has sometimes been an issue of struggling to set one's agenda in a situation where outside forces have strongly interfered with this effort.[7] Finally, in the same way that

6. By using the term "cultural sphere" there is no intention to maintain that the West would be a culturally monolithic unit. I rather refer to a relative proximity of cultural traditions and a high level of acculturation between the cultures in the West. I need to emphasize this partly because of my "marginally European" background speaking a non-Indo-European language, which resembles in some ways much more the Bantu languages than most of the European ones.

7. See Mugambi, *From Liberation to Reconstruction*, 39–40. "The shift from liberation to social transformation and reconstruction begins in the 1990s. This shift involves

it can be said that western cultures struggle to reconcile postmodern pluralism with the modern concept of truth, it can be maintained that Christian theologians face similar challenges everywhere, albeit in different forms. In Africa and Asia, this challenge tends to culminate on the issue of how to encounter African and Asian traditions. Christianity in Africa and Asia is divided, sometimes even bitterly, on this issue.[8] In Latin America, the cutting-edge theorizing has tended to be more on the side of social injustices, even though the cultural dimension cannot be dismissed in many of the contexts.[9]

The western modern concept of reality was founded on the remains of the theologically and philosophically constructed classicist view of one universal truth which was out there to be discovered.[10] Transposed into the modern worldview regarded the natural sciences as the highest model of attaining knowledge. So permeating was the idea of the one universal truth, and the certainty that Europeans have the deepest understanding of it, that during the high tide of colonialism there was hardly any doubt of the legitimacy of the western Christianizing and civilizing mission on the other continents. This conviction was shared even by those who felt the highest degree of tension between the scientific and their Christian worldview, like traditionalist Roman Catholics and conservative Protestants. Thus, the missionaries and colonialists came with a similar mindset, even if they did not always agree with each other concerning the means of implementation and the final goal of the enterprise. Needless to say, this view of truth was very much defined by its context of high colonialism and modern scientific advances which brought about a scientific optimism.

Interestingly enough, while the western mind gained more self-confidence because of scientific discoveries, academic advancement, and political and economic world hegemony among other things, western philosophy was gradually undergoing a number of developments which would eventually dig ground from under the feet of western self-confidence. While nominalism had already introduced a certain level of methodological suspicion in western philosophical thought in the medieval ages, it was only British

---

discerning alternative social structures, symbols, rituals, myths and interpretations of Africa's social reality by Africans themselves, irrespective of what others have to say about the continent and its peoples" (40).

8. See, for example, Mugambi, "Evangelistic and Charismatic Initiatives," in which Jesse Mugambi protests strongly against the evangelical trends, which he considers to represent western cultural imperialism on this continent.

9. See, e.g., Boff and Boff, *Introducing Liberation Theology*.

10. This idea was typically that of Aristotle, see Aristoteles, *Metaphysica*, 981b 14–982a 6.

Empiricism in the seventeenth and eighteenth centuries that brought it to a level of crisis in terms of trust in the concept of reality. British empiricists wanted to apply scientific criteria to philosophy as well. They expected for everything to be empirically proven. The outcome of this was that philosophical ideas grew increasingly skeptical from Locke through Berkeley to Hume—to the extent that at the end even the idea of causation was pointed out not to be empirically verifiable. Immanuel Kant tackled this problem of the uncertainty of our knowledge and produced a model of reality in which the human mind plays the role of the integrating link between reality as it is and our perception of it. The human mind would, in turn, be considered to work in a universal way. In the late nineteenth century, however, Friedrich Nietzsche questioned the universality of human patterns of thought and wondered whether knowledge could be a human creation and truth a communal myth. The foundational questions of postmodernism were thus expressed.

Approaching the twentieth century, western civilization was shaken to the core: the two World Wars during the first half of the century, together with scientific findings like Niels Bohr's quantum theory, Albert Einstein's theory of relativity, Werner Heisenberg's uncertainty principle, and many others, began to dismantle the certainty of possessing the highest degree of truth, or even of science being a teleological path towards a clearer vision of the world.[11] Scientific advancement began to look like a series of revolutions in which the past structures were demolished. Meanwhile, colonialism, Christian missions and later cultural anthropology, accumulated views on the immense variety of human cultures. Gradually, some Europeans were able to begin to see other cultures not only as backward, but also as genuine alternatives for the human attempt to make meaning of reality and cope with it. The earlier ethnocentric, so-called classicist, understanding of culture had to give way to more plural modes of understanding cultures. Ancient Greece and Rome and their heirs could no longer be considered the yardsticks of cultural evolution—why not choose Axum, Egypt or China instead?

The last essential factor leading to the dismissal of the absolute claim of western cultural superiority in the intellectual circles was the independence of most of the former European colonies after the Second World War, as well as the emergence of an outspoken intellectual elite of the "Third World." At that point, the West began to see itself only as one geographical

11. The question of how to relate to the sciences is a vivid discussion in the West. In Africa, it has been much less debated but not completely ignored. See Tshibangu, *Théologie africaine*, 74 on the need of taking these scientific developments into account in African theology.

and cultural area. This development was amplified by the political divisions of the Cold War, which also emphasized deep divisions in worldviews and led to the recognition of the western inability to maintain peaceful relations among nations.

Thus, gradually, a more pluralistic and accommodating mind began to permeate western thought. This change was labelled postmodernism. The main idea of postmodernism was that there exists no universal truth.[12] Another way of expressing this is that the time of grand narratives is over, grand in the sense of making universal truth claims.[13] All intellectual work would then be relegated to dealing with competing interpretations. In this intellectual climate, the idea of western cultural supremacy, and a certain denominational and culturally limited interpretation of Christianity being the final truth, began to seem ridiculous.

Traditional western theology had been constructed in such a way that theologians were considered to produce objective, universal truths. The idea of the context influencing the thinker's theological considerations was not particularly central. However, simultaneous with the rise of postmodernism, there was a gradual growth of contextual theologies—both from the majority world and from affluent countries. Thus, the space for these theologies was created by these intellectual, social, and political developments. These theologies no longer expected the interlocutor of theology to be a middle-aged middle-class European white man, but the points of view introduced women, the poor, Africans, Asians into the field.[14] The options of interpreting social realities were classically understanding and explaining whether human reality should be understood in a causal and mechanistic manner or whether it should be explained in a teleological manner.[15] What is common to both of these approaches is that they consider the truth as something attainable in itself.[16] In postmodernist approaches, the point of view shifts from understanding or explaining the reality to interpreting the realities. The reality and truth of a young poor rural African woman is not the same as that of a well-to-do male urban bourgeois middle-aged European professor.

---

12. However, this proposition seems to carry the weight of a universal truth to a considerable extent, in which case it would be self-contradictory.

13. See Lyotard, *Postmodern Condition*, 37–41.

14. See Frostin, *Liberation Theology*, 2–11.

15. See Ricoeur, *Time and Narrative*, 132.

16. This, however, does not completely exclude the possibility of admitting the personal influence of the thinker on the outcome. However, this influence is not considered something central, and could rather be seen as a kind of interference.

This shift from universal knowledge towards the interpretation of personal realities has two basic influences on our understanding of theology: First, it gives ample room for pluralism in the theological field by admitting that the influence of diverse contexts is not only acceptable, but also inevitable. Thus, contextual theology, be it African, Asian or whatever, does not need to make excuses for its existence. It can no longer be considered as a deviation of the norm, because the previous norm has become just another possible point of view. European theological tradition cannot, thus, claim any special treatment in the plethora of equally valuable interpretations of Christian faith in various contexts.

Second, as the concept of truth is blown up into pieces, each constituting a personal subjective reality, the concept of the norm collapses. Thus, in such a situation, it becomes impossible to set any criteria for, let us say, *Christian* theology, because *my* way of experiencing the Christian faith is just as legitimate as anyone else's. An outsider cannot come and set any criteria as to what is Christian and what is not because she cannot possibly know what *my Christianity* looks like. If my understanding of Christianity was condemned as a heresy at a point church history, that does not matter because the church cannot lay claim on the final truth because it does not exist.[17] Previous norms, like the Bible and the creeds and confessions, simply become sources of working material for one's innovative theological creativity.

It is because of this second outcome to theologizing that many church leaders seem to be wary of postmodern influences in their churches. Yet, can one afford to reject the challenges of postmodernism, even in Africa, where its influence is still limited to a few urban scholars? One could maintain that there are aspects of African social realities that could well enhance the spread of this trend of thinking in the continent. One might even argue that some aspects of life in Africa already contain ideas suited for postmodernism, ideas and practices that were there before the invention of the whole concept in the West: religious pluralism taking form as syncretism, dual religious practices and remarkable religious tolerance (especially from the side of traditional religions).[18] There is also a remarkable ability among some Africans to cope with different levels of reality without making them

---

17. Thus, for example, Heikki Räisänen can consider Marcion's efforts to make sense of his Christian faith legitimate, albeit in part outdated today. Räisänen, *Marcion, Muhammad and the Mahatma*, 76–80.

18. See, for example, Wijsen, *There is Only One God*, 69–70, 79; Schreiter, *Constructing Local Theologies*, 144–58.

collide.[19] Thus, one might maintain that a strain of "postmodernism" is already there in Africa without it needing to be introduced.

Furthermore, is it viable to continue to consider a theology of the West as the final model for the interpretation of reality, valid also in other contexts? If yes, on what grounds? If this is not a plausible option, one might consider the necessity of making Christianity at home in other contexts, too. In the case of rejecting the postmodern refutation of the universal truth, one needs to point out what is precisely the universal truth of Christianity, which needs to be reinterpreted (or only reworded?) in the other contexts. Is it a certain denominational confession, an ecumenical creed, or a certain interpretation of the foundational narrative of Christianity (the gospel)? However, in the final analysis all these cognitive solutions based on different documents, or even their interpretations in the West, must be seen as products of particular culturally conditioned developments. One may, of course, maintain that these culturally conditioned documents reflect the universal content of Christianity in a specific manner. Thus, what needs to be done is simply to "translate" this universal message into the African cultural context.[20] However, as it is impossible to sift out the western cultural heritage from the universal truth it supposedly carries,[21] the task easily turns into the abovementioned "translation."[22] In this case, western Christianity still remains the yardstick of genuine Christianity.[23] One may pose a further question and wonder what grants western Christianity, in particular, this normative role.[24] Finally, which brand of western Christianity should be taken as the most genuine model of the universal truth?

19. Thus Tcherkézoff, "Black and White Dual Classification," 62.

20. On contextualization from the point of view of translation see for example Sanneh, *Translating the Message*.

21. For example, classical Christology and Trinitology were formulated using Greek philosophical terms. Although the meanings of these terms were in some cases redefined to fit the needs of Christian theology, and usually at least slightly modified, one cannot avoid the conclusion that Greek cultural heritage from which the terms were derived, also contributed to their meaning and connotations. Thus, deciding what actually belongs to the truth the Church Fathers wanted to express, and what belongs to the means to express that truth, is a matter of interpretation. Furthermore, one may well ask whether it was possible for the Church Fathers to perceive the universal truth as it is without any "interference" from their cultural and social background. See for example Dulles, *Survival of Dogma*, 160.

22. For different alternatives on constructing contextual theologies see Bevans, *Models of Contextual Theology*; Schineller, *Handbook on Inculturation*, 14–27.

23. Criticism of western denominational theologies as norms: Dickson, *Uncompleted Mission*, 161.

24. The frank answer to this question seems to be simple: western Christianity is the type of Christian heritage that managed to spread over most of the African continent,

Thus, while the challenge of postmodernism brings with it a certain inconvenience by denying the legitimacy of traditional Christian claims of a universal normative truth,[25] a total abandonment of postmodern suspicions of the social constitution of the idea of truth and the use of truth as a means of domination leads to another inconvenience: This would make it more difficult for the majority world Christians to claim an equal footing with western Christians. A danger of hegemony and subordination lurks behind every human universal truth-claim.[26] Thus, an African or Asian theologian, and any context-sensitive theologian willing to remain Christian in a traditional normative sense, remains between the Scylla of postmodernism and Charybdis of western normative claims.

On the Nature and Role of Tradition in Today's Theology

Sometimes there is a tendency among the Protestants to juxtapose Christian tradition and the Bible, maintaining that while the Protestants pledge faithfulness to the Bible, the Roman Catholics stick to the (human constituted) tradition. Hence, many Protestants would ideally consider themselves to be following *only* the Bible and no tradition.[27] The historical accuracy of

---

mostly in connection with European colonialism. This leads one to wonder whether might is right also in the Christian community.

25. Knitter, *No Other Name?* 219: "The new model reflects what our pluralistic world is discovering: no truth can stand alone; no truth can be totally unchangeable. Truth, by its very nature, needs other truth. If it cannot relate, its quality of truth must be open to question. Expressed more personally, I establish my identity, my uniqueness by showing not how I am different from you but how I am part of you. Without you, I cannot be unique. Truth, without 'other' truth, cannot be unique; it cannot exist. Truth, therefore, 'proves itself' not by triumphing over all other truth but by testing its ability to interact with other truths."

26. Within postmodern philosophy especially Michael Foucault has dealt with the concept of truth as a means of exercising power, thus, bringing Nietzsche's work to its logical conclusion. Foucault, *Discipline and Punish*, 27: "We should admit rather that power produces knowledge . . . that power and knowledge directly imply one another; that there is no power relation without the correlative constitution of a field of knowledge, nor any knowledge that does not presuppose and constitute at the same time power relations." Feminist thinking has also thoroughly analysed the use of the concept of truth as a means of male domination. Schüssler Fiorenza, *In Memory of Her*, xvii: "Mainstream language and science do not give an objective, value-neutral account of reality. Rather, by making marginalization and stereotypes appear as 'natural' or 'common sense,' they interpret, construct, and legitimize reality from the perspective of elite western men and in the interest of relations of exclusion and domination." However, the realization that knowledge and domination go hand in hand does not necessarily mean that this is inevitably the case, as Foucault suggests.

27. Gadamer (*Wahrheit und Methode*, 250–74) points out that Enlightenment

this view is more than questionable, and a quick look into the major confessions of the mainline sixteenth century Reformation suffices to prove this—they begin almost invariably with a statement of continuing to hold the ecumenical creeds and, in many cases, their argumentation is supported by references to revered texts of Christian tradition outside the Bible, such as the Patristic writings.[28] Thus, the slogan *sola scriptura* is not tenable if understood as referring to the Bible as the only source of theology.[29]

The other possibility of reading *sola scriptura* is to consider it to mean that the Bible is the measure by which all other tradition is assessed.[30] Also in this case, when one tries to argue that the Protestant point is that the Bible is the highest authority above tradition, one needs to agree with the Roman Catholic argument that the Bible must always be interpreted (and should preferably be interpreted in the light of genuine Christian tradition). This point is related to the observation that it is impossible to refine any pure gospel, free from any cultural influences. However, the weakness of the Roman Catholic position, visible already in the days of sixteenth century European reformations, is that the preferred tradition is culturally specific which leads to a near idolization of Greco-Roman cultural heritage. This issue has been tackled, for example, by Asian Roman Catholic bishops who feel the pinch of cultural estrangement in their churches.[31] And, after all, the creation of the biblical texts proceeded from oral tradition to written forms.

No interpretation of the gospel is pure, in the sense of not building on previous traditions and, thereby, contexts as well as the present context at hand. Likewise, biblical narratives are formulated in their respective contexts and are heard and read in our own contexts. Thus, there is always a minimum of two cultural contexts involved. This means that, the *sola Scriptura*-principle cannot be taken to literally mean that the only basis for our theologizing could be the Bible as it is. Additionally, especially considering the late definition of the biblical canon (sixteenth century council of Trent for the Catholics, and reactions to Trent for the Protestants) as well as the fact that many respected early Christian texts were not included in it, it does not seem reasonable to draw a sharp division between the Bible and the rest of the Christian traditions. That would require an inspiration theory, in

---

discredited *Vorurteil* (prejudice) which is, however, a necessary precondition for knowledge-production in the sense of interpretation. This fact calls for a rehabilitation of tradition.

28. Vähäkangas, "Doctrinal Relationship," 71–73.

29. In this case, the last vowel of *scriptura* is read short, *scriptura* being in nominative.

30. Then the last vowel is read long, turning *scriptura* into ablative, referring to its instrumental role.

31. See Phan, "Asian Christian?" 70–73.

which the revelation that ended up in the Bible is qualitatively different from the rest of the Christian texts of the time, and that the council or Protestants deciding about the canon were inerrant. Naturally, all of the decisions about the canon across denominational boundaries cannot be infallible because the canon differs, for some parts, between ecclesiastic traditions.

One of the undeniable outcomes of historical-critical study of the Bible has been that the Bible is seen as a collection of writings which evolved during a long process of formulating the sacred texts of religious communities.[32] When seen in this light of gradual formation, it becomes evident that one can no longer consider the Bible and the trends of early Christian tradition as opposing realities, but as dimensions of the attempts of early Christians to narrate their faith in written form. Thus, from a purely historical and social point of view, the Bible is a part of our early Christian tradition. It is a matter of theological evaluation whether we want to elevate the Bible onto a different qualitative level from that of rest of tradition. Yet, we interpret the Bible largely through the agenda set by the tradition of previous generations of Christians.[33]

Christian denominational communities have often tended to consider their stand in doctrinal issues as the last word presenting the authentic interpretation of the Christian faith. Thus, the Lutherans consider themselves to be the champions of the doctrine with which the Church stands or falls (salvation by grace alone), the Roman Catholic teaching authority (Magisterium) sees itself as the true interpreter of the Christian doctrines, the Eastern Orthodox churches consider themselves to be true heirs of the Apostolic faith, the Pentecostals claim that the Holy Spirit is genuinely at work in their communities, and so on. In each of the cases, the concept of the Christian faith (that is believed, the content of faith) tends to be seen as something unchangeable, something that has been set out from the times of Jesus. Furthermore, it is objective, universal in its contents and normative for all. Thus, the ideal picture of tradition is that it does not change.[34]

However, a closer look into the history of dogma reveals the following: First, the wording of traditional Christian dogma has not always remained the same. Thus, in Antioch, a local council denied in 268 that the Son would be "*homoousios*" willing to reject Unitarianism. Just fifty years after the Council of Nicaea (325) maintained that the Son was "*homoousios*" with

32. Compare to the Muslim understanding of the receiving of the Quran: Räisänen, *Marcion, Muhammad and the Mahatma*, 118–23. Some Christian ways of interpreting the birth of the Bible could be considered as ways of "Quranifying" the Bible.

33. Note that even rejection of an agenda is still influenced by the agenda through negation.

34. Bergmann, *Gud i funktion*, 61; Dulles, *Survival of Dogma*, 153, 157–59.

the Father. Thus, there can be changes in the wording of dogma (which does not necessarily mean that the factual content would change radically just because of the change in wording.) Second, while the wording of a doctrinal statement might remain the same, its interpretation might undergo serious changes. Thus, "outside the Church there is no salvation" (*extra ecclesiam nulla salus est*) was taken in its literal exclusivist sense in the medieval ages while today's Roman Catholic magisterium interprets it in an inclusivist manner.[35] Among Protestants, there is a divided opinion on the validity of that statement.

Finally, even if the believing community would honestly strive to maintain the wording of a specific doctrine and its interpretation unaltered through generations, there is no guarantee that the way the believers understand that doctrine would ultimately remain the same. At any rate, the historical, cultural and other changes in our environment mold us and change the way we perceive reality. Even if we tried to stick to the ways of the past, like the Amish in Indiana (USA) or other conservative Mennonites in Canada, we cannot resist change in our environment: What was normal a century ago is a sign of ultimate conservatism today. Driving a horse-cart today is not only a means of transport: it is also a visible manifestation of one's attitude to the modern world, which it was not a century ago. Thus, as social and historical creatures, our worldviews under constant transformation, we cannot keep our sacred traditions intact. In fact, we may try to petrify the expressions of faith of our community, but this will gradually estrange our religious language, ultimately rendering it pointless in everyday life.[36]

In Africa, from the side of African traditions, there is a particular pressure to understand expressions of Christian faith as sacrosanct unchangeable pieces of revelation, very much in the same manner as the ancestral traditions were considered in the traditional religions.[37] However, ironically, this African approach is simultaneously an approach that threatens to suffocate the growth of African theological thinking. That said, African pre-Christian traditions, as well as some African Instituted Churches, have a much higher level of flexibility in their traditions due to the oral nature

---

35. Dulles, *Survival of Dogma*, 59–162.

36. On the inevitable nature of contingency and changeability of cultural forms and patterns see Sahlins, *Islands of History*.

37. Yet, the ancestral traditions reflected the changing context, as well despite the ideal picture of unchangeability. See Wijsen, *There is Only One God*, 67; Middleton, *Lugbara Religion*, 215–16; Vähäkangas, "Ghambageu Encounters Jesus."

of transmission. Orality provides the opportunity of gradual editing of the tradition while retaining the sense of immutability.[38]

To provide a basis for contextual theology, one needs to define Christian tradition in a manner that would, on one hand, safeguard the continuity of the faith (an attempt towards universality) and, on the other hand, facilitate the flourishing of genuinely contextual thinking within the Christian faith-community. Thus, we need to balance between universality and particularity. The churches tend to be very conservative, erring rather on the side of universality and tradition, rather than change and innovation. Thus, Steve Bevans encourages churches to "gamble for the sake of the Gospel" and not to be too afraid of syncretism.[39]

This seems to require us to discard the concept of an unchangeable Christian tradition.[40] Thus, one would no longer need to consider the whole of the history of dogma as a constant straightforward march towards an ever-clearer understanding of the universal normative truth. This means that we will basically need to abandon a strict propositional understanding of revelation. Thus, we could no longer consider revelation as a deposit of divinely delivered doctrinal statements, like the view of revelation which gained a dominant position among the theologians from the medieval ages onwards.[41] However, this does not remove us from the dilemma of universality and diversity, from the quest for Christian identity amidst other identity claims in the surrounding context.[42] Therefore, we proceed to more closely inspecting the role of contextuality in the process of constructing theology.

---

38. See Vähäkangas, *Between Ghambageu and Jesus*, 148–49.

39. Bevans, "Models of Contextual Theologizing."

40. This would be based on two arguments: First, the theoretical difficulties attached to the notion, viewed from a historical point of view, and secondly the practical issue concerning the need of freedom of thought for contextual theologies. Rigid propositional understanding of doctrine and a historical approach have also collided in the past. See Kerr, "Yves Congar and Henri de Lubac," 112. Historicity could even be maintained to be a specific phenomenon of Christianity (as well as the other monotheistic religions of the Near East). Thus, the historical argument also gains some theological weight. Lubac, *Catholicism*, 140–41; Eliade, *Myth of the Eternal Return*, 104–5. Lubac, *Catholicism*, 166: "[H]istory is the necessary interpreter between God and man."

41. Dulles, *Models of Revelation*, 36.

42. This field of tension has given Küster (*Theologie im Kontext*, 52) impetus in drawing his hermeneutical circle of contextual theology where there are two twin poles: text and context as well as identity criterion and relevance criterion.

Ways of Constructing Contextual Theologies

Above, it has been indicated almost *ad nauseam* that any human intellectual endeavor is seasoned by its context in various manners.[43] One may then wonder, what the use of discussing contextual theologies is if all theologies are inevitably shaped by their contexts. Thus, the whole concept of contextual theology could be contested by pointing out that it contributes to the marginalization of theologies from outside the academic status quo by implying that there is, on one hand, (real) theology and, on the other hand, contextual theology. While acknowledging that the concept contextual theology is a bit unfortunate in this sense, it has a relatively long pedigree and is so established that its use is justified so long as some clarifications are made. First, by contextual theology one means theology that is conscious of its context and its contextual limitations as opposed to theologies that are imagined as universal and, thereby, lack the understanding of their contextuality. Additionally, a contextual theology is a theology that actively addresses the context of its origin. The second dimension of the clarification does not suffice to define any theology contextual, in the proper sense, because one may simultaneously engage with one's context and imagine that context as universal. Therefore, both consciousness of contextual limitedness and engagement with the context are required for a properly contextual theology.

Another critical remark against contextual theology is that it is too limited: it is not enough to theologize only in one context. As a solution to this, concepts like intercultural or intercontextual, or even interreligious, theology have been proposed.[44] One needs to keep in mind, at any rate, that even if one combined several cultural or religious contexts, one could not produce a universal theology but, rather, theology that may have a slightly wider application. Furthermore, what could be counted as intercontextuality is subject to the question of how precisely a context is limited. Context could, in its most limited sense, refer to an individual's life world or, in its broadest sense, western or majority world context. In both extremes, the definition of the context might prove fruitless for theologizing. The first produces an extremely limited point of view which is, however, philosophically

---

43. A strong and relatively early voice in this was Wingren, *Växling och kontinuitet*, 23: "Evangelium är *alltid* färgat av lokal, mänsklig, begränsad miljö."—"The Gospel is *always* colored by a local, human, limited context." The concept of context was not yet applied in systematic theology at the time but I find it to be the best (albeit somewhat anachronistic) translation for "miljö/milieu" in this sentence.

44. Bevans, "Models of Contextual Theologizing" discusses different ways of approaching contextuality, thereby encountering this question.

speaking defendable as no-one else has exactly the same experiences as I do. In the latter case, the context is defined as so large, that the greatest common denominator may prove to be too limited.

Regarding interreligiousness and interculturality, suffice it to note at this point that all theology is, by necessity, interreligious and intercultural, as will be argued below. It needs to be noted, that in spite of any theology being contextually shaped, it does not mean that it would not have some intelligibility and relevance in many other contexts. Additionally, it is possible to theologize contextually both in an open and a closed manner. An open way of contextual theologizing is inclusive in character and opens up for interpretations in other contexts as well whereas a closed contextuality in theology excludes and turns inwards. Context sensitivity does not mean insularity but contextuality should balance with catholicity in the sense of openness.

The demographic shift of the centre of gravity of Christianity to the South has launched a quest for a similar shift within Christian theologizing. This quest is directly linked to the developments of our understandings of reality described above. There has been a great variety of proposals on how it should be done. In the next sections of this book I will attempt to outline the range of different proposals. What needs to be remembered is that because the varied contexts of theology differ vastly and there exist such a great number of philosophical, theological, and confessional traditions and preferences as well as personal contributions to the discussion, what is done below is an attempt to fuse a number of classifications of contextual theologies.[45] The variety of terminology connected with these classifications complicates the situation.[46] In addition to the variety of terminology, each term also tends to be interpreted in various ways by different theologians. Below, I will use the term "contextual" to refer to the whole range of theologies in which the context is consciously taken into account. The term "contextual theology" was, in fact, coined in 1972 by WCC Theological Education Fund to cover the field of theologies which consciously take context into account. It was first used in discussing theological education in the majority world, but it soon gained wide acceptance as a term among Protestants both in WCC and Lausanne movement. Roman Catholics, on the other hand, were initially less willing to make use of this term.[47]

---

45. The classifications referred to here are Schreiter, *Constructing Local Theologies*, 6–16; Bevans, *Models of Contextual Theology*, 37–137; Küster, *Theologie im Kontext*, 18–52.

46. Thus, also Küster, *Theologie im Kontext*, 25.

47. Roest Crollius, "What is so New About Contextualization?" 3; Fabella, "Contextualization." In this I follow Justin Ukpong's (*African Theologies Now*, 5–6), Robert

Types of Western Missionary Approaches towards Non-Western Cultures

The missiological terms below, describing the ways of constructing local theologies, have mostly been developed by expatriate missionaries and missiological theoreticians. Thus, they have previously been used as tools of dealing with "non-Christian" cultures. The question of their own culture was not regarded that pressing by many of these missionaries, because they thought of themselves as coming from "Christian" cultures where there were no major problems in this field.[48] It is only later, in working on views on contextual theology, that, for example, Africans have contributed to the issue. However, the emphasis has been on theologizing, rather than building theories about theologizing. Today there is a gradually growing opinion also among theologians of the West that contextualization is a task for all theologians—and that the best western theologians have always been contextual in their surroundings, even before the invention of the term.

One of the basic dividing lines among theologians willing to contextualize has been whether the gospel, or its essential core, can also be perceived separately from its cultural expressions.[49] Let us first examine the terminology connected with the conception of a possibility of also considering the gospel separate from culture. In this view one maintains that, whereas in Christian faith there is a good deal of culturally relative elements, the kernel of the gospel is universal and above cultures. Among others, approaches of this basis have been called translation, adaptation, accommodation, and indigenization.

The concept of translation suggests that the interplay between cultures and the gospel is analogous to the translation of, for example, the Bible.[50] Just like in translating the Bible the original message can be conveyed to other

---

Schreiter's (*Constructing Local Theologies*), Stephen Bevan's (*Models of Contextual Theology*) and Volker Küster's (*Theologie im Kontext*, 46–47) use of the term.

48. However, in some other circles this discussion could sometimes even be rather topical, like in Søren Kierkegaard's criticism of contemporary Danish Folk-Church or in European considerations on socio-cultural change and theology during the time of rapid expansion of science.

49. See Nkéramihigo's ("Inculturation and the Specificity of Christian Faith," 25) rejection of "docetism" that tries to isolate Christianity in its essence from its cultural expression. See also for example Roest Crollius, "What is so New About Inculturation?" 7.

50. Sanneh (*Translating the Message*) is an ample study on the way translation has influenced the theological developments within early Christianity and modern Christianity in Africa. Sanneh's approach seems to oscillate between the notions of linguistic and cultural translation.

languages, the gospel in, let us say, a European form could be translated into an African form. One could also conceive of variations of the translation model according to the understanding of the concept of translation one holds. On one hand, one may stick to literal translation and, subsequently, to only a meagre degree of contextualization. On the other hand, one subscribing to the modern method of translation, dynamic equivalence, tries to look for the original meaning of the text and then convey it in a dynamic way that might be considerably different from the original wording.[51]

Bible translation does not necessarily have to reach this culture-free point of view, because the attempt is to translate different culturally conditioned biblical texts and not the gospel itself. However, translation as a solution to contextualization suggests that one is able to grasp the meaning of the gospel from a culture-free point of view and convey this into a new cultural setting. However, it is difficult to see how one could reach this culture-free understanding of the gospel when the gospel, even in the Bible, is thoroughly embedded in ancient Mediterranean worldviews. Furthermore, in this approach, one is tempted to see too close an analogy between culture and language.[52] Culture is a much more complicated issue than the grammar of a language, or even vocabulary. Robert Schreiter argues that this kind of a view tends to reduce cultures' richness in variations by viewing them as roughly similar without prior studies. Schreiter also considers translation as the lowest stage of contextualization but considers it necessary in the initial stages of evangelism when no other possibilities are available.[53]

Indigenization is a term which was popular among Protestants. It was rarely theologically defined, but often connected with Venn and Anderson's three selves formula. Thus, it contained a rather practical orientation to and ideas about decolonization.[54] The use of this term has become varied recently and today it can also be taken to even denote a very deep-seated mental and spiritual decolonization. However, it is not very widely used in this sense.[55]

51. On the approaches to Bible translation in the case of Namibia see Laukkanen, *Rough Road to Dynamism*.

52. Yet, structures of language can shed a lot of light on the logic of a given culture, as a comparison between Aristotle (Aristoteles, *Metaphysica*) and Kagame (*La philosophie bantu-rwandaise de l'Être*) shows. Thus, language is never just an objective medium of communication.

53. Schreiter, *Constructing Local Theologies*, 6–9. See also Bevans, *Models of Contextual Theology*, 37–53.

54. Küster, *Theologie im Kontext*, 29. Ukpong (*African Theologies Now*, 23–25) uses the term indigenization as an umbrella term for ways of constructing local theologies (but compare p. 6 where contextualization serves as such).

55. Aleaz, "Indigenization." Also, Bevans, *Models of Contextual Theology*, 55 uses indigenization in this, more radical, sense.

Robert Schreiter's three-stage taxonomy climbs higher into adaptation models. The terms adaptation and accommodation have been used almost synonymously in Roman Catholic missionary circles in the past. In that kind of approach, the missionary or educated local Christians formulate a philosophical construction of the local worldview. This construction is used to provide a framework for a contextual theology. At best, the outcome is an intellectually sophisticated theological system that makes use of local worldviews, but basically conforms to the western medieval ideal of theology (and philosophy). Academic appearance and conformity to western standards have been identified as the shortcomings of this approach. This approach was already used during late medieval ages in China (Matteo Ricci) and India (Roberto di Nobili).[56]

Classifying Contextual Theologies

The highest level of Schreiter's classification belongs to contextual theologizing (contextual proper—the previous ones have been just stages towards the fullness of contextuality). According to Schreiter, the starting point is the context, the needs experienced by the people. Contextual theology would then be theology from below, starting from the questions of the people whereas in previous approaches, the point of departure was top-down, namely the gospel above culture. Contextual theology contains two currents: liberation theology and inculturation.[57]

The term inculturation evolved in Roman Catholic theological circles, first as few occasional uses of the word without clarification of its content in detail. The term was more widely adopted by Roman Catholic theologians the in mid-1970s especially among the Jesuits. The term gained final acceptance among the Roman Catholics after it was used by Pope John Paul II in his exhortation *Cathechesi Tradendae* in 1979. African bishops had proposed incarnation to serve as the paradigm for contextualization in the Roman Synod of 1974, but the proposal was encountered by Pope Paul VI's emphasis of universality.[58] The African proposal probably seemed too

---

56. Schreiter, *Constructing Local Theologies*, 9–11; Roest Crollius, "What is so New About Inculturation?" 3; Küster, *Theologie im Kontext*, 25–29.

57. Schreiter, *Constructing Local Theologies*, 12–15. Schreiter uses the term "ethnographic approaches" instead of inculturation.

58. Shorter, *African Christian Theology*, 150–52; Roest Crollius, "What is so New About Inculturation?" 2; Küster, *Theologie im Kontext*, 29–30; Martey, *African Theology*, 66–68. The term entered into Jesuit use in the 32nd General Congregation of the Society of Jesus (1974–75) in which cultural anthropological term "enculturation" was used in Latin in the form "inculturatio" because the prefix en- would have violated the

pluralistic. Jesuits' proposal for the term inculturation was more welcome, perhaps not purely because of the difference between the concepts but also because of the proposing party.

Just like the concept of incarnation, inculturation proposed a deeper process than adaptation. While adaptation could be seen as a relatively extrinsic tinkering of peripheral issues in western Christian thinking to adapt it to new cultural surroundings, incarnation proposed a much more radical acceptance of non-Roman cultures. Inculturation denotes that there is a dual process whereby authentic cultural values are transformed by the integration of Christianity into the culture while, simultaneously, Christianity is rooted in various cultures. In this view, the gospel would become the transforming soul of a culture by getting incarnated within it. In many definitions of inculturation the term is interpreted through incarnation. Some interpreters of the term also stress that inculturation is an open process, unlike adaptation.[59] Thus, eventually African bishops got what they wanted, at least in principle. The similarity between adaptation and inculturation was that the preoccupation in both was in the sphere of culture.[60] Contextualization, for its part, left the possibility open to also emphasize the political and economic questions. Thus, contextualization was more readily accommodating liberation theological approaches.

It is noteworthy that lately also some Protestants have adopted the term inculturation. This means that inculturation can no longer be automatically seen as a term that comprises Roman Catholic theological and philosophical presuppositions. Thus, its meaning has somewhat relaxed. However, this development has been useful in the sense that now there exists a relative consensus of the use of contextualization as the umbrella term for liberation and inculturation. Thus, contextualization could be seen as covering all the local theological approaches that take the socio-cultural context seriously and reject the possibility of extracting a non-cultural gospel. This kind of a definition still leaves us with quite a variation of possible approaches to local theologies. So, it remains worthwhile to look more closely into this problematic.

Latin language (Roest Crollius, "What is so New About Inculturation?" 5-6, fn 14). In anthropology, enculturation refers to a person's growing into a culture, or socialization. However, the term can already be found in Protestant G. L. Barney's article of 1973 ("Supracultural and the Cultural").

59. Schineller, *Handbook on Inculturation*, 6, 17; John Paul, *Redemptoris missio*, § 52; John Paul, *Post-Synodal Apostolic Exhortation*, § 60, § 87; *The Church in Africa*, 43, 44; Roest Crollius, *Teologia dell'inculturazione*, 7-11; Küster, *Theologie im Kontext*, 30. See also Martey, *African Theology*, 67-68; Nkéramihigo, "Inculturation," 25.

60. This is clearly manifest for example in Roest Crollius, "What is so New About Inculturation?" 5-18.

Stephen Bevans has attempted to bring clarity to the question of contextualization by classifying different approaches to it under six models. The models are (starting from the least open approach in terms of culture and ending with the most open one): countercultural[61], translation, synthetic, praxis, transcendental and anthropological models.[62] As the translation model has been dealt with above, we can proceed directly to the synthetic model.

The synthetic model is quite popular among Roman Catholic theologians as a middle-of-the-way solution. It strives to retain the essential traditional doctrinal formulae while being open to the surrounding culture. It is not happy with only adapting to the cultural situation or translating the western traditional thought and, yet, it is significantly cautious about how to proceed. It is often proposed as the standard definition of inculturation and gains plenty of support from Roman Catholic official documents.[63] Bevans points to Aylward Shorter's definition of inculturation as an example: "[I]nculturation is . . . the on-going dialogue between faith and culture or cultures."[64] Thus, the central characteristic of this model is dialogue, the ongoing cross-fertilization between the cultural background of the church and the new cultural surroundings.[65] According to Bevans Charles Nyamiti serves as an African example of this model.[66]

Bevans's praxis model is also an open, on-going process. It differs from the previous model in that, whereas the synthetic model stresses the dialogue with culture, the praxis model chooses the social situation as its counterpart in dialogue. Furthermore, the praxis model is less interested in authentic being, in the sense of cultural identity, but it rather emphasizes

---

61. It has to be noted that the countercultural model is not anti-cultural or critical towards cultures in a cultural imperialistic manner (Bevans, *Models of Contextual Theology*, 118–19). In that sense, I hesitate to place it on this continuum.

62. See the figure of Bevans, *Models of Contextual Theology*, 32.

63. Bevans, *Models of Contextual Theology*, 88–89.

64. Shorter, *Toward a Theology of Inculturation*, 11; Bevans, *Models of Contextual Theology*, 90. Thus also Roest Crollius, "What is so New About Inculturation?" 9–11; Küster, *Theologie im Kontext*, 30.

65. See Bevans, *Models of Contextual Theology*, 88–102. These new cultural surroundings must not be understood as something "non-western" or exotic from the point of view of western so-called high cultures. Rapid social change has alienated especially the historical churches also in the West. The traditional approach of these churches is still that of people leading an agrarian monolithic communitarian way of life, even though urbanization, industrialization and pluralism have become the parameters of the society. Likewise, for many African churches it is no longer sufficient to only consider how to relate to the traditional village societies.

66. Bevans, *Models of Contextual Theology*, 96.

social action to transform the society to rid it from sinful and oppressive structures. The shift of emphasis is from being to action. For praxis-oriented thinkers, like liberation theologians, it is no longer sufficient to believe correctly (orthodoxy) but to act correctly (orthopraxy). The praxis model often contains a hermeneutical circle, or a process of interpretation, where there is a rotation between reading the Bible and reflecting on it, analyzing the social situation, acting committedly to change the situation (praxis) and analyzing the outcome of the action, reading the Bible again, and so on.[67]

The transcendental model in Bevans's classification builds on the philosophical and theological developments based on Kant's epistemological conviction that the truth is not out there to be perceived as such, but that the observing mind always creates its own reality. However, the outcome of the Kantian system is not relativistic pluralism due to Kant's view that humankind is fundamentally similar as there are some set (*a priori*) rules of thought. These produce a similar result in thinking provided that the starting-point is correct, and one's thinking is without fault. In theology, especially in so-called transcendental Thomism (Karl Rahner, Bernard Lonergan), this Kantian pattern of thought has been further developed to fit theology. Kant's basic epistemological view is endorsed and is coupled with a Christian view of God who wants to reveal herself to humankind. As a creature a human is basically open to transcendence (God's reality) and in this encounter God calls humans to conversion.

The proper subject of theological thought would then be an authentic, that is, converted, person. This person is called to reflect on her experience of God as an individual. As such, the main objective is not to construct contextual theology by asking how one should think in this particular situation. Rather, the starting point is universal, based on the common ground of humanity. At the same time, the starting point is extremely particular because it is subjectivistic and individualistic. According to Lonergan "[g]enuine objectivity is the fruit of authentic subjectivity. It is to be attained only by attaining authentic subjectivity."[68] This means that only a person who is radically and authentically subjectivistic can reach true objectivity.[69] In Lonergan, this authenticity is reached in self-transcendence. This is achieved through intellectual, moral and religious conversion. The last is needed for all authentic subjectivity because God is implicit in all our reasoning. Religious conversion serves as the final criterion of all thinking. In this way, a person can escape both rigid cultural conservatism by sticking

---

67. See Bevans, *Models of Contextual Theology*, 70–87.
68. Lonergan, *Method in Theology*, 292.
69. See Lonergan, *Third Collection*, 144.

only to the Mediterranean formulations of Christian faith and the bottomless swamp of all-permeating relativism.[70]

This thoroughly subjective objectivity produces contextual theology as a kind of side effect. This is because a person can never be only a universal thinker making use of only *a priori* patterns of thought. Simultaneously, this thinker is a product of her culture and even if the basis is universally valid, the resultant theological work is bound to be contextual. Even in this model, theologizing is seen as an ongoing process. Lonergan considers this understanding of ongoing theologizing to be based on the understanding that culture is also a dynamic process.[71]

The model in Bevan's classification that is the most open towards cultures is the anthropological model. The starting point for this model could be expressed in Max A.C. Warren's words:

> Our first task in approaching another people, another culture, another religion, is to take off our shoes, for the place we are approaching is holy. Else we may find ourselves treading on men's dreams. More serious still, we may forget that God was here before our arrival. We have, then, to ask what is the authentic religious content in the experience of the Muslim, the Hindu . . . [72]

The creation, humans included, is basically good, and there exists a continuum between God and Her creation. Thus, creation occupies a central position in this kind of theologizing. The outcome is that one may view cultures in a very positive light. In fact, in approaching foreign cultures, a Christian is called to conversion into learning from the cultures the ways God has spoken in them, rather than converting and teaching. Finally, conversion into Christianity should not mean that one abandons one's culture but that one's cultural being reaches fulfillment in Christ.[73]

The countercultural model engages with (usually western) cultures in a respectful but critical manner. Here one attempts to be relevant and intelligible but not lose the edge of the gospel. The gospel challenges profoundly among others the secularist and consumerist inclinations of the western cultures. There is a basic incompatibility between the gospel and any given

---

70. Lonergan, *Method in Theology*, 104–7, 217, 282–84. On Lonergan's definition of conversion see *Method in Theology*, 130–31.

71. Lonergan, *Method in Theology*, xi. On the transcendental model see Bevans, *Models of Contextual Theology*, 103–16.

72. Warren, "General Introduction," 10.

73. On this model see Bevans, *Models of Contextual Theology*, 54–69.

culture, well captured in Lesslie Newbigin's book title, borrowed from Paul, *Foolishness to the Greeks*.[74]

While Bevans's classification of models in contextual theology gives a wide picture of different approaches to constructing these theologies and is useful as a general map of the field, its shortcoming lies in that the approaches, grouped as models, belong to different categories. Transcendental and praxis models are theological methods, whereas anthropological and synthetic models could best be described as general attitudes towards cultures and religions. The translation model, on the other hand, could be said to deal with the general question of how to contextualize. Thus, it is an approach to contextualization. It seems that the discussion on the taxonomy of theologizing in context must be carried forward.

Furthermore, much of the discussion on contextualization has concentrated on the conscious, more or less academically oriented, theological programs and processes. However, it seems that one of the theological consequences of the Christian center of gravity moving to the South is that the role of academic theology is diminishing at the expense of less academically formulated and systematically thought practical theologies at the grass-roots level. This is linked to the expansion of Pentecostal and Charismatic Christianity where it is not uncommon to suspect or ignore academic theologizing. Much more emphasis is laid on spirituality and the practical demands of the situation. This does not, however, do away with the fact that the socio-cultural context has a major role in the interplay between the context of the faith community, the Bible and the rest of the Christian traditions. Therefore, the approach below will attempt to formulate a model so general that it will be applicable to these more practical-minded theologies, too.

---

74. On the model, see Bevans, *Models of Contextual Theology*, 117–37.

5

A Model of the Contextual Process

AFTER HAVING MAPPED OUT the general trends in perceiving contextuality in theology, we proceed to drafting a more detailed picture of the process of interchange between a context and a Christian message. The earlier approaches have not been casting that much light on the dynamics at play in the contextual process and I hope that the following proposal will contribute towards that goal.

To begin with, as has already been noted when dealing with the praxis model, several theologians have proposed that within theologizing there exists a so-called hermeneutical circle—an ongoing process of interpretation.[1] Because contextualization can be seen as a process rather than a product, I opt to join the large company of theologians embarking from the hermeneutical circle. Fulkerson expresses the nature of the process succinctly: "Theological reflection is not a linear form of reflection that starts with a correct doctrine (or a 'worldly' insight) and then proceeds to analyse a situation; rather it is situational, ongoing, never-finished dialectical process where past and present ever converge in new ways."[2]

The model of the contextual process presented in this chapter builds on the foundation of the hermeneutical tradition. Some representatives of hermeneutics have emphasized the role of the interpreting subject to the extent that the text interpreted almost loses its significance. While acknowledging the role of the interpreter one cannot dismiss the central role of the text either. So, a happy medium between the objectivistic approach

---

1. Robert Schreiter has proposed a spiral type of a circle where the poles are Church tradition and culture (Schreiter, *Constructing Local Theologies*, 25) whereas Clodovis Boff's circle rotates between theory and praxis in different forms (Boff, *Theologie und Praxis*, 225–31); see also Küster's interpretation of both, Küster, *Theologie im Kontext*, 23) and Volker Küster draws the circle between text and context between the identity and relevance criteria (Küster, *Theologie im Kontext*, 52).

2. Fulkerson, *Places of Redemption*, 234.

to the text, that is, the belief in the human capacity of reading the text as it is, and an extremist hermeneutical subjectivism is sought here. In some instances, this kind of an approach is called objectifying hermeneutics.[3] Another theoretical starting point for this section is that the human being is not approached as an individual, but always as a member of several communities.[4] These communities have their traditions that mold the way the members experience and interpret the text at hand.

The Hermeneutical Circle

In the theological hermeneutical circle, we can constitute two poles: theory (the text understood as Christian tradition and/or the Bible) and praxis (the action informed by theory rising from the felt needs born in the context). The Bible or Christian tradition is interpreted within and through one's experiences in a particular context. This interpretation, in turn, molds one's way of reading the Bible or understanding the Christian tradition. In liberation theology, there is an emphasis on praxis, which is often understood as the active transformation of one's context to be less oppressive and more humanizing. This praxis changes the context. So, we can see that both poles are in a dynamic transformation as the hermeneutical circle rotates onwards. One could view this process also as if in a still picture, trying to identify the different factors contributing to the process of theological interpretation at any given moment. Here I attempt to analyze a snapshot of this ongoing process from the point of view of contextualization.

The variables to be dealt with here are five: the gospel, a worldview, social and cultural context, choice of themes and a theological method.[5]

The gospel can be understood as the Jesus-story, as it is expressed in the Bible and understood in the broad tradition of Christian community or, alternatively, as it is understood by the person in her community as a result of previous interpretations.[6] What is noteworthy is that the story "as it is

3. Alvesson and Sköldberg, *Reflexive Methodology*, 94–95.

4. Emphasis on individuality heightened in Enlightenment and through modernization processes which deconstruct(ed) many traditional dimensions of communality. Late modern thought has questioned this emphasis on the individual. For me, however, the significant discussion partners in terms of individuality and communality have been the African theologians.

5. For an example of a somewhat similar hermeneutical circle consisting of several factors in literature studies see Palm, "Att tolka texten," 196–202.

6. It has to be noted that by this "broad tradition" I refer to the whole corpus of Christian traditions, which has been directing our understanding of the Christian message. What must be properly taken into account is that this tradition has never

expressed in the Bible" is a kind of a limited reality or almost an imaginary entity. To grasp the gospel as it is in the Bible, one would need to be one of the writers of the Bible. In fact, to grasp it in its totality, one would need to be all of the writers of the Bible. Furthermore, when they were writing, they would have to have been fully conscious of all the revelational dimensions of the texts they were writing—an idea that even a Fundamentalist may contest. Revelation, when transmitted to another person, must be expressed in words or signs. Thus, the limitation introduced by interpretation is inevitable. This limitation would probably be the smallest in the case of a member of the early Jesus-movement expressing its faith orally with the tradition eventually evolving into the Biblical writings and other early Christian writings. Even then, it is questionable whether the original message would be the untainted gospel. This is because of the limitations of expression imposed by the original language and culture in the Biblical writings, as well as the personal intellectual, linguistic and cultural limitations of that person. So, the expression "as it is expressed in the Bible" should not be understood here in a fundamentalist manner but, rather, as an expression of the fact that the Bible is the closest one can get to Jesus of Nazareth today. The Biblical texts have their limitations having been written in specific languages and within the parameters of specific cultures. The interpreters' limitations and preferences add another layer of limitations distancing the reader further from the full understanding of the Word incarnate. Even if one would in some miraculous way be able to go beyond the text to the actual experiences of the writers of the Biblical texts, even those experiences would also be limited and directed by the cultural, social, psychological etc. premises of the writer. Even an experience is an interpretation.

Concerning the other dimension of the starting point in the gospel is the question of tradition. As mentioned above, creating an artificial separation between the Bible and tradition is not historically tenable but would presuppose such theological moves that require intellectual somersaults. The interpretative horizon of each reader of the Bible is limited even though studies in Biblical scholarship and various interpretative traditions help fuse

---

been purely European or Hellenic but has always been lived out in other contexts as well (already since the antiquities among the Jews, Aksumites, Babylonians, Indians etc.). Indeed, the heartlands of Christianity were outside of the western cultural sphere well into the medieval ages. The demographic center of gravity was probably outside of Europe at that time as well. Today, the center of gravity has been outside of the western cultural sphere for a couple of decades. One may conclude that the western hegemony in Christianity lasted almost a millennium, the second Christian millennium which both started and ended with West not being on the top. Frankopan, *Silk Roads*, 38–44; 54–62; Jenkins, *Lost History of Christianity*.

some of the horizons.⁷ However, our view of reality is always limited. To be able to produce the broadest possible Christian tradition to understand the gospel would call for a bird-eye view of reality. Unfortunately, this kind of a universal view is not attainable to humans as context-bound beings.⁸ This limit-entity called the "gospel" is, however, no imaginary "pure gospel" in the sense of being a non-cultural or culture-free Christian message. The gospel is always transcribed, experienced and interpreted within a culture and a social context. In this case the shorthand "the gospel" refers, on one hand, to the gospel as it is contextually expressed in the Biblical writings and, on the other hand, the various Christian communities—both contemporary and historical. Theoneste Nkéramihigo expressed this sentiment well:

> Christianity is not a universal abstraction which must be concretized in every culture; it is a specific concreteness which must be universalized by proclaiming the Gospel of Jesus Christ to all peoples. Christianity is the singular specificity of the man Jesus of Nazareth who has a universal destiny by reason of his power to break all other specificities.⁹

The second variable in the contextual hermeneutical process dealt with here is worldview denoting the basic way one perceives and interprets reality. It is used here in the sense of the culturally, socially and personally developed patterns of thinking by which one produces order and knowledge out of perceptions. Worldview is a deep dimension of culture which could well be defined in Clifford Geertz' words as "a set of control mechanisms—plans, recipes, rules, instructions (what computer engineers call 'programs')—for the governing of behaviour."¹⁰ Thus, worldview would be the partly conscious and partly subconscious intellectual dimension of culture that finds its expressions through the processes in which culture is lived out in visible cultural phenomena.

---

7. See Vessey, "Gadamer and the Fusion of Horizons." See also Gadamer, *Wahrheit und Methode*.

8. This does not mean that we would have absolutely no chance of understanding phenomena outside of our native cultures. Rather, we have a limited scope of reality, which we can expand on by getting to know other cultures and ways of thought. At any rate, however large our view of reality would be, it can never span all of reality and become universal.

9. Nkéramihigo, "Inculturation," 25. It could be noted here at the outset that this position distances itself from purely narrativistic solutions claiming a text an independent status. On this kind of a solution in Frei see Comstock, "Truth or Meaning," 126–27, 130–31.

10. Geertz, *Interpretation of Cultures*, 44.

Third, there is the social and cultural context in the sense one experiences it. Again, social context is not thought of as an empirical reality, but something which is experienced and interpreted by each individual in their own way.

Fourth, a theologian uses different criteria when choosing topics to be dealt with. No theology can cover all possible information, nor is it necessary. For instance, Thomas Aquinas, in his *Summa Theologiae*, deals with the question of how the sex of a fetus is determined.[11] Thomas felt that he needs to cover this in his theological magnum opus together with several other questions today seen to belong to natural sciences. Probably theology as the queen of sciences was supposed to provide a total view of the reality because theology deals with creation, too. Today, theologians tend to address only such questions of natural sciences that have existential or ethical consequences or shed light to the relationship between religious faith and science. Natural determination of the sex of a fetus hardly ever belongs to that category today while it had such dimensions for Thomas.

Finally, any theologian, implicitly or explicitly, uses a theological method. By method is meant a consistent approach to dealing with the sources of theology and analyzing them as well as constructing theological ideas.

Even though the variants are many and the interplay between them even more complicated, one cannot maintain that this model would cover the whole of theological work. Rather, the issue here is just about the relation between context and theologizing. To gain a fuller picture, one would need to add the third dimension of theological systems to this two-dimensional (flat) image. This would be the time dimension extending to the third dimension.[12] Thus, the figure below could be seen as a still picture of a series of developments behind the figure itself.

---

11. Aquino, *Summa Theologiae prima pars*, q. 99 §2.

12. On this time-dimension and the continuous chain of interpretation see, e.g., Gadamer, *Wahrheit und Methode*, 250–52.

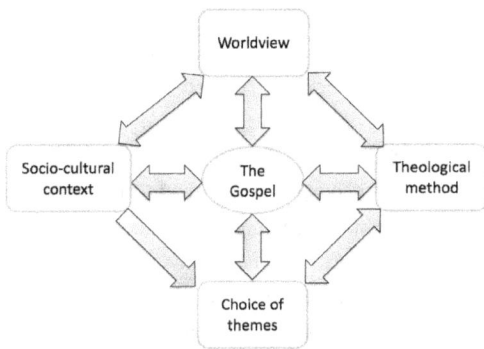

Reading the gospel: The interplay between the variants of contextual theologizing.

The Gospel and the Worldviews

A good starting point for the interpretation of this model is to consider the interplay between the gospel and one's worldview first. H. Richard Niebuhr's *Christ and Culture*[13] could be seen as a classic in this field. He deals with western theologians' understandings of how Christ (or perceptions of Christ, interpretations of the gospel message) is related to culture. Even though the point of view of the study is limited to the West, Niebuhr's understanding of culture and human views of cultures is not ethnocentric.[14] Thus, Niebuhr's classification remains of value when Christian theologians ponder the relationship between the gospel and their cultures around the world. In our figure, Niebuhr's classification seems to fit in the two-way arrow between the gospel and worldview. Also, Bevans's anthropological and synthetic models would fit there. It must be noted that by "culture" Niebuhr refers to a larger entity than "worldview" in this picture. In my reading, Niebuhr's use of culture extends beyond worldview and the rest of the intellectual side of culture, to social patterns and the material dimensions. Furthermore, Niebuhr's models have their implications on some other parts of our picture as well. Finally, his development of the theme is a still picture, capturing a momentary situation. He also notes that his model is a simplification of reality as most theologians would span multiple categories

---

13. What follows will be a brief summary of the main arguments in this book.
14. Niebuhr, *Christ and Culture*, 31: "[C]ulture as we are concerned with it is not a particular phenomenon but the general one, though the general thing appears only in particular forms, and though a Christian of the West cannot think about the problem save in Western terms."

simultaneously.[15] Additionally, because of theological argumentation and maturing, a theologian is bound to move from one position to another over the course of time. In my figure, the two-way arrow denotes a dynamic relationship.

When we discuss Christ and culture we are in fact dealing with the ways the Christ perceived by us relates to culture or worldview.[16] This is simply because the way we perceive Christ also defines the way we understand his relation to our worldview or culture. Niebuhr points out that our conceptions of Christ are varied and limited and cannot reach the level of analytical definition of the "essence" of Christ.[17] Thus, our understandings of Christ could be adequate, but not sufficient pictures of Christ, which can only serve as complements and correctives to each other.[18] These conceptions of Christ, in turn, have already been influenced by our worldview and our context. Thus, here we look into a moment in an ongoing dynamic and open process. Niebuhr disclaims that the types of relationship between Christ and culture he sketches do not directly match any theologian. Rather, they represent the great motifs that are found in different theologies in various combinations.[19] The types Niebuhr lists could be organized as follows, the doubt or negativity against culture increasing towards the left and acceptance of culture increasing towards the right:

Niebuhr's typology of Christ and culture

Christ against culture	Christ above culture			Christ of culture
	Christ and culture in paradox	Christ the transformer of culture	The synthesis of Christ and culture	

The conception of Christ as being opposed to culture, found on the far left, departs from the observation that all humankind is sinful and corrupt. As a result, human culture is bound to be sinful and corrupt as well. Thus, culture needs to be suppressed and avoided as "the world." The outcome is

---

15. Niebuhr, *Christ and Culture*, 43–44.

16. Note that I limit the discussion here to the worldview—the term culture also covers the rest of the four factors around the gospel.

17. Niebuhr, *Christ and Culture*, 12–14.

18. Naturally, not every portrait of Christ is compatible with the Christian views of Christ. Here we are confronted then with the question of Christian identity (which Küster calls identity principle, *Theologie im Kontext*, 50), which defines the limits of acceptable Christian understandings of Christ.

19. Niebuhr, *Christ and Culture*, 43–44.

often very legalistic. This solution does not actually provide much room for consciously contextual theologizing. If we believe that our culture is completely in a discontinuity with the extraterrestrial gospel, we need to stick also to the form of the gospel, not only the supposed content. This, in fact, leads to cultural conservatism. Christians often consider a certain period in the church history as normative, like the Apostles' time in the way it is narrated in the Acts (e.g., Pentecostals), the Reformation(s) (e.g., many Lutherans), or the Great Revival (e.g., many American Protestant Christians). In this kind of thought, one imitates this paradigmatic historical context and imagines that the theological, ethical, and other solutions of that particular context would be universal. There is no criticism towards the culture of the paradigmatic period, and one's view even to contemporary cultural questions is stifled. Furthermore, one overlooks the fact that we cannot perceive the past realities as they were perceived at that time: even the most detailed research on the context of that time is bound to contain a degree of modern interpretation. Finally, especially in non-western contexts, this kind of an approach tends to disvalue the local cultures and try to replace them with a supposedly Christian Anglo-American revivalist subculture.[20] Therefore, the Christ against culture position is not usually intellectually consistent.

The following type, Christ above culture, covers the whole range of approaches between total rejection and total acceptance of culture. Thus, it is understandable that in practice the majority of Christian theologians can be found here, balancing between their Christian and cultural identities. In this group in the middle, the universality and radical nature of sin is not denied and grace is provided as the solution to sin. Christ is, thus, seen clearly as the Son of God, the Redeemer.[21] Niebuhr further divides this type into three subtypes: Christ and culture in paradox, Christ the transformer of culture, and the synthetic solution. What is common to all of these subtypes is that they want to affirm the absolute lordship of Christ above culture, while acknowledging that culture can have a positive function in the life of a Christian. Each of the three tries to resolve the tension between the gospel and culture in a different way. It should be noted that, especially within this type, theologians combine subtypes in varying ways and the subtypes often supplement each other easily. Thus, even if Niebuhr uses Luther as an example of the paradox-solution, he also points out that Luther's approach includes tendencies towards the transformative solution as well.[22]

---

20. See Niebuhr, *Christ and Culture*, 45–82 for his description and analysis of this type. See also Mugambi, "Evangelistic and Charismatic Initiatives," 115–16; 121–25.

21. Niebuhr, *Christ and Culture*, 116–20.

22. Niebuhr, *Christ and Culture*, 151–52, 188–89, 209.

When the relationship between Christ and culture is seen as a paradox, one tries to safeguard centrality of Christ's atoning work for Christianity. This presupposes that the reality of sin may not be underestimated. In this way, one strives to underline the specificity and meaning of Christianity in the world of religions and ideologies. This solution is based on the conviction that there exists a conflict between us humans and God, a gap between holy God and mortal sinners. Christ is the redeemer and the bringer of reconciliation to this conflict. We receive God's grace through Christ. This grace never becomes our own, but always remains alien to us, i.e. God's own proper work. Because God's grace remains alien to us, we continue to be sinners regardless of whether our efforts are considered worthy or unworthy by our fellow humans. Thus, whatever we do is perverted by sin, culture included. Niebuhr describes the follower of this solution:

> When he speaks of the sinfulness of the law-abiding man he does so as a Paul who has been zealous in observance of the law ... When he speaks about the corruption of reason, he does so as a reasoner who has tried ardently to ascend to the knowledge of truth. What is said about the depravity of man is said therefore from the standpoint and in the situation of cultured, sinful man confronting the holiness of divine grace.[23]

Thus, we could consider that an African follower of this solution would not condemn her culture in favor of another. Rather, she views herself, culture included, in the light of divine judgment. One subscribing this view consistently observes her culture with suspicion. Luther (and Paul, in a different manner) escapes a purely negative approach towards culture by making a sharp distinction between the kingdom of God and the kingdom of the world. These two kingdoms are not separate, as in the first type, but they somehow represent two dimensions of the same reality. Just as a believer is a sinner and a saint at the same time, her world is also a world of sin and redemption. We are called to follow Christ within our cultures and reason within our worldviews, no matter how fallen and corrupt our world, our cultures or worldview is. Nevertheless, the world is the stage of the great play of redemption. The demands of God and the Spirit of love continuously challenge our cultures and our ways of conduct. Only the alien grace of God can purify the human heart from self-love and hubris, to make the tree good to produce good fruit. The cultural sphere, at its best, can provide us with laws and customs that force and lead us towards decent life. However, even the decent life is tarnished by sin if it is not cleansed by Christ. In this subtype, one does not propose a final solution to the tension between Christ

---

23. Niebuhr, *Christ and Culture*, 153.

and culture but retains it within this paradox. Dealing with paradoxes is a task demanding a great deal of care: on one hand, we may twist the paradox into an illogical anomaly and, on the other hand, we may resolve the paradox—thus, ending in one of the extremes. In the latter case, we either only view culture as bad and see no difference between the creation and the fall, or we emphasize the value of culture to the extent that the reality of sin is overlooked. Paradoxes provide us with possibilities for constructing dynamic patterns of thought. However, if this dynamism is spoiled the outcome is a poor one-sided theology.[24] Bevans's countercultural model would probably come closest to this approach.

The type that sees Christ as the transformer of culture only narrowly misses the paradoxical position. This serves in Niebuhr's typology as the central tradition of Christianity. Here, Christ is seen primarily as the Redeemer, just like in the previous positions. The view of humankind's depravity and sinfulness is endorsed too. This position differs from paradoxical thinking in that the goodness of creation is not so much overshadowed by the fall. The view of culture would be that it is not evil but, rather, a perverted good—just like the fall perverted humans but did not make human nature evil. Thus, the crux of the question of culture is its conversion or transformation into conformity with God's will and not its rejection. Just as humans are lifted and transformed by Christ in his likeness, so is culture. Furthermore, Christ was present and active in the creation with the Father and the Spirit, and so he is present in the world. When Christ converts and transforms humans spiritually, also human societies improve.[25]

The third option under the category of Christ above cultures is the most accepting towards culture out of the three subtypes. To this point, the question about culture has been posed as if it were a choice between Christ and culture. This subtype maintains that the question is incorrect, and we should strive towards a view in which both Christ and culture could be affirmed. Therefore, Niebuhr calls the outcome synthesis. Christ is introduced to culture as the fulfillment. For example, Thomas Aquinas represents this solution in both theory and practice. In his theology he managed to make a great synthesis of Aristotelian and Platonic worldviews and the Christian faith. He picked up Aristotelian teleology, which pointed out that each being's nature is directed towards its reason of being and its purpose. For Aristotle, humans were rational animals and the purpose of the human was to use his reason. Aquinas would accept this point of departure and yet reform it by placing the purpose of humans in God, just like Augustine had done

24. See Niebuhr, *Christ and Culture*, 149–89.
25. See Niebuhr, *Christ and Culture*, 190–229.

centuries before. Thomas's solution was brilliant in the sense that he underscored that God is omniscient and therefore the summit of all rationality. Thomas considered that there are, in fact, two levels of goals: the natural ones and the supernatural ones. Thus, one's cultural activities are good and direct one towards natural happiness. That said, one also needs to be guided by grace towards supernatural happiness.

Here culture is granted a great degree of prestige: it becomes the vessel of God's activity in the world. God's will (at least in terms of natural goals) is manifested and fulfilled through culture. However, we are sinful regardless of whether God confronts us with His demands in our hearts and we respond to those demands in the way we live, thus shaping cultural standards. How can we be certain that that which is demanded from me by my culture or by my way of thinking is not perverted by sin? What kind of criteria should one use to create a relationship of critical solidarity[26] to one's culture? Furthermore, if the solutions of Thomas Aquinas to the questions of Christian life in this world are correct and represent the right incarnation of the gospel in the world in which human culture and the gospel are not divided nor mixed, what is the value of my culture? This solution in its openness to culture also opens up the chances for cultural imperialism of the Mediterranean. In order for this solution to serve Christians of the majority world, it demands a fresh take and it might need to be modified to accommodate a more pluralist view of cultures. In fact, this has taken place in some works of Roman Catholic African theologians. However, the question of the relationship between Christ and culture is then replaced by the question of the relationships between cultures and truth claims of culturally defined theologies.[27] This is, in fact, the way Bevans's synthetic model of contextual theology has set the question. It could be seen as an updated form of Niebuhr's synthetic subtype.

Anthony Balcomb purports that Kwame Bediako's understanding of the relationship between faith and culture should be seen as another category to be added to Niebuhr's typology, namely, "Christ behind culture." This model should probably be placed as the fourth alternative under the midway solutions. In this model, Christ is anterior to culture and must be found behind it. Therefore, this model deals with cultures in non-Christian

---

26. In post-Apartheid South Africa "critical solidarity" became a buzzword in ecumenical theology. For criticism on its uses, see Vellem, "Ecumenicity and a Black Theology," 178–79. In spite of the critique, I find the term applicable in relation to one's culture in a situation where one is balancing between criticism and acceptance.

27. See Niebuhr, *Christ and Culture*, 120–48. On the question concerning the relationship between cultures within a synthetic solution to the matter see Vähäkangas, *In Search of Foundations*, 210–18, 251–55.

contexts and is of a type less visible for Niebuhr, who was viewing this question from the perspective of Christendom. It is in the process of translation (an idea gleaned from Lamin Sanneh[28]) into the vernacular that Christ is revealed and a dynamic relation between culture and Christ takes place.[29] In this process of translation and transmission of the gospel, Christ is not brought to the context but found within it. This idea has its roots in the *logos spermatikos* idea of Justin the Martyr where creation and redemption are not seen as discontinuous. Rather, creation by the triune God meant that the divine Word is found everywhere in the creation.[30] Here, culture as a dimension of the sphere of creation, is a special seat of God's presence through Christ. This model has its connections to Geertz' definition of culture quoted above. Culture is seen there as the organizing and meaning creating entity of human reality. Christ, understood as Logos, also stands for the divine order of things in the creation and for the divine wisdom (Sophia). Therefore, this Logos could also be seen as the deepest ordering reality behind cultures, giving them their cohesion and integrity. This thought will be developed further later on in the section on incarnation as the basis of contextualization.

The most accommodating view in terms of culture is called Christ of culture. Here the tension between the gospel and culture is resolved by interpreting the gospel in terms of culture. Thus, the conception of Christ becomes a picture in full conformity with culture. The values of culture are projected directly onto this interpretation. Cultural Protestantism of the nineteenth century produced a Christ who was fully human, functioning mostly as an instructor of the morality of enlightened European bourgeoisie. Similar kinds of cultural Christs could be produced in the majority world as well. The positive side of that kind of theologizing is that one could possibly avoid cultural imperialism and, were the resulting conception of Christ culturally convincing, people could find Christ acceptable to them. However, this kind of an approach does away with the starting point, the Bible and the broad tradition of Christianity. The gospel becomes only a message that agrees with anything that a culture has to offer and, thereby, loses its edge and ceases to be the gospel.[31] The risk of this kind of an uncritical gospel is

---

28. Sanneh, *Translating the Message*.

29. Balcomb, "Faith or Suspicion?" 12.

30. And, of course, this concept has another dimension of continuity between creation and Christology—it was probably adopted from Platonic philosophy. At least Numenius used the same term but it is not known whether he antedated Justin or not. Edwards, "On the Platonic Schooling of Justin Martyr," 21–23. Compare Price, "'Hellenization' and Logos Doctrine in Justin Martyr," 20–21.

31. See Wingren, *Växling och kontinuitet*, 23–25.

that it becomes a tool for oppression. Culture is a system in which meaning is created, and the ones with power have the greatest say in the definition of meanings. Christ of the culture could, at worst, become the puppet of the powers that be, something that has occurred often.

In Stellenbosch, South Africa, some theologians of the past created theology legitimizing Apartheid thereby making the gospel into an Afrikaner political-cultural tool.[32] According to Wingren, a balance between the creation-based wide openness to society and culture and the radicality of the (redemption-centered) gospel creates a tension that contributes to theological strength in Christianity. The Christ of culture is only the Christ of creation, whereas the Christ against culture would resolve the creative tension for the benefit of the redemption only.[33]

Furthermore, the Christ of culture model does not create an open process of contextualization as it is a static one-way affirmation of one's culture (and of the distortion of the gospel) in which the outcome is defined by one pole.[34] Bevans's anthropological model comes close to this position. However, even in this case, one could maintain that while the basic orientation looks similar, the setting of the question has been modified. In Bevans's description of the anthropological model, there is space for dynamism and a degree of dialogue between the ecclesiastic culture and the present cultural context. However, according to Bevans, there exists a danger of cultural romanticism and irrelevant theologizing that disregards the present cultural dynamism when emphasizing the traditional forms of culture. Furthermore, one may also question the extent to which this model actually reflects the local cultures and to what extent it mirrors western ways of approaching foreign cultures.[35]

This kind of a perception of the relationship between Christ, or the gospel, and culture also easily leads to many kinds of real or fictitious conservatisms. Cultural romanticism easily becomes a vessel of injustice and a way of purging the unequal patterns of social action of the past. It is understandable that we tend to admire the most spectacular cultural monuments: Zanzibar Stone Town (*Mji mkongwe*), Colosseum in Rome or the Great Wall in China. In this admiration we tend to forget that much of the wealth of Zanzibar, producing the fabulous Stone Town, was created through slave

---

32. Vosloo, "The Bible and Justification of Apartheid." It needs to be noted that not all Afrikaner theologians supported Apartheid, and even some of those who did, did not buy the argumentation on the Biblical basis of Apartheid even though it became the position of the Dutch Reformed Church.

33. See Wingren, *Växling och kontinuitet*, 179–84.

34. On this type see Niebuhr, *Christ and Culture*, 83–115.

35. Bevans, *Models of Contextual Theology*, 59–61.

trade and the work of slaves in clove plantations. Likewise, when marveling at the impressive Colosseum, one does not easily remember the human blood spilled on its sand in brutal shows. Moreover, the magnitude of the Great Wall may overshadow the fact that it could only be built by a highly centralized and unequal political system.

Cultural romanticism is often consciously used by oppressive regimes and structures to justify the status quo. In some cases, there is also cultural romanticism that uses fictitious past for justifying patterns of oppression. Male chauvinist politicians, churchmen and other figures of power, sometimes present African traditions as univocally oppressive towards women. This is used as an argument legitimating the marginalization of women. While it is true that some African cultures have been, and still are, oppressive towards women, in some cases there was a gentle balance of power between genders which was often destroyed by colonialism. On the other hand, in some African societies the role of women is far more equal to men than male chauvinist propaganda would like to consider as truly African.[36] After all, the selection of the real culture that should be counted as the classical yardstick of a cultural sphere is always a matter of choice and often also a value judgment between the culture of the rulers and the ruled. Culture is never just there but it is always perceived, selected and interpreted by someone. It is never monolithic and fully functional but, rather, a varied and uneven playground of interests of different groups where rules are kept, bent, and changed according to the circumstances.

The anthropological model as described by Bevans runs also the risk of becoming isolationist in a manner that can be against the interests of the people. It may be overlooked that cultural change and exchange has always existed. Thus, the question should not be whether intercultural connections should take place but rather what kind of positions of power are embedded in them.

However, the relationship between our worldview, in the sense of our pattern of thought, and the gospel is always an open process of interchange between the two. The gospel proclaimed to us may result in a conversion in which our worldview may undergo thorough changes. For example, many thinkers with Christ and culture in paradox type of tendencies have come to that kind of thinking as a result of a conversion process.[37]

The influence of the broad tradition of Christianity and our own understandings of it based on our worldview may also be a gradual process. The gospel contains an edge that challenges our thinking and our values.

---

36. Oduyoye, *Daughters of Anowa*, 92–98.
37. See Niebuhr, *Christ and Culture*, 153.

However, at the same time it is always an I or a we who perceives, listens to, interprets, and reacts to the gospel. When I understand the gospel, I understand it within and through my way of thinking. Even if the result is a major change in my worldview, even that changing worldview is a part of the process. So, the arrow points, not only from the gospel to my worldview, but also from my worldview to the gospel. When I interpret the gospel in a certain manner, I get involved in an open dialogue with the broad tradition of Christianity. In this, there is not only an encounter between me as a cultural creature and God, but also a cultural encounter between my worldview and the cultures of the broad tradition, including at least the Biblical cultures (Israelite/Jewish and Hellenistic cultures). In most cases there will also be more or less normative interpretations of the Bible, provided by different authorities from a number of cultures that guide my understanding. In many cases this interchange is quite subconscious, but one may also seek a more active role in this by seeking to widen one's understanding of the different trends of thought within the broad tradition of Christianity. If the Bible belongs to the core of theologizing, all Christian theology is, thus, always intercultural by definition. My understanding about the interactions between cultures and between my worldview and the gospel adds yet another loop of exchange through which my worldview, my understanding of the gospel and eventually even my theological method are refined.

The Dynamics of the Socio-Cultural Context

A worldview is never created in a vacuum. It is a product of learning and the socialization process. This process is largely guided by the socio-cultural context. On one hand, the general socio-cultural context covers the cultures and cultural influences in a given place and time, as well as the political system, communal patterns and so on. In addition to this multifaceted reality, the position of an individual, and of a group in a community, has a vast bearing on their specific context. It is different to be a female child slave in nineteenth century Zanzibar than an elderly male sultan on the same island. These two are bound to experience the socio-cultural context in different ways, not only because of individual differences but also because of differences in social and cultural standing: the slave is young in a society that values experience. She is female in a context where men dominate. She is a slave owned by a freeman. She does not have a socially accepted religion in a society ruled by Muslims. Her cultural background is not appreciated in a political and economic system that gives preoccupancy to the Arabs. She has dark skin in a setting where light color of skin is valued. She lives in a rural setting while the important decisions are made in town. The list could continue, and the sultan could serve as the prime example of the opposite qualities that constitute an intersectional view of the positions of these two persons in the society.[38]

It is clear that while both of these people live on the same island at the same time and, thus, participate in the same society, their worlds of experience are thoroughly different. Therefore, it becomes clear that we cannot take even the socio-cultural context as a given, but also should see it as it is experienced and interpreted by the person herself. Our culture, social standing, education and many other factors, influence the way we think. Also, the way we personally perceive our socio-cultural position affects the way we relate to it. In movies, it is a cliché that a waiter considers her situation temporary because she is really an artist or a singer, for example. Additionally, a position that is a fulfillment of dreams for one can be an unpleasant means of bare survival for another. Furthermore, we do not think and experience as individuals but as members of different groups: of a family, of a religious community, of a group of colleagues, of a generation, of voluntary organizations, and so forth. Thus, in a way, one could describe an individual as a meeting point of different groups and their interests and influences.[39] As a result, while there are real differences and inequalities in the socio-cultural positions, these positions should not be regarded in an essentialist manner as if there would be a standard, normal or even inevitable meaning these positions carry for the persons in them. How we experience them and what we make out of them differs vastly.

Tracing the arrow in the other direction, our worldview influences the way we interpret our socio-cultural reality. The developments in pre-revolution Ethiopia could serve as an example. Arne Tolo maintains that the Protestant missionary endeavor served unintentionally as a catalyst for the Marxist revolution in Ethiopia. As we have noted, the gospel influences our worldview. Protestant proclamation among non-Amharic peoples of Ethiopia asserted to these oppressed peoples that they too were important in God's eyes and, in fact, that they are equal to the ruling Amharic elite. This shift in worldview also transformed their perception of social structures. Perhaps they were more prepared to recognize the oppression that was exercised in the society. At any rate, this change in thinking helped to create the critical mass to launch the revolution that would replace Emperor Haile Selassie. Thus, their change in worldview not only changed their

---

38. See Collins and Bilge, *Intersectionality*.

39. However, to consider a person only as such a junction, thus, deconstructing the notion of person (see, e.g., Mbembe, *On the Postcolony*, 14–15) sounds far-fetched.

understanding of social structures, but also served as an impetus to bring thorough political and social changes.[40]

In academic theological work there is another crucial dimension of social context: choosing one's discussion partners. The way we write and argue is influenced by our concept of discussion partners. In fact, this issue is so important that Per Frostin lists it as the first emphasis of the liberation theological paradigm.[41] There will be a notable difference in approach if one chooses to construct an African theology for Africans or if one constructs African theology for export only. Argumentation is an activity of convincing others. Convincing, in turn, depends largely on the generally accepted premises of thought among the interlocutors. What is taken for granted among people of a certain time, culture, social class, gender or religion can be a ridiculous statement in another context. According to Peter Berger, each social and cultural context has its ways of rationalizing what is credible. He calls these plausibility structures. Social and cultural changes can make a certain claim self-evident, or reduce it to a matter of opinion or even deny it credibility in the eyes of the majority.[42] Therefore, the existing or imagined partners of dialogue are of utmost importance for a theology in making, because they provide the framework of argumentation—what goes without supporting argumentation and what needs to be defended with particular care. And, naturally, the interlocutors also define what is possible to say or write at all.

The social context is also in a relationship of interchange with the interpretations of the gospel. The question of slavery and racial oppression can serve as a case in point. Different types of slaveries have been legitimized either by suppressing the message of liberation and human value inherent in the Christian tradition[43] or by purposefully manipulating the scientific opinion.[44] This kind of action to justify oppression is understandable, because it seems that humans generally need to see their actions as morally acceptable. Therefore, in order to justify themselves, one resorts to

---

40. Tolo, *Sidama and Ethiopian*, 272–74.

41. Frostin, *Liberation Theology*, 6–7.

42. Berger, *Sacred Canopy*, 150.

43. At the same time, one needs to note that even if the message of liberation and human equality has been seen as a core value of Christianity, especially in the early Jesus-movement, a strong tendency of authoritarianism and oppression has also been present in Christianity since early on as an adaptation to the surrounding patriarchal society. Schüssler Fiorenza, *In Memory of Her*, 80–92.

44. This was the case, for example in physical anthropology, where different physical measurements were taken to produce the results desired. Montagu, *Man's Most Dangerous Myth*, 104, 123–40.

various kinds of self-deception. Montesquieu describes this quasi-scientific myth-mongering ironically: "It is impossible for us to assume that these people [black slaves] are men [sic] because if we assumed they were men one would begin to believe that we ourselves were not Christians."[45] Another alternative to perpetuate oppression was by tinkering the content of the gospel. At worst, oppressive systems have done the both: for example, the Afrikaners produced both an Apartheid ideological interpretation of Christianity and an ideological racist anthropology.[46]

However, the influence also occurs in the other direction. It is hardly a co-incidence that it was just Christian revivalists that exercised such a strong pressure on the British government that it abstained from the highly profitable slave trade and eventually fought to abolish it in areas under its control, including East Africa. The revival brought a renewed moral consciousness, which was transformed into action and change in the social context. The renewed social consciousness was more likely to shake the economic logic of the society because the Clapham sect (the derogatory name given to the anti-slavery revivalists by their opponents) was also otherwise in radical breach of some of the social norms due to its strict moral code. For a theologian very close to the powers that be, radically prophetic action is much more difficult than for someone who is already in the margins. In a similar way, it has been reported that the East African Revival brought about the amelioration of women's conditions in some areas. This revival also promoted a radical break with the existing cultural patterns it perceived sinful.[47]

Theology, just like any other branch of human knowledge, attempts to deal with themes and topics which are considered to be central to its field. It is interesting how social context influences the choice of theological themes.[48] Political questions and the issue of the relationship between the church and the state were an important area of discussion for Luther, at least partly, because without political support the Reformation could not have survived too long. In the time of Lutheran Orthodoxy these issues were

---

45. Montesquieu, *Spirit of the Laws*, book 15, ch. 5. See also Montagu, *Man's Most Dangerous Myth*, 73.

46. Note that here anthropology stands for one's understanding of human nature, not for the academic discipline. Ahonen, *Transformation*, 42–44. For a detailed description of the roots and development of this ideological theology see Bosch, "The Roots and Fruits of Afrikaner Civil Religion." This was the case also with Anglo-American slavery in which the slave owners and traders interpreted slavery as their divinely ordered task. Montagu, *Man's Most Dangerous Myth*, 69, 74–75.

47. Nlwagila, *From the Catacomb*, 259–60; Sahlberg, *From Krapf to Rugambwa*, 124.

48. See, e.g., Bevans, "What Has Contextual Theology to Offer," 12–13.

considered to have already been addressed and occupied a much less important position. Only the social and political changes of last century, with influences from liberation theology, have revived an interest in these issues.

In cases where the ecumenical discussion partners of the Lutherans (or Presbyterians or the like) are high church Anglicans or Roman Catholics, questions of ordained ministry and church order tend to get emphasized whereas discussions with Pentecostals bring the issues of baptism and faith to the fore. Moreover, the theologian's standing in society contributes to the choice of themes: naturally, if one belongs to an oppressed group, the theme of oppression would not be overlooked. A critical question to academic theologians is the issue of transcending one's social context. To which extent are we able to feel with others? Another dimension of this question is to which extent we can actually empathize with the others at all. Do we construct our theologies among ourselves or do we seek avenues of coming out of isolation and looking for ways of contributing to society? A Christian theology that is created in a cocoon of likeminded for the likeminded with no intention to communicate and be in communion with any others is an anomaly. It is a communal version of what Luther describes as a human basic sinful directness human being *homo incurvatus in se ipsum* (a human curved inward on oneself).[49] An individual or a group only lives true her or its nature as the image of the triune God when yearning communion with the other humans and the whole cosmos. This insight is not only Christian but widely held in many cultures not permeated by Enlightenment. For example African theologians have a strong tendency to emphasize communality. Openness to the other does not, however, need to mean letting down one's community but rather finding ways of opening up towards the others,

No matter how eager I might be in building bridges with others and in trying to understand them, and even to work on their behalf, it will hardly be possible for me to construct a theology for someone else. Unless I can deeply identify with the others, to the extent that the others become "us" for me, there cannot be a possibility of my theologizing for the group. However, there is always the possibility of entering a fruitful discussion with the other thereby lowering the dividing fences and expanding my horizons.

The choice of themes does not usually directly influence the sociocultural context. Rather, this happens through the changes the scrutiny of these topics causes in the general interpretation of the gospel. For example, several theologians, including some Roman Catholic bishops[50] took up the

---

49. Luther, *Martin Luthers Werke*, 56:304, ln. 25–29.

50. *Documento de Medellín*, especially 28–45, 115–20; "La evangelización," especially §15–§149, §316–§339, §470–§562, §1128–§1310.

issue of the fate of the poor and oppressed in Latin America. The political change that followed in some countries, for example in Nicaragua, did not take place just because the theologians would have chosen to deal with questions of justice. Rather, their contribution was in their liberation theological thinking which, in turn, helped to raise awareness and create a liberating intellectual culture that helped the democratization process.[51]

No matter how contextual we become in theologizing, we still need to listen to the Bible and the Christian tradition if the resulting theology is to be Christian. Theologizing which ignores the Biblical witness of God's action in the world, cuts itself off from its roots and either gets suffocated or becomes something else than Christian theology. A theologian is bound to lend an ear especially to the Bible. The Bible is Christian tradition par excellence and can serve as a directing guide in setting an agenda for our theological enterprise. Naturally, many things have changed since the times the Bible was written. However, from the Bible we can learn about the richness of themes that a Christian theologian has to deal with. The Bible is not only a collection of books on the salvation history of human souls nor is it only about socio-cultural liberation, or ethics, or miracles etc. We are challenged to revise our naturally evolving agendas in the light of the Bible. However, it is almost inevitable that we have our favorite books or passages of the Bible, which match with our pet topics. That said, the Bible should be given the opportunity to challenge us. Thus, those books and passages that do not fit with our conventional patterns should be taken seriously. Likewise, because we always read the Bible in the light of previous interpretations, we are challenged to listen to those interpretations. However, because the context of the other theologians is different, we need to remain critical as to what best clarifies the gospel message for us today.

The way one selects the topics in the Bible, or the Christian tradition at large, produces a new interpretation of the gospel. For example, Pietism, while struggling to deepen the Lutheran understanding of believing and Christian life, sometimes introduced a highly individualistic interpretation of the gospel. This trend was again strengthened by the Evangelical revivals in the Anglo-Saxon Christianity.[52] As a result of this, and many other developments, the broad tradition of Christianity got a strong push towards the focus on individual salvation of the soul. Social Gospel can be seen as a reaction against other-worldliness and individualist piety. In it, the social

---

51. See Álvarez, "Future for Latin American Liberation Theology?" 92.

52. However, it would be unfair to claim that this is the whole picture. The Christians empowered by the Evangelical revival were the driving force behind the abolition of slave trade in Great Britain and Pietism contributed to diaconia in the Lutheran churches. The revivalist communities were, at times, anything else but individualistic.

concerns of the industrialized world were brought to the forefront. Pietism, Evangelical revivals and Social Gospel all had their influences on the societies in Europe and North America exemplifying how the selection of topics can change the socio-cultural context through the changes in the interpretation of the gospel.

The difference between revivalist individualism and Social Gospel can partly be recognized behind contemporary US politics—not least in the tug of war about Obamacare, the attempt to widen the coverage of health insurance to the poorer segments of the population and the subsequent Trumpian reaction. Obamacare is definitely in line with Social Gospel and supported by socially active church-going people. The opponents in the Republican Party argue that it limits the individual's freedom. These economic and social libertarians are usually not liberal in sexual ethics and other areas of strong regulation in revivalist Christianity. The Christian Right was and, partly, still is able to strongly influence American politics and, thereby, change some selected theologically motivated dimensions of the US legislation. Thus, their choice of topics has been a strongly changing factor vis-à-vis the American socio-cultural context.

The choice of topics can also be influenced by the thinker's worldview, either directly or indirectly. As noted above, one's interpretation of the gospel influences the choice of themes, while the interconnection between the worldview and the gospel has also been established above. Other indirect ways of influence take place, naturally, via the socio-cultural context and theological method. However, because the value we place on different things, qualities, persons, ideas, and phenomena is largely defined by our worldviews, the connection between worldview and the choice of the topics is also direct. This is because no one usually decides to work on a worthless or irrelevant question. Thus, those topics that our worldviews make visible and important to us tend to imprint our theological agendas.

Theological Method

Here, theological method refers to the system or basic principles which a theologian uses as methodologically or instrumentally normative tools for theologizing. It is not normative in the same sense as dogma or the Bible are considered to be by many theologians. In this kind of normativity, the norm is considered to have been given from outside as a fact. Theological method is normative in the sense that it sets the norm within the theological system. It is a matter of a theologian's choice based on her understanding of reality (worldview). Worldview and the theological method are deeply interconnected, because one's worldview sets the criteria for the choice or development of one's theological method. For example, someone subscribing to Kant's philosophical premises can opt for transcendental theological methodology (described by Bevans as a model of contextual theology).

Theological method can also influence one's worldview. When a theological method has been adopted and is used consistently, it tends to yield results that not only produce theology but also mold the theologian's worldview in conformity to the method. This can be a matter of improving the consistency of one's worldview, but also of a more profound change in cases where a theological methodology has been adopted from outside rather than created by the theologian herself.

Theological method can also be influenced by social context, by influencing one's worldview or via influencing the choice of themes of theology, as well as the interpretation of the gospel, which, in turn, influence one's theological method. For example, experiences of oppression can lead one to interpret the world as a battleground of social classes, which would best be understood by Marxist social analysis. This kind of a worldview fits well with praxis-type theological methods (Bevans's praxis-model). On the other hand, the situation of acute oppression brings issues of social justice and the like to the center of theological discussion. While these issues can be dealt with other methods, praxis methods have been developed exactly for that kind of work and would, thus, be easily adopted in that situation. Theological method, in turn, directs the theologians' views of what is interesting and what is important. This often occurs subconsciously. Someone using a praxis method is more likely to tackle issues of social conflict than someone applying transcendental methodology.

In theology, the amount of space devoted to a topic or the number of times that a topic is mentioned by a specific theologian does not necessarily indicate that the topic would be more essential for the theologian than another topic. Rather, the way the topics and the theological method interact produce the specific emphasis of the theologian. For example, even if I would remember to mention the importance of women's rights on every page, that question will be more crucial to a feminist theologian who constructs the entirety of her thinking on methodology revolving around that matter.

Finally, the way we understand the gospel should play a major role in establishing a theological method. Our interpretations of creation, sin, redemption, grace, and so on, influence our choice of methodology. It seems that especially the way we conceive of the relationship between creation and redemption, or nature and grace, is of pivotal importance to our choice and use of theological method. For example, the young Karl Barth subscribed to a radical break between nature and grace and worked following dialectical theological method, which juxtaposed the gospel and culture, God and human, grace and law etc. Thus, his way of perceiving nature and grace went hand in hand with his theological method. On the other hand, in academic theology in Africa there is often the opposite tendency, in which one attempts to see continuity between the gospel and African cultures. This kind of an understanding of the gospel does not provide much space for dialectical methods.

A Closer Look at the Hermeneutical Circle

As stated above, this illustration of contextual theologizing is a snapshot of a moment in an open process. To allow the illustration movement, we could imagine time as the third dimension of the picture. The gospel in the middle, understood as the interpretation of the Christian faith, could then be seen as a growing and developing theological process. In fact, the center of the image already contains the depth-dimension of theologies of the past and width dimension of the broad tradition of Christianity which are in a constant dialogue with our interpretations of the gospel. In the same manner, our worldviews, understandings of our social contexts, our theological methods, and choices of themes are in a constant change and interchange with each other.

Finally, if this figure of the contextual reading of the gospel is understood as a description of a genuinely organic type of a process, the different elements should not be understood as separate (even if they appear so in the graphic presentation of the figure) but, rather, as dimensions of a complex process. They have just been distinguished here to illustrate the interconnections of the same reality.

Now, we have reached the point of summing up this chapter so far: The figure below has been interpreted above. As can be seen in this version, Niebuhr's typology has been placed on the two-way arrow between the gospel and the worldview. Bevans's anthropological, synthetic and countercultural models could be seen to fit in here roughly representing three of Niebuhr's types. Bevans's transcendental and praxis models have been placed under theological method. Bevans's translation model cannot be easily placed within this image because it presupposes a propositional understanding of revelation. This means that revelation is seen as a deposit of statements of faith, which are perceived to be correct and unchanging statements. The issue in translation in its most simple and conservative form is simply to translate these statements into new cultures. Thus, the translation model presupposes a specific type of understanding of the "gospel" in the middle of the figure. At the same time, it leaves the other parts of the process relatively free. In principle, in the translation model, one is left with a great variety of options of working on the process of contextualization, depending partly on the context of theologizing and the way one understands the content of the gospel to be translated.

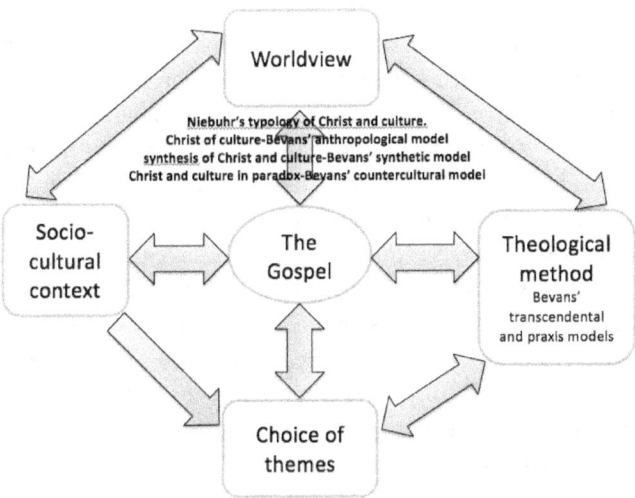

The hermeneutical circle revisited

This process has been discussed as a contribution to understanding constructive academic theology. That could be understood as rather an elitist approach to interpreting the contextual process of Biblical interpretation. However, only the elements of choosing the themes and theological method do not naturally belong to non-academic reading of the Bible. Yet, even there one chooses, often subconsciously, which topics feel relevant and understandable in the Biblical text. Additionally, each reader of the Bible has their strategies and approaches to the Biblical texts. Again, they are often subconscious and tend to build on the reader's understanding of what the Bible is, as well as on examples of Biblical interpretation in one's tradition, most commonly as it is done in the church services.

At a closer inspection of the figure, changing "gospel" into "text" and "theological method" into "method," shows that this figure could describe any reading of a classic text. Any classic text carries with it a tradition of interpretation. Likewise, any reading of a text involves one's worldview and socio-cultural context, and if the text is used as a fountain of renewed thought of any sort, one needs to choose themes and develop them further methodologically. So, what makes this figure here specific to a theological process? The obvious answer is that the text in the center is the gospel. The whole process revolves around the foundational text, the foundational story, of the Christian community.[53]

However, anyone else may read the Bible as well. Furthermore, it is not just a question of restricting the reading of the Bible to a faith community, because also Muslims can read the Bible as a faith community despite believing that some parts of the Bible have been corrupted and do not describe the past as it was (like the narration on Easter). However, this is the case with some Christian exegetes, as well. Should one prescribe a set of doctrinal criteria to measure the Christian quality of the readings of the gospel? This is what has often been done but, in fact, this truncates the process because it is no longer an open process but one with a fixed beginning and end. Furthermore, this kind of a solution either logically requires the possibility of separating the cultural and universal elements of Christian faith or demands that any Christian needs to adapt to (some of) the Jewish and/or Hellenistic (and in the churches of the West also Roman) patterns of thought, whether they are compatible with one's cultural background or not. This closes the path of open investigation about the possibility of contextual theologizing right at the outset.

A handy solution in the history of philosophy and theology in questions like this has been to look for a *deus ex machina*, a god to save our thinking. Here one might propose that the real Christian reading of the gospel always presupposes the presence of the Holy Spirit. Without the help of the Spirit, no one can grasp the gospel. The Holy Spirit makes Christ present in the dead letter of the gospel, bringing it to life as the saving message of God. While this theological view may be seen as correct, at least from the traditional Christian point of view, it has some weaknesses as a solution to the question at hand. First, one would need to presuppose that the Holy Spirit acts only among Christians or ones being converted into Christianity.[54] While there are many (Protestant and Pentecostal) Christians who would agree with this view, a great number of Christians and churches,

---

53. See Ricoeur, "Toward a Hermeneutic of the Idea of Revelation," 25–27 dealing with a similar question, namely the difference between the Bible as revelation and any text as revelation (in an analogous sense). He proposes that the specific Christian character of the Revelation rises from the fact that the "forms of discourse [of the Bible] are referred to the Name which is the point of intersection and the vanishing point of all our discourse about God, the name of the unnameable" (26).

54. On this kind of a question see Comstock, "Truth or Meaning," 126–27.

the Roman Catholic Church included,[55] would not subscribe to this proposal. Furthermore, for example the traditional Lutheran understanding of the means of grace—the word and the sacraments—could be seen as a challenge to this kind of exclusivism. According to the traditional Lutheran teaching, God has committed herself to the means of grace. This being so, the Bible and any Christian message always contains the openness or the possibility of becoming the living Word of God. Thus, in any reading of the gospel the Holy Spirit may be at work, whether one is a Christian or not. That said, we sinful humans turn away from God and shun her saving word, be we Christians or people of other persuasions. Second, if we see the Holy Spirit as the criterion of Christian identity and theologizing, we encounter the problem of verification. We may refer to the fruits of faith and yet we know that there are many people of other faiths who lead morally commendable lives, while our Christian life is sometimes a scandal. So often "[t]his is how everyone will know that you are my disciples, if you have love for one another." (John 13:35) looks like irony.

It seems that the solution must be sought elsewhere. First, it should be noted that the dividing line between believing Christians and the nonbelieving world need not be seen in such a stark contrast as many Christians tend to. The gospel itself must be seen as inclusive rather than exclusive. The Christian message of welcoming all people with Christ's open hands on the cross often turns into a theoretical and practical construction of beliefs that we use for segregating purposes. Thus, the dividing line between Christianity and the world need not be overly emphasized, especially when this emphasis is often used for externalizing evil and avoiding facing our own sinfulness.

Second, a more open way of affirming the Christian identity must be established. Robert A. Jenson has proposed that we should understand Christians as people who identify themselves with the gospel, the foundational story of the Christians.[56] This solution could be understood as a more open approach because the point is not in how to exclude someone from Christianity, but how to establish a Christian identity. This solution lifts the notion of narrative onto the center of the stage. Thus, to proceed, we need to take a closer look at the notion of narrative.

---

55. *Gaudium et spes*, § 22.

56. Jenson starts from the gospel of Christ in defining his understanding of God rather than from philosophical considerations as has often been done. Jenson, *Systematic Theology*, 42. Naturally, Jenson is not alone in this as there are also many other theologians whose position could be described as narrative. See Comstock, "Truth or Meaning," 121 (especially footnotes 11 and 12), 137–38.

Narrative and Reference to the Truth

Many majority world cultures, including African ones, are traditionally predominantly oral cultures with a high respect for storytelling. Many of the stories told mold or define some dimensions of the identity of the narrator and the listeners. Some of these stories can be openly fictitious, like those in which a clever rabbit manages to manipulate or cheat the stronger animals. Despite the story being understood to be fictitious, it analogically reflects the values and aspirations of the community from which it originates. There are also stories that are mythical in character. In many cases, they are myths of origin of the world or of a specific group. Traditionally, they tend to be taken as real representations of the past incidents that form the manner of existence today. There are also many stories that are told as representations of historical incidents, as oral history. It is not possible to draw a clear line between purely historical narrations and myths, because over time historical narrations get dramatized and loaded with mythical elements or meanings. In some cases, historical incidents also grow into myths, accounts of why things are the way they are, during the life-span of the story. The shift from historical narration into a mythical tale often happens, according to Jan Vansina, during the first few generations after the event.[57]

Building one's identity on myths and mythically presented historical accounts is not only an African peculiarity. The importance of stories for one's identity seems to be a common human element and the difference between the ways we use stories for building our identity largely reflects our cultural differences as well.[58] It can be justifiably maintained that Christianity (and also Judaism) is defined by its story. To be a Christian is to base one's identity on the story of Jesus of Nazareth, crucified and risen. On the other hand, this Jesus of Nazareth identified himself with the story of the Jews, followed the God of Abraham and Isaac, again, within the perimeters of a historical-mythical narrative.

One cannot avoid the conclusion that the story of Jesus looks mythical in character. However, since the beginning of the Jesus-movement and subsequent Christianity there has been a strong tendency to emphasize the historicity of the story of Jesus. The four canonical Gospels already show signs of historical consciousness. There are attempts to anchor the good news of Jesus the Christ in the profane history of everyday life. In fact, there is a strong historicizing tendency in the Christian story.[59] In modern west-

---

57. Vansina, *Oral Tradition as History*, 19–21, 136.

58. Ricoeur, *Soi-même comme un autre*, 137–98.

59. On the relationship between the common religious "myth of the eternal return" and Jewish-Christian historicizing tendency see Eliade, *The Myth of the Eternal Return*.

ern theology there have been constant debates on the extent to which the four Gospels are mythical and to what extent they are historical, in the sense that modern western academics understand historicity.

Thus, despite the understanding of identity formed in and through stories, one needs also to consider the way in which the story of Jesus the Christ can be considered true. This task is there not only because of the Christian claims of historicity, but also culminates in the question of the legitimacy of Christian religious expansion in the majority world.[60] Or, to put it in other words: do we only designate meaning to the Christian narrative or both meaning and truth? Should we perceive the Christian narrative as not referring to the world in a manner that could also be meaningful to the people outside our group or does the Christian message contain something that could be counted as truth for any person?[61]

Thus, the question is whether God created the human being and her community in her image or whether human communities create their gods in their images. If the latter Durkheimian thesis is correct, Christianity has no specific rationale in expanding in the majority world. Why should one import another set of myths to replace African or Asian myths? One can only legitimize the Christian missionary endeavor in the majority world only if they can show that it is plausible to believe either that the practical outcome of Christianization is better than other alternatives[62] or that the Christian story is, or can be (at least from the point of view of those who adhere to it), a reflection of the truth. Thus, reference only to one's personal commitment to a Christian identity, referring to the good news of Christ, cannot serve as a proper basis for a majority world Christian theology. Secondly, if one wants to purport that there is a possibility for genuine majority world theologies, one will need to consider the possibility of the reinterpretation of the story.

---

60. For critiques of this expansion from a pluralist point of view see Eboussi Boulaga, *Christianisme sans fétiche*.

61. On this question in connection to narrative theologies see Comstock, "Truth or Meaning."

62. This conclusion would be difficult to reach, indeed. After the crusades, inquisition, slave trade, the two world wars, the Holocaust, evils of Communism, ethnic hatred in Europe (former Yugoslavia, Chechenia etc.) and African predominantly Christian countries (like Rwanda and Burundi), Christian-run Apartheid and so on, there is little to convince one of the moral superiority of Christians. One may argue that these developments were actually against Christian principles and some, like Communism, were directly anti-Christian in nature. Yet, the religious context in which these incidents took place was predominantly Christian and, in many cases, Christian argumentation was used to support these atrocities.

It is almost self-evident that each one of us as an intellectual recipient of a story understands it in her own way. This means that the story is interpreted and reinterpreted over and again. In this, the context of the listener and the narrator plays a significant role. However, the crucial question is: to which extent and how does this reinterpretation reflect the truth? Is truth only an internal conviction of a person, or is it a fact "out there"? And what is the specific relationship between a person and the truth?

To address the question above, we examine the phenomenon of syncretism from a theological perspective in the next chapter and proceed thereafter to propose how to claim a foundation for theology while remaining receptive to the realities of religious pluralism and syncretism.

6

On the Inevitably Syncretistic Nature of Christian Theology

THE QUESTION OF CONTEXTUALITY in theology, even if it may be considered problematic by some theologians, is not generally seen as threatening in many theological and ecclesiastic circles. That may partly be a result of not paying enough attention to the consequences of contextualization or of resorting to some easy solutions that are not intellectually tenable. In this chapter, I will discuss the interreligious dimension of contextuality in theology maintaining that Christian theology is inevitably syncretistic and this state is theologically not only acceptable but actually in line with the basic doctrine of much of Christianity, namely incarnation.

Religion Is Naturally Syncretistic

For pious people it is often very difficult to admit that their religions are actually amalgamations of different religious-cultural elements—they are syncretistic, so to speak.[1] Only a few theologians seem to be prepared to consider their faith and theology as resulting from religion's historical metamorphoses and the borrowing and reworking of religious ideas.[2] Yet,

---

1. Of course, one may object to this wide use of the concept syncretism pointing out that this wide meaning makes it useless, and to refer to syncretism as a process (thus, Maroney, *Religious Syncretism*, 168). This argument becomes pressing, however, only after the syncretistic nature of the religions is accepted.

2. One such theologian was Gustav Wingren (e.g., *Växling och kontinuitet*, 7–8). Wingren, *Växling och kontinuitet*, 141: "En viss pluralism svarar emot den kristna trons historiska art."—"A certain pluralism reflects the historical nature of Christian faith." More recently, Pannenberg (*Systematic Theology*, 147–48) has acknowledged the reality of syncretism in all religions but, in my opinion, that acknowledgement has not led to sufficient changes in the general theological approach.

religious studies take it for granted today that there are no "pure" religions. Heikki Räisänen's magisterial work on the formation of the early Christian faith shows in a convincing manner how multifaceted and varied the process of formation of Christianity was.[3] Unlike in the popular pictures of the ecumenical tree showing how different Christian denominations grow from the same root—often referred to as "Jesus"—and divide into various branches, the beginnings of Christianity were not that uniform. Even a fairly casual reading, especially of the Acts, indicates the bewildering variety of understandings of the message of Jesus the resurrected, as well as the resulting practices that were to become Christian. Gustaf Wingren points out that even the fact that the Bible contains four Gospels witnesses to the fact of the plurality of interpretations from the very beginning.[4]

The fact that every religion builds upon the others and is, in that sense, not pure and unique is also a logical necessity: no religion can ever begin from a *tabula rasa*. Even if one were to believe like Christians and Muslims that God's Word came directly from God, either as a person or as dictation, one builds on previous religions. In the case of Christianity, on Judaism (which, in turn, is based on several Middle Eastern religious traits) and in the case of Islam on Judaism, Christianity and the old Arabian religions. There is always a religious tradition through which the purported new revelation is interpreted.[5] Actually, what one should rather debate about is how that syncretistic process happens: is it a matter of bricolage, hybridity, amalgamation or something else?[6] The central theological question here would be what is the *novum* of the purported new revelation, what novelty does it bring to the world of religions.[7] Or, in Christian vocabulary—what makes good news into news? The question can also be reformulated to direct itself to the special character of Christianity: what makes it Christianity?

What makes it so difficult for many theologians to consider their religion syncretistic? First, syncretism has a very pejorative ring to it, at least in Christian theology, especially in the Protestant dialectical one. It has been defined, among other things, as the "illegitimate mingling of different religious systems."[8] Here one needs to ask who defines the mingling

---

3. Räisänen, *Rise of Christian Beliefs*, 56–76.

4. Wingren, *Växling och kontinuitet*, 23–24, 104–5.

5. See, for example, Boff, *Church, Charism & Power*, 92–93, 94; Pannenberg, *Grundfragen systematischer Theologie*, 268–70.

6. This debate has mostly taken place in social sciences, for a theological pondering of the alternatives see Boff, *Church, Charism & Power*, 90–91.

7. On the gospel being news see Wingren, *Växling och kontinuitet*, 23–25.

8. Kraemer, *Christian Message*, 203. This is actually Kraemer's description of the usual Christian or Protestant position of the time. Kraemer himself considered

illegitimate. At any rate, not the one who mingles! Secondly, according to Michel Foucault, in western cultures one tends to seek the truth of a phenomenon through its *Ursprung*, its origins, albeit in vain.[9] This seems to address the nature of much of Christian theology. Many a theological program, which could be described as *ad fontes*-movements, can be considered to follow such an idea, for example: Lutheranism (the Bible against tradition), Neoscholasticism (scholasticism against modernity), or *la nouvelle théologie* (patristic theology against scholasticism). In each case, one claims to have recaptured something original that was lost through the course of church history. In each case, one could hardly speak of a naïve belief that one may delete the previous history and return to the roots but there was an understanding of varying levels of the historical intricacies involved. However, the idea is that the earlier understanding of faith was more profound and genuine and that there remains a possibility of grasping (some of) its genuine nature and ideas. Returning to the ideals of the past would, thus, redeem the fallen contemporary form of Christianity. However, subscribing to the view that there never was a sole original Christianity but, rather, a multifaceted and plural phenomenon, closes that route to a theological bliss of certainty and purity of faith.

Agreeing that there never was the ideal Christianity of the past to be replicated liberates theological imagination of today as well. The insight of plurality belonging to Christianity from the very beginning facilitates a bolder approach to the plurality of faith in Christianity today, also in relation to the contextual process in theology. Theologians should rather discuss the nature of Christian syncretism and the kinds of theological conclusions it leads us to, rather than what is pure Christianity.[10] Before we have a glance at some of these theological conclusions, we will view some of the contemporary conditions for such conclusions.

From Imperial Religion to Heretical Imperative

A century ago, Christianity was, at least from the point of view of European religious elite, still a relatively easy phenomenon to define, because of its centrality in the ideological map of the hegemonic national cultures. The

---

syncretism normal, even inevitable for religions. However, he made a separation between religions and faith. The latter, as a gift of God, was able to remain uncorrupt by syncretism and human sinfulness.

9. Foucault, "Nietzsche, Genealogy, History," 242–43.

10. See Fridlund and Vähäkangas, *Theological and Philosophical Responses to Syncretism*.

idea was that Christianity has its kernel and bulk in the western Christendom, and most so in one's own country and national culture, and that it expands from there, especially to the colonies. "The West is the best and may evangelize the rest." Naturally, this view has never been an adequate description of reality, because there have always been strong Christian churches outside of the western cultural sphere.[11] The same applied to the doctrinal content of Christianity: that which was either held by one's own denomination or generally considered as the common Christian heritage in the churches of the West, or in the largest conceivable terms European Eastern Orthodox churches, was taken as the yardstick of true Christianity. The pre-Chalcedonian oriental churches like the bulky Coptic churches in Egypt and Ethiopia were routinely left out of consideration, not to speak of the ancient Near Eastern or South Indian churches. The consensus of Christianity had, therefore, either a West European cultural consensus behind it, or at least a consensus of the Greek philosophical heritage. However, even the European reality was more diverse, with several ethnic groups not belonging to the Indo-European linguistic and cultural family on the fringes. Yet, that plurality was not very visible because the European theological hegemony was also imposed on those groups.

An idea gradually developed in Roman Catholic theology that considering the so called *dogma non-necessaria*, less central teachings, it was sufficient for a Christian to believe whatever the religious authority had decided, even without understanding or knowing those doctrines.[12] In this way, the church was able to deal with religious plurality in its backyard when the general level of theological knowledge among the European Christian population was not at a satisfactory level. This move was also partly an outcome of the realization that many people were non-Christians only due to not having heard the gospel, like the peoples in the newly discovered America. This resulted in a need to re-examine the faith of the non-Christians, and to appreciate it as *fides implicita*, faith that was not adequately formulated, or faith that was implicit in the sense that even if it exists, it is not visible.[13] The intention behind this was quite generous, namely, to assess the non-Christians theologically in a positive light. In this way, also they could be counted to belong to the community of salvation in Christ. However, concomitantly this meant the climax of religious authority, or its understanding of itself. Thus, it would be better not to think and to know those doctrines, rather

---

11. For a popular introduction to the history of non-western Christianity see Jenkins, *The Lost History of Christianity*.

12. Ott, *Fundamentals of Catholic Dogma*, 6.

13. Dupuis, *Toward a Christian Theology of Religious Pluralism*, 99–100, 114–16.

than to know them and formulate one's own opinion. Theological thinking became superfluous for the ordinary Christian, and her task was simply to submit to the doctrinal authority of the church. Thus, the essentially inclusive and benevolent attempt to approach religious diversity actually functioned to gloss over religious differences as irrelevant—as long as the ecclesiastic hegemony went unchallenged. Choice and freedom of thought were not a part of the package.

To choose or to have an opinion is, in fact, the literal definition of *haireioo*, the Greek verb behind the term heretic. Despite efforts to the contrary, heretics like Martin Luther, who thought for themselves, were always present. His Biblical interpretation went against some of the magisterial teachings of the Catholic Church which earned him condemnation as a heretic. He gained followers, both those who took his interpretation as the new true teaching, thus, replacing a pope with another, and those whom he inspired to become heretics of their own account. In some areas, Lutherans, Reformed and Anglicans could reach hegemonic positions which, alongside the Roman Catholics, facilitated them becoming dutiful oppressors of those they labelled as heretics, like Anabaptists, or of each other.

The Protestant Reformation turned against *fides implicita* teaching that everyone should know the true doctrine. This move was accompanied with a strong emphasis on folk education, in terms of reading and the content of the Protestant doctrine. By this way, the problematic religious plurality, usually interpreted as ignorance and superstition, could be overcome in the Protestant plans. This necessitated the opportunity for everyone to read the Bible in her own language, a principle that also called for Bible translation into vernaculars. This availability of the Bible in one's mother tongue, with the emphasis of everyone as a theological agent in terms of having to understand the central tenets of the Christian faith, actually opened the Pandora's Box of theological-religious pluralism within Protestantism. However, the homogenous cultural context and the state-church cooperation could keep the lid largely closed. The ecclesiastic, social and cultural pressures to concur with the majority kept the theological variation at a relatively low level in spite of the regularly occurring revival movements that could produce groups of dissenters. Putting it in a pointed way, one may say that the Protestant authorities taught that one must learn to understand the Christian faith, to ruminate it, and eventually believe as the church taught. Pietism, the mother movement of Protestant revivalism, can be understood as the strengthening of this principle: You are supposed to decide to follow Jesus—the way we teach about him. This means that one was simultaneously supposed to think and believe personally, and to choose *(hairein)*, but not to become a heretic by choosing differently from the dominant doctrine of the faith community.

Contemporary western societies are undergoing a twofold process of increasing pluralism. The first, most discussed, mode of increasing pluralism is fueled by immigration and increased intercultural connections. The more immigrants there are, at least statistically, the higher the level of cultural and religious diversity there is. However, this diversity may result in a ghetto-type situation in which the degree of diversity is expressed in the multitude of encapsulated parallel monolithic realities.[14] This is the case when immigration does not lead into an integrated society. This seems to be the vision many immigration critical thinkers dread most. However, if this criticism stems from the fear of losing national and cultural identities, the alternative of integrated immigration is actually much more threatening for cultural purists. Integrated immigrants are in close contact with the indigenous population, leading to much deeper and wider processes of cultural change and diversification, something that is happily referred to in South Africa as the rainbow nation irrespectively whether this is a dream or reality.[15] However, in both cases pluralism increases, more dramatically in the latter.[16] That kind of cultural change does not often seem so threatening, though, because the changes take place in oneself and are, thereby, more acceptable. My practices of Yoga and eating sushi are not quite as dangerous in the eyes of xenophobic spectators as the appearance of different looking people in their neighborhood, even if the former may signal a deeper change in society.

Simultaneously, there is also an autochthonous dimension to the increase of pluralism. Pluralism has grown partly from within western cultures. The Enlightenment has encouraged us to take our fates in our own hands. This can be considered a continuation and logical consequence of the Protestant idea of personal faith which is not, in principle, dependent on ecclesiastic or governmental authorities. Enlightenment ideals encourage us all to be heretics. It should not come as a surprise to the Protestant religious authorities that in a context of free individual consideration, the majority does not produce a unified outcome in favor of the church establishment. That is related to the modern person's inescapable necessity of choice. This is

---

14. This kind of development is visible in many American cities.

15. This concept was popularized by Archbishop Desmond Tutu. Buqa, "Storying *Ubuntu*," 1.

16. The wish simply to absorb the newcomers without any changes in the recipient culture is naïve. There are no pure cultures and additionally, (neo)colonial encounters increase the cultural hybridity. See an interpretation of Bhabha's views on hybridity in Childs and Williams, *Introduction to Post-Colonial Theory*, 123, 133–37.

described by Peter Berger as the "heretical imperative."[17] Individual choice has become the norm for our societies, making pluralism a built-in value as such. One simply cannot expect everyone to make the same or even similar choices in the long run. Thus, pluralism in our societies has dual roots based, on one hand, on the increased cultural exchange and, on the other hand, the modern basic value of the freedom of choice. Pluralization in the West is accelerated by the fact that there is no longer a homogenous culture to keep the religious and cultural pluralism in check.

In Christianity, we also need to account for the third dimension of pluralism, that stemming from the Christian tradition. Although Christian leaders of each persuasion have tended, and often still tend, to present themselves as the authoritative representatives of the authentic Christianity, Christianity itself is a seedbed of pluralism. There has never been a time of unified Christianity. Christians have never had a common interpretation of their faith. Furthermore, what many consider as the fundamentals of Christianity, namely the Bible, also causes that plurality.[18] There are four gospels in the New Testament, with considerable differences in emphases.[19] Different epistles further increase the pluriformity of New Testament theological views. Even the doctrine of the Trinity refers to the multifaceted character of reality. If God, the ultimate Reality, is not a simple unity, then our earthly reality need not be conceived as such.

Actually, pluralism permeates the whole of the western sphere of life from worldview to the most trivial decisions in everyday consumption. No humans have ever been as free as the affluent inhabitants of the industrialized countries—if we narrow down freedom into choice the way advertisements want us to do.[20] We have endless choices, from the most minuscule consumption decisions to greater decisions in life like the choice of our life partners, having children or not and so on. However, one may question how real the choices concerning the true questions of survival of our planet are. To which extent can individual humans freely choose whether to annihilate the living conditions of the majority of the poor human population in the world as well as vast sections of global natural habitat through the consumerist culture that devours global resources and accelerates global warming? Through which kinds of choices could each individual effectively contribute to a more just distribution of wealth in the global scene, where

17. Berger, *Heretical Imperative*, 23–28.

18. Räisänen, *Marcion, Muhammad and the Mahatma*, 191–93. Of course, it is also the other way around: Because there were varying views among the early Christians, the Bible became a book of many voices.

19. See Wingren, *Växling och kontinuitet*, 23.

20. See Berger, *Heretical Imperative*, 1–3.

multinational corporations dominate the market with the backing of a few strong governments?[21] Each of us can make choices to cut down on consumption and direct it to ethically produced items, but those choices are constantly in the danger of being reduced to individual actions not leading to any major global changes because the global, regional and national structures do not change. In that case, freedom is limited only to individual choice. Furthermore, considering the social pressures, cultural norms and the continuous market-driven bombarding of preferences through advertisement and consumer culture, one may even question whether even individual choices really exist. And, here above, we have considered only the simplest and most prosaic dimension of freedom, namely choice. Western pluralism and capitalist organization of the societies is thus no guarantee of freedom, not necessarily even as free choice.[22]

In many majority world contexts, one has never even had the luxury of major individual choices in consumption. Nor has one had the possibility of imagining a monolithic homogenous culture but different languages, cultures, religions and traditions have intermingled in communities. There are, of course, also some contexts where only one culture, language and religion have an absolute hegemony. However, this hegemony often masks the variety of silenced cultures. In the pluralistic majority world contexts, the only possible way of creating a theological hegemony is to form insular reality bubbles where one may attempt to maintain the unified correct faith. This is, in fact, a not so uncommon approach. At any rate, the pluralistic situation poses similar challenges to the absolute truth claims of faith communities everywhere.

The increasing importance of choice has led us to view almost everything through the lens of economic free competition, as we can see for example in international, EU and national politics. This kind of freedom in the sense of free market economy—which actually is not quite as free as it claims to be—has been successfully and partly forcefully exported to the rest of the world.[23] Thus, in this light it seems natural that even religion is seen

21. See Klein, *Shock Doctrine*.

22. Compare Friedman, *Capitalism and Freedom* and Klein, *Shock Doctrine*. For Friedman, capitalism and freedom tend to go hand in hand for which he gives only some anecdotal evidence. Klein presents dozens of well documented cases where Friedmanian principles coupled with American imperialism have been destructive to freedom in the sense of democratic political rights and even economic alternatives of the local populations. According to both Friedman and Klein, capitalism builds on a hyperindividualized view of a human being (Friedman, *Capitalism and Freedom*, 1–6; Klein, *Shock Doctrine*, 52–53) which, however, is a skewed understanding of human nature, especially from the point of view of most non-western cultures.

23. On the forceful exportation of this economic model and its accompanying

as another market in which the consumers make use of rational choice.[24] In this situation it has become impossible not to choose. So, viewing from the western capitalist point of view, we have arrived to a situation of the heretical imperative in pluralist societies. The heretical imperative can be seen as a child with pluralism and market ideology as its parents. Both of these parents are strongly molding our world and forcing us in the position to choose, even if nominally.

Within religion, this change means that it is no longer possible to believe just the way the others believe—there is no longer any norm. To follow a strict religious authority is a choice just as much as to select the most fitting religious ideas in one's worldview. Even the secularist agenda cannot claim a definite hegemony. Any way of relating to religious questions involves a decision and not dealing with any religious questions is a decision as well, at least if it is conscious. This is "the heretical imperative" in the religious realm.[25]

In a certain manner the heretical imperative should be a positive situation for the Protestants, and definitely at least for revivalist Christians. The emphasis on Jesus as the "personal savior" could not be more fitting to any other situation. When any religious commitment or even non-commitment denotes a personal choice, Jesus cannot be but a personal savior or not a savior at all. Yet, among Protestants, revivalist or not, it is very common to hear lamentations about secularization and the rise of new non-Christian forms of religiosity in the global North, as if it were to be expected that everyone freely makes the same choices they do.

Christian Religious Authority Is More Splintered Than Ever

Meanwhile, the face of Christianity has changed considerably. As stated before, the majority of Christians have been found outside of the West already for a couple of decades. The most rapidly growing churches tend to be charismatic local churches of the South which do not depend on western denominations. Among charismatic Christians, one often conceives religious authority as a direct gift from God in the power of the Spirit. That means that, in principle, anyone can become a religious authority irrespective of

---

ideology and the logical and practical flaws related to its alleged freedom, see Klein, *Shock Doctrine*; Wahl, "International Financial Markets"; and Terreblanche, "American Empire."

24. See, e.g., Stark, *Rise of Christianity*, 166–89.
25. Berger, *Heretical Imperative*, 23–28.

her gender, education, family background, social standing and other factors which are often used by religious elites to limit access to leadership.

Previously, even if, for example, Lutherans and Roman Catholics could not accept each other as true Christians, they still had common ground: the traditions and creeds of the early Greco-Roman church as well as the common western European cultural background. Today, however, it is quite possible to find churches that do not subscribe to the ecumenical creeds and still see themselves as thoroughly Christian. This is the case in some post-confessional congregations which often, in fact, subscribe to rather generic Anglo-Saxon Evangelical traditions. Simplified Biblicism belongs to that tradition and easily leads to the idea of not needing anything else than the Bible and, thus, becomes post-confessional. One can, naturally, also break away from both the language and the contents, as is the case of the Olumba Olumba church in Nigeria. The founder of the church considers himself the incarnation of the holy Trinity.[26] In western theology, however, one tends to rather stick to the traditional theological language while modifying its meaning considerably.

Thus, the Pandora's Box is completely open today. New churches are founded on a daily basis and there is hardly anything apart from the Bible (albeit in thousands of translations in various languages) that binds them together.[27] Even the role of the Bible can be totally different in the churches. How should one classify those African churches which read only read the Torah as their Bible—despite only having historical ties to Christianity, not Judaism?[28]

It is clear that religious authority is increasingly splintered in Christianity: there is no one to define the limits of Christianity, true teaching, or heresy, except in a communally limited, less than ecumenical way. Therefore, although there are many very autocratic religious leaders within Christian churches and Christian-inspired religious movements exercising unlimited authority, even to the extent of leading to mass extinction, like in the Ugandan Kanungu,[29] the authority of the leaders is usually strictly limited to the group. Those rejecting the authority of the leader must simply leave the group. In that case, the leaver will naturally be regarded as a backslider, but is hardly more of a heretic than the rest of the world outside the boundaries

---

26. Sabar and Shragai, "Olumba Olumba in Israel," 206.

27. Wingren, *Växling och kontinuitet*, 30 points out that the continuity in Christianity, i.e., between different historical forms of Christianity, is continuity based on the text. This notion could be expanded to also cover different contemporary variations of Christianity.

28. See Turner, "Typology for African Religious Movements," 8–10.

29. On the Kanungu case, see Vokes, *Ghosts of Kanungu*.

of the group.³⁰ Therefore, regardless of how strict the definitions of the boundaries of Christianity might be, their relevance is usually very limited.

While it is true that even in the past there was no single Christian doctrinal authority, there were regional religious hegemonies, as there were religiously almost monolithic states or areas. In that context, adherence to that type of religion in a specified manner did not necessarily denote choice, whereas opting out was a clear choice, often at a high personal risk. Such a person was definitely a heretic in the surroundings where religious plurality was either suppressed or minimal. This lack of plurality was strengthened by the fact that media and other forms of communication with people representing other faiths were very limited. Today, even the most significant religious leader of the world, the Pope, cannot claim such hegemony about any area. Rather, his authority is a contested authority among others, that spreads wide but thin over almost all world. In some areas the authority is thicker (stronger) than in others, but nowhere truly hegemonic any longer.

No Clear Boundaries for Christianity

What do the boundaries of Christianity look like in this world of splintered religious authority? Grossly simplifying, one could say that belonging to a religion consists of two dimensions: that I define myself as belonging to a certain religion and that the other members of the religion accept me as one of them. So, basically that belonging revolves around identity and membership, or personal and group dimensions of religious identity.

The situation becomes more complicated when dealing with groups like churches instead of individuals belonging to definable religious groups. There is no official entity called "Christianity" which can accept or turn down the churches' applications to belong to Christianity. Such discussions about membership take place in the World Council of Churches, like that of the Kimbanguist church accepted as a member in the 1960s after a thorough screening.³¹ Today, one wonders whether that church should be excluded because it has begun to openly teach that the founding prophet, Simon Kimbangu, was an incarnation of the Holy Spirit.³² They subscribe to all

---

30. This does not suggest, however, that leaving the group would be easy especially if the leaver's family still belongs to it. In those cases when the group is, sociologically speaking, a sect, the members' relations to the rest of the world have been seriously limited which creates a strong dependency on the religious movement. In such a case leaving the group means losing practically all existing social relations.

31. On the Kimbanguist Church written by a WCC delegate sent to assess it see Martin, *Kirche ohne Weisse*.

32. Kongo Dumbi, *Doctrine du Saint Esprit*, 63: "Simon Kimbangu est de la même

the ecumenical creeds, but have additional beliefs on top of that, like that of Simon Kimbangu as the incarnation of the Holy Spirit. They have a strong Christian identity, but other Christians tend to look at them with suspicion in the best case. Whatever the fate of the Kimbanguist Church in the WCC, the WCC can hardly be considered to represent Christianity as such. Churches belonging to the WCC only represent a fraction of the world's Christian population, and, yet, it is arguably the most inclusive Christian organization, if one does not take into account the Catholic Church which claims about half of the world's Christians as its members. However, the Catholic Church is more limited than the WCC, in the sense that its doctrinal basis is relatively strictly defined. Therefore, its approach is bound to be more limited too. Even if one combined these two most likely candidates to represent world Christianity, a considerable chunk of world's Christians would remain marginalized. Therefore, there is no one to represent the global Christian voice in defining the criteria of inclusion and exclusion from the community.

For many, the label "Christian" as an epithet of a religious group appears so positive that it is easy to see how the Kimbanguists would like to be considered Christians. The opposite is more difficult to grasp. However, Jonas Adelin Jørgensen, a Danish missiologist, analyses a mirror image of the Kimbanguist case in his research. In Dhaka, Bangladesh, there are Jesus-imandars who claim to be Muslims even though they believe in Jesus as their savior and include many elements that, for an outsider, appear to be highly contextualized Christian rituals in their worship life. Yet, they rather see themselves as Jesus-believing Muslims. Furthermore, in Chennai, India, Jørgensen studied Christ-bhaktas, Hindus believing in Christ, representing a similar approach to the Jesus narrative as well as Christian ritual life. While there is a great temptation to define these groups as Christian, they reject this definition themselves.[33] Thus, there are groups who do not consider themselves as Christian, although many Christians would be tempted to do so.

I have analyzed the metamorphosis of the myths of the North Tanzanian Sonjo, known also as Batemi. For almost seventy years, Lutherans, Catholics and later even Pentecostals have tried to convert them. There are relatively few baptized Sonjos and very few of them are active in the churches. However, the apotheosized cultural hero of the Sonjo traditions, Ghambageu, has gradually absorbed so many dimensions of the Christ-message

---

nature divine que le Père et le Fils. Les deux natures sont unies sans confusion en lui. Il est donc le Saint Esprit."

33. Jørgensen, *Jesus Imandars and Christ Bhaktas*.

that today Sonjo leaders claim that after he died and resurrected among the Sonjo, he went to the Europeans as Jesus! Thus, Sonjos have neither a Christian identity nor explicit faith in Jesus. Even so, they have absorbed major portions of Christian faith.[34] Thus, here we have a case in which the people belonging to an ethnic group and, thereby, their traditional religion do not claim to be Christians as a group—some individuals in the ethnic group do—and they do not practice a clearly Christian ritual, nor do they claim to be Jesus' followers except as followers of Ghambageu. Yet, we have here a case of increasing absorption of the Biblical stories and even Christian approaches to moral questions. Theoretically, one might raise the question: How much of Christianity can one appropriate without becoming Christian?

When some people claim not to be Christians, while subscribing to the central Christian doctrines like Jesus-imandars and Christ-Bhaktas, others both claim to be Christians but believe in a heterodox way like Kimbanguists or Mormons, and others just absorb Christian values and teachings without using Christian expressions like the Sonjo, it seems impossible to draw clear boundaries for Christianity without subscribing to a very rigid set of criteria.[35] To be able to draw such boundaries in a more flexible way, one would need to define the essence of Christianity[36] through which one could evaluate all groups under the title of Christianity. However, such an essence of Christianity would always be a product of a certain culture, historical context and even personal choice. Therefore, setting the boundaries of Christianity by defining its essence is a futile effort. Gustaf Wingren argues against such essentialization of Christianity by pointing out that it is the concrete manifestations of Christianity that make it what it is, not an abstract idea of its essence.[37] One could even claim that Christianity is a floating signifier because it gets different meanings depending on the context and the one that uses the signifier.[38]

To conclude, one simply needs to acknowledge that the multifaceted nature of Christianity and its splintered state of authority result in the

34. Vähäkangas, *Between Ghambageu and Jesus*.

35. The diffuseness of the boundaries of Christianity has been pointed out before: According to Heim, *Salvations*, 46 this is the position of Wilfred C. Smith. See also Bauer, *Orthodoxy and Heresy*.

36. The title of Adolf von Harnack's book *Wesen des Christentums* points out to this need to define the essence. His approach banks on the search on *Ursprung* discussed above (Harnack, *Wesen des Christentums*, 17–18).

37. Wingren, *Växling och kontinuitet*, 28–29.

38. For an example of the use of the term in theology/philosophy of religion see Topolski, "Spinoza's True Religion."

impossibility of clearly defining its borders. Therefore, the borders of Christianity must be seen as porous, with a wide grey zone where it depends on the position of the observer and her preferred criteria whether a certain group should be counted as Christian or not. Additionally, it also depends on which dimension of the group in question one assesses. If one extended this kind of an exercise to individuals, the result would be even more confusing when issues of multiple religious belonging, pick and mix religiosity and dual religious practices entered the picture.

Translatability Makes Christianity Global and Diffuse

What is notable in contemporary Christianity is that it has become a veritable world religion. While Hinduism is marked by its Indian cultural heritage, and Islam bound to Arabic as a language and thereby to Arabic cultures, Christianity has found its expression in a myriad of cultures. That is referred to as "translatability" by the Gambian theologian Lamin Sanneh.[39] However, this difference between Christianity and other religions should not be overestimated to the extent of maintaining Christianity to be *sui generis* in this sense. There are culturally rigid forms of Christianity attempting to exercise cultural imperialism over others. On the other hand, there are some forms of Islam, often regarded as very culturally bound, that are highly adjustable to new cultural surroundings. This especially applies to many forms of Sufism which have spread to various parts of Africa and Asia.[40] Sanneh compares, most of all, Christianity and Islam which are the most relevant religions in his native Gambia. While one can argue, on the practical level, against Sanneh's thesis and note that there is only a difference of degree between these two religions in adjusting to the local context, Sanneh's point is stronger when applied to the theological imagination of these religions.

Due to the notion that in Islam one cannot translate the Quran, what an outsider calls translations of Quran are interpretations in the Muslim perspective. This idea in Islamic theology contains very deep and genuine observations on the nature of language, knowledge, and translation. Every translation is inevitably a matter of interpretation. There is no translation that can fully capture the meaning of a text. Words and syntaxes are never

---

39. Sanneh, *Translating the Message*.

40. Waardenburg, "Official and Popular Religion in Islam," 321. Waardenburg points out that in the past, Islam tended to be more culturally adaptable even if there always have been tensions between what he labels as "popular" and "official" Islam (Waardenburg, "Official and Popular Religion in Islam," 318, 330, 332).

fully equivalent, especially when considering all the nuances, double meanings and connotations. This is all the more so regarding poetic and religious language such as Quran. Therefore, the only viable option to maintain certainty is to subscribe to an inerrant divine revelation as text in the original language. A precondition to this is, of course, that there is only one authorized text variant. According to the Muslim traditions, this was achieved during the caliphate of Uthman by lifting one version above the others and destroying the rest of the text variants.[41]

Christian Fundamentalism attempts a form of Quranification of the Bible by adhering with verbal inspiration theory, through which an idea of an inerrant Biblical text can be established. To get over the countless text variants and to allow for the use of a translation that deals with the three languages (Hebrew, Aramaic and Greek) and a mass of text easier, an intellectual somersault is required: the declaration that the King James Version is inerrant as a translation inspired by the Holy Spirit. Here, these often so anti-Catholic Protestants come scarily close to the Catholic medieval position on Vulgate translation. This fundamentalist move may be psychologically assuring, but comes with a price even without considering the credibility of this position. In the fundamentalist position, the anchoring of the truth in the form of the text results in virtual declaration of the inerrancy of the cultural forms of expression behind the Biblical messages. In forms of Fundamentalism where one Bible translation is elevated over others as the correct one, simultaneously, one interpretation is offered as the right one. Thereby, the sphere of interpretation is narrowed to the imagination of England of times past. Much of the dynamism belonging to Christianity is lost.[42] In the following, I will be discussing the dimension of the translatability of Christianity from the point of view of the dynamics that I consider to be inalienable from the gospel.

Translatability does not only mean that you can translate the Bible, but that Christian faith can find its concrete forms, become Christianity, within different cultures. And that does not necessarily mean that something is lost in this process.[43] Therefore, one cannot and should not seek the true nature of Christianity in its *Ursprung* but, rather, in the dynamic process of the re-creation of Christian message in the variable contexts. In this sense, although Sanneh may not be pointing to a qualitative difference between Christianity and Islam in terms of comparative religion, he may be

---

41. Saeed, *Qur'an: An Introduction*, 43–44.

42. See Wingren, *Växling och kontinuitet*, especially 69–70.

43. Boff expresses a similar idea using the term "catholicity": "The catholicity of the Church is the power to be incarnated, without losing its identity, in the most diverse cultures." (Boff, *Church, Charism & Power*, 98).

pinpointing a quality in Christianity that is related to the theological fundamentals of Christian faith. Therefore, for him, Islam would be more of an *Ursprung*-directed religion that has Quran as the *Ursprung*-foundation, whereas Christianity is more directed to the process of translation than sticking to the *Ursprung*. At any rate, in any translation, some dimensions are lost while, at the same time, new vistas are opened. Thus, because translatability of Christianity rises from its theological quality rather than from translatability being the same kind of a phenomenon in all religions, one needs to approach this question theologically, rather than from the point of view of comparative religion.

When we add the temporal perspective and historical changes in culture and thought, the inevitability of contextualization of the Christian faith becomes clear. It would be absurd to claim that the faith of contemporary Christian churches, even in "old Christian" countries of Europe would be the same as a thousand years ago.[44] As indicated above, even in cases when the wording remains the same, the meaning of the text changes along with a transforming social and cultural context. What once was a radical departure from the status quo of male hegemony, like Jesus' ban on divorce, can, in another context denote a strong support of male hegemony.[45]

In debates about contextual theology, it has long been argued that all theology is contextual, and that no one can theologize from a universal point of view.[46] Each of us is situated somewhere in terms of culture, history, society, economy and so on. That means that in all theology, one not only includes her own theological innovations but that these innovations grow from a soil that is already a mixture: in which one not only encounters the present challenges, but also the historically-constructed religious-cultural traditions which, in turn, are mixtures of Christian and non-Christian influences. For the *Ursprung*-type of a theological purist this is, naturally, unacceptable. But where would you find pure Christianity when even the Bible is a meeting point for various religions and cultures? Thus, even the most rigorously Biblicist theology cannot avoid a certain level of syncretism.

This view has been accepted in liberal theology for quite a long time. The conclusion was often that one no longer saw Christianity as the only true religion but, rather, that all religions were dimensions of the same phenomenon. However, Christianity was often perceived as the highest echelon

---

44. See, e.g., Wingren, *Växling och kontinuitet*, 15–17.

45. See A. Vähäkangas, *Christian Couples*, 69–70 on Tanzanian Chagga understandings of marriage and divorce and M. Vähäkangas, "Gender, Narratives and Religious Competition" on the Sonjo Christian women's view on divorce as a liberating practice in their traditional cultural background.

46. See, e.g., Bergmann, *Gud i funktion*, 16.

of the evolution of religion—and within Christianity, liberal theology without doubt the most sophisticated type of thinking.[47] Unfortunately, liberal theology can claim relatively little support among the majority of Christians, most of whom are found outside of the western countries. In the Global South, one does not necessarily share the Enlightenment background, and the reading of the Bible tends to be literal, even if it is interpreted in different cultural contexts.[48]

Dialectical theology attempted to deny the liberal theological argumentation by claiming that Christian faith is not a religion, while Christianity is. Strangely enough, in that view, true (Christian) faith and religion do not necessarily belong together.[49] Thus, one strove to preserve the idea of Christ as the only savior when one could not reject the fact that various religions had so much in common. This is an ingenious solution, in the sense that no empirical finding can disprove it: If one finds syncretistic elements in Christianity, it is not a matter of a genuine Christian faith but of sinful human influence within the religion of Christianity. Thus, syncretism in Christianity was not seen to have anything to do with the Christian faith.[50] But faith cannot be a mere abstract idea—faith that finds no expression in life is rather a play of ideas, not a faith. Thus, one must anyhow tackle some empirical realities. Here, the dialectical theologian will begin to classify between acceptable and unacceptable contextualization. Which contextualization preserves the Christian uniqueness? In so doing, the dialectical theologian places herself above the others and makes universal truth-claims.

But, as seen above, the crisis of religious authority in Christianity makes it difficult for anyone to place oneself above the others and claim to be the universal authority in a convincing way. Yet, there are numerous theologians, religious leaders, self-appointed prophets or apostles and other who do so—which only serves to underscore the crisis of authority. Thus, it seems that no one can define these borders.

Contextual theology often emphasizes the openness and spontaneity of the process.[51] Following from that, the result can never be known in advance. That means that we cannot have any recipes for safe contextualization—safe in the sense of being manageable and controllable by ecclesiastic hierarchies and theological specialists. As a result, the diffuse boundaries

---

47. See Heim, *Salvations*, 63; Jørgensen, *Jesus Imandars and Christ Bhaktas*, 71–74.

48. Jenkins, *New Faces of Christianity*.

49. See Jørgensen, *Jesus Imandars and Christ Bhaktas*, 74–81.

50. Heim, *Salvations*, 61, 108 directs similar criticism towards Wilfred C. Smith who makes a division between faith and religion much in the same way as the dialectical theologians, albeit to serve a different theological agenda.

51. E.g., Schineller, *Handbook on Inculturation*, 12.

of Christianity appear to be natural—if the result is not known in advance, one cannot expect each outcome to fit neatly into a preconceived idea of traditional Christianity.

Furthermore, the relations between Christianity and other faiths, as well as between followers of Christian and other faiths, are not one-dimensional and do not allow for easy categorization into exclusivism, inclusivism, pluralism and relativism, or any other neat classification.[52] This is, firstly, because in real life these categories do not work separately. For example, it is quite possible to include something by exclusion. When an African Charismatic preacher condemns dimensions often related to traditional worldviews, the action looks first like outright exclusion. A closer look reveals, however, that this exclusion actually indicates the endorsement of the traditional worldview by letting it set the agenda for preaching. Additionally, some of the preaching will conform to the traditional worldview—like the condemnation of witchcraft—an opinion shared by the traditional religions too. Furthermore, some dimensions of the worldview are simply renamed, and so benevolent spirits are baptized as angels and malevolent ones as demons.[53] Some other dimensions, like ancestral veneration, are (sometimes) rejected but in a way that their veracity or efficacy is not disputed but, rather, they are not considered compatible with the Christian faith. Finally, in some dimensions, a functional substitution takes place. For example, Christian preachers have taken over the functions of the traditional healer to such an extent that there exists a discourse on whether some of the preachers who used to be traditional healers remain as such, or whether the conversion was genuine.[54] Thus, exclusion suddenly proves to be predominantly inclusion in this case.

Secondly, relating to other religions is not a single-level reality, nor does a believer's relationship to another religion happen as a direct application of a single theological-philosophical principle. Again, Jonas Adelin Jørgensen's study provides useful material and analysis. He shows that a Jesus-imandar or a Christ-bhakta can be simultaneously an exclusivist, an inclusivist and a pluralist in different dimensions and levels of her life and faith. Because of the varying levels and dimensions, the multifaceted approach need not be illogical at all. For example, a pluralist or an inclusivist liturgical life does not need to rule out an exclusivist Christology.[55]

52. Heim, *Salvations*, 4: "Its categories treat religious traditions as reified."
53. Adogame, "HIV/AIDS Support and African Pentecostalism," 478.
54. Sermon in the Lingala-speaking service of Siion congregation in Helsinki, Finland, 6th September 2008.
55. Jørgensen, *Jesus Imandars and Christ Bhaktas*, 428–36.

Thus, just like the boundaries of Christianity cannot be neatly drawn, neither can the theologies of religions—when they refer to real life—be neatly delineated. The different taxonomies of theologies of religion may have some heuristic value, but their practical applicability is very limited. Like all theological thinking, also theologies of religions must be more closely related to empirical realities. Theological thought should not distance itself from life to the extent that it becomes pure speculation.

The Pilgrim Church, Tradition, and Flexibility

Does the above-presented view on the syncretistic nature of Christianity mean that, from the view of Christian theology, everything should go? Have heresy and orthodoxy lost their meaning? I would answer no, but that heresy and orthodoxy need to be seen in a new light.

The history of theology is abound with examples of theological ideas and theologians who have been considered heretical or bordering on heresy, but that have later become almost normative. A case in point is Thomas Aquinas, whose utilization of the pagan philosopher Aristotle—who also happened to be a thinker until then known mostly only to the Muslim world—was regarded with great suspicion. Yet today, he is among the greatest theological authorities in the Catholic Church and beyond.

Traditionally the Roman Catholic Church has posited that the revelation grows, but does not change to the extent that some older dogma must be rejected. However, that very thing has taken place. For example, the *"extra ecclesiam nulla salus est"*-idea has authoritatively been interpreted so that it is incompatible with today's magisterial teaching. Faith does change.[56] As noted above, even when the formulations remain the same, their interpretations and meanings in their context change. The point in statements of faith is not that one believes in these statements in and of themselves. Rather, those statements of faith, like confessions, refer to the realities believed in. Therefore, the confessions can only be understood to be of importance insofar as they refer to the realities of faith. These formulations are human attempts to express that which goes beyond the human language and capacity of understanding. They are limited in time and place, bound to their contexts and therefore meaningful and understandable. It is through their limitedness that they gain communicational value. The infinite can become expressed and intelligible in a limited manner only by becoming temporarily finite. Resulting from this, the nature of doctrinal statements should be

---

56. Discussion on the changeability of dogma see Dulles, *Survival of Dogma*, 158–62; D'Costa, *Meeting of Religions and the Trinity*, 136.

understood as indicative rather than propositional. Rather than timeless expressions of eternal truths, they should be seen as contextually limited indications on how to interpret the Mystery. Exactly because of this nature, they can have continuous value for generations to come—not in the sense that future generations should chain themselves to antiquated worldviews and incredible forms of faith but, rather, as examples of how the generations past have grappled with the mysteries of faith.[57]

Therefore, churches should reject the image of Christianity as a fortress to be defended, or as a collection of dogmas to be fought for.[58] This kind of an understanding of Christian faith is not only propositional, but petrified and dead. It lacks life and freedom. It also creates the wrong type of antagonism between the world and the Church. Instead of facing and opposing evil, the Church creates antagonism between its formulae of faith that should be received with a fideist mind on one side and inquiring mind on the other. While the cross, that is to say suffering and persecutions, were a mark of the true Church for Luther, ridicule because of superstitious nonsense[59] should not be taken as a criterion for true Christianity.

A better metaphor for Christianity would be that of a road to follow.[60] The one who has followed the paths among the sheep on the Mediterranean mountains knows that they are not quite like motorways with parallel lanes, where one speeds towards a single destination. Churches and Christians could rather be seen as sheep and groups of sheep of a greater flock on a mountain path, with meandering bypaths here and there. This means that, despite great pluralism, there might be a common direction.[61] Some may

---

57. See Barth, *Learning Jesus Christ*, 21.

58. Italian philosopher Gianni Vattimo considers that a proper understanding of *kenosis* taking place in the incarnation leads to the abandonment of ontologically based unchanging dogmas. Vattimo, *Credere di credere*, 40–41.

59. Naturally, what a rationalist may consider to be superstitious nonsense from the outside may make perfect sense to the believer. In that case, however, the believer has a communication issue at hand. While Christian faith cannot be reduced back to rational statements, its foolishness to the Greeks can, however, be expressed in a way that does not require a total sacrifice of reason. The dimension of mystery is always present in the message involving the Infinite, yet as long as the Christian message is Logos-centered, there is a relation to human reason, too. Language of faith may need to make use of paradoxes and images not readily open to reason, yet the task of a theologian is to attempt at clarity and intelligibility as great as possible.

60. This is—of course—no new idea because even the Gospels depict Jesus as calling himself the Way.

61. Thus, while one may doubt the philosophical adequateness of the pluralist position in theology of religions (see, for example, the argumentation in D'Costa, *Meeting of Religions and the Trinity*, 19–95 and in Heim, *Salvations* up to p. 126), pluralism appears as an attractive approach to Christianity as a multi-faceted phenomenon. Phan's

be wandering off to the left and right, and the ones avant-garde today, may be left behind by the main group tomorrow. The Clapham sect's approach to slavery was definitely avant-garde before they got through to the British public opinion and, thereby, formulate anti-slavery legislation. Their position against slavery, as well as that of others, gradually became the new norm, not only in Britain, but globally. Today's Christian activists for the rights of sexual minorities are also certainly avant-garde but may well find themselves in the center of the flock as the journey goes on. The picture of *ecclesia viatorum* (the wayfarers' church) grants us the dynamism and flexibility needed today for our understanding of Christianity and its doctrines. The limits of a flock of sheep may be diffuse, but that does not do away the fact that the flock exists.[62]

This kind of flexible view can be experienced as threatening by many Christians. Who is then the one who knows the general direction and has the authority to assess the others? What we have are the Bible and the tradition, both of which show us where we come from. Were Christianity regarded a bastion, tradition becomes a prison. In that case, one is manacled in the ancient doctrinal formulations, behind the lock of inerrant unchangeability. The formulations to express the faith of the Church turn into the content of faith.

However, if Christianity is the people on the way, tradition is the path trailing behind us, and can, to some extent, point where to go. The way behind is only an indication, and the very recent past cannot give the sufficient picture. When viewed in totality, covering the whole of Christian history and considering the broad tradition of Christianity, one scrapes together a general idea of how Christians have tended to understand the Christ-message.

However, which turn to take is the decision of *sensus communis*—the common view of the flock. Each Christian community trusts that they are led more or less by the Holy Spirit, usually believing that my community is led more by the Holy Spirit than my neighbor's. The directions these communities take vary considerably. A part of this variation can be explained by their contextual differences. However, one cannot explain away the differences between the views of the communities. In some questions, the differences may be relatively superficial and cover the underlying deeper consensus and in other cases they might be relatively irrelevant theological

---

emphasis of the inherent plurality of Christianity through the ages is in line with the view on Christianity as this kind of a way. See Phan, "Doing Theology in World Christianities," 115–16.

62. This view of the borders of Christianity as porous and changing comes close to, e.g., Seyla Benhabib's view of cultures. Benhabib, *Claims of Culture*, 184.

duels which function to keep up the dividing fences. However, in many cases the differences are substantial and real. In such a case, one may perceive different groups in the flock as taking differing routes, sometimes in completely opposing directions. In the longer run, it is possible to identify general trends out of this mishmash of theological opinions, debates and doctrinal announcements. Such a general tendency can be understood as the *sensus communis ecclesiae viatorum*, which means that it is always something provisional, changing, developing and never completely clear-cut. Thus, doctrines are no longer fortresses to be defended but, rather, maps or road signs of the past that support the Christians of today in their deliberations on issues of faith and morals.

When *sensus communis* is seen in this manner, orthodoxy and heresy are relativized. Even if specific churches still have, quite legitimately, their doctrines and views of right doctrine and heresy, in the larger picture right faith is relativized. In the long run, then, *sensus communis* becomes the approximate direction of faith of the previous and the present generations of believers. It cannot be dictated by the big men in shiny gowns because too much of pressure from their side leads to splintering of churches. While this does not correspond the present views on democracy with one person one vote it still is far from the powers that some of the ecclesiastic princes imagine to possess. A widely held grass-roots' theological position is not easy to wipe away by the ecclesial elites as the case of the Kimbanguist leadership's attempt to protestantize the Kimbanguist faith in the 1960s and the 1970s proves.[63]

Understood in this way, tradition, the Bible being tradition *par excellence*, is an invaluable asset supporting the today's faith journey instead of a roadblock on the way forward. Inasmuch as different faith communities' monopolistic and conflicting declarations on the ownership of truth—and thereby of the Holy Spirit—cannot be taken at their face value and because there is no Archimedean point from where to issue objective judgments on the conflicting views, one has to be content with postponing conclusions and admitting a level of uncertainty about the present. At the same time, one may still believe in the guidance of the Holy Spirit in the general process of Christian wayfaring. This does not necessarily prevent anyone from believing in the guidance of the Holy Spirit in one's own Christian community. However, all such views should be taken as provisional and subject to further assessment, which endows the believer with the humility and flexibility

---

63. For this, see Broggi, *Diversity in the Structure of Christian Reasoning*; Vähäkangas, "How to Respect the Religious Quasi-Other?"

needed for a decent common life, within the confines of Christianity and beyond.[64]

In this view heresy, in the sense of dissenting and independent thinking, is nothing negative in itself but a prerequisite for a living faith-tradition. After all, as suggested above, in the time of heretical imperative and rapidly changing contexts, one inevitably becomes an independent thinker—a heretic. This independent thinking may lead one further from or closer to the *sensus communis*. It may be avant-garde or backward looking or off on the sides. Orthodoxy, in this picture, would mean a relative and changing, always hard to define *sensus communis* of which each and everyone has a slightly different opinion. Yet, it exists, not as a rigid yardstick of doctrinal soundness but, rather, as a moving point of reference with which one can situate oneself within the flock. It is only afterwards that one gains a fuller understanding of what orthodoxy was at a given time. For example, as noted above, whether *homoousios* is the correct way of describing the relationship between the Father and the Son varied in time and between different factions of the church, depending on how the term was interpreted and what the political balance of power was in the church.

Balancing between Normativity and Neutrality

Today, balancing between normativity and neutrality may be harder than before for theology. Theologians are in the field of tension between faith communities and the academia. In other words, the tension traces the space between internal Christian relevance and external credibility. If theology loses its relevance to the faith communities, it cuts off its roots and will dry and wither away. If it turns into an uncritical mirror of the convictions of faith communities, it loses its *raison d'être* in the public square. It would also mean being unfaithful to its critical role vis-à-vis these faith communities. An uncritical mirror shows the person as the person wants to see herself and, thus, provides nothing else but a false sense of certainty. A true mirror shows the person the way she is and can, thereby, contribute to a better knowledge of oneself and perhaps a change in lifestyle. The analytical role of theology, that of analyzing a certain theology, can make great contributions to faith communities by making them face the facts of their faith and background. Where the metaphor of the mirror breaks is that in theological analysis, there is no possibility of providing a completely neutral view but

---

64. This proposal contains an element of postponement resembling John Hick's eschatological verification discussed above. Hick, *Faith and Knowledge*, 178.

the analyst's convictions and preferences always influence the outcome in some way.

As for the constructive task of theology, the theologian must likewise balance between the two audiences. For the academic, increasingly post-Christian, audience, theological constructive thought needs to be formulated in such a manner that it makes sense and is, to a certain extent, acceptable even without much prior knowledge of Christian doctrine or commitment to a Christian community. At the same time, if a theological work is rejected by all Christians, it is reduced to a curiosity in the theological language game. Therefore, a theologian is a kind of middleman between two audiences and two sets of needs. This tension can also be expressed with reference to the ideals of neutrality and commitment.

On one hand, no neutrality in the strict sense of the word exists, because each researcher is situated somewhere and has her background influencing her work. On the other hand, normativity is also a difficult position to maintain in a pluralistic situation like ours. Accepting the syncretistic nature of Christianity, while acknowledging the diffuseness of its boundaries, limits the possibility for the theologian to be normative about the real nature of Christianity and its limits. She cannot be normative in a rigid and petrified sense. However, at the same time, one can still maintain a kind of an emic approach to Christianity as a theologian. This emic type of approach in this case denotes a limited normativity—such normativity which accounts for the pluralistic context while not necessarily applying relativistic principles within the theological system itself.

This solution may be helpful in interreligious encounters because the popular notion of relativism as the ideal starting point for interreligious encounters is not the only desirable, or even the most fruitful, starting point. The relativist relativizes not only her religion but that of her dialogue partner as well. Thus, the counterpart is latently expected to be another relativist. The fact that one considers her faith as normative to herself does not necessarily rule out openness to followers of other faiths, so long as this normativity is not of a rigid and exclusive type. The preconditions are that one does not consider their faith so absolute that there is nothing to learn from the faith of others, and that one is ready to give space to others' claims of the normativity of their faith too. The idea of the syncretistic and transitory nature of the Christian faith and faith statements facilitates the openness required.

Incarnation as the Doctrinal Basis for Christian Syncretism

It was alluded to above, that the syncretistic nature of Christianity which becomes visible in the contextual process and translatability may be intrinsic to the Christian theological imagination. To support such an argument, one must examine the question in the light of central Christian teachings. Since incarnation is the Christian doctrine through which inculturation and contextualization have been defined theologically and, perhaps, the most central dogma for the vast majority of Christians, it is the point of departure for the way in which syncretism in Christianity is approached here. In other words, the question is whether the concept of incarnation could serve as a basis for defining the nature of syncretism in Christianity. If so, one may pose the further question of whether this syncretism is something that follows intrinsically from the concept of incarnation and is, thereby, a natural dimension of any form of Christian life or whether it is a side-effect of incarnation that merely needs to be tolerated.

If we sharpened the definition of syncretism to even fit the taste of the most purist defender of Christianity being completely separate from other religions, syncretism could be taken to mean the combination of incompatible religious elements. For a theological purist, this approach to syncretism would range between total negativity towards human cultural traditions (an intellectually untenable position as the gospel must be expressed in and through a culture) and the traditional Catholic approaches. In them, the cultural and religious elements of a given culture are selected according to their suitability in the light of the gospel as well as purified and elevated to be included in the Catholic faith.[65]

The basic principle of incarnation is the union of the incompatible. The *novum* of the Christian message was that the transcendent God crossed the gap between the Creator and the created, the pure Spirit incarnated in the flesh with its limitations. In theories about contextual theology, one often draws an analogy between the incarnation and contextualization. Like the Word was incarnated in the flesh, so must also the word of the Christian message incarnate in concrete contexts.[66] As has already been argued before,

---

65. A good example of such an approach which balances between generous openness to the cultures and the vigour to conserve the doctrinal purity is Prof. Nyamiti who does it meticulously and with an uncommon level of precision and critical thought. For a detailed analysis of Nyamiti's fundamental theology see Vähäkangas, *In Search of Foundations*.

66. Boff: "We are dealing with the 'law of incarnation' proper to Catholicism, whose present reality and future destiny are determined by its capacity to syncretize." (Boff,

it is not possible to depict the pure gospel—in the sense of being devoid of any cultural expressions. In the human reality, the revelation is always mediated in some way. This mediation is inevitably a cultural mediation, whether it is a question of language or other forms of expression—or even human thinking not expressed to anyone else. Divine presence in the world requires mediation, and when that mediation is human, it is inevitably cultural because humans are essentially cultural beings. Whatever is human is cultural. Therefore, there is no way of escaping the cultural mediatedness of the Christian message.

Especially in Protestant views on contextual theology and in mission contexts, one has often had the tendency to separate culture from religion. A Protestant missionary can have a positive view on culture but encountering other religions in a positive manner is often more challenging. Therefore, contextualization comes to denote the inclusion of as many cultural traits as possible, as long as one keeps the foreign religion out of the picture. Thereby, the purity of faith, in the sense of not being syncretistic, was purportedly safeguarded while making Christian faith indigenous. However, as pointed out in the discussion on the role of theology in a secular state, religions cannot be isolated from the rest of culture as cultures and religions are intrinsically interwoven. As cultural beings, humans are simultaneously religious beings even if the religious dimensions of culture have a different significance to different people.

Finally, the use of an umbrella category of religion is also questionable. The problematic nature of this category is partly revealed through the notorious difficulty in defining the concept, or at least reaching a consensus thereof. Most scholars want to extend the definition even to forms of Buddhism which do not subscribe to any deities. Yet, some football clubs or the North Korean Communist Party are not considered religious organizations although their ideologies and ritual practices, at least, border religiosity. Just think of the commitment and piety, songs and rituals in football stadiums. "You never walk alone" proclaims one football club, and football club emblems can even be found on tombstones. At the same time, not all of the churches' activities, for instance in the Church of Sweden, appear to be that blatantly religious. The church's social work may have few, if any, visibly

---

Church, Charism & Power, 89, see also 102). See, e.g., Ukpong, *African Theologies Now*, 27; Schineller, *Handbook on Inculturation*, 6, 20–21. Pannenberg points out: "Darin daß das Christentum in besonderem Maße synkretistisch ist, äußert sich also nicht etwa eine Schwäche, sondern die einzigartige Kraft des Christentums." (Pannenberg, *Grundfragen systematischer Theologie*, 270, fn. 33). He does not, however, give here the theological grounds for his statement, neither does he figure out how Christian tendency towards syncretism might be "einzigartig."

religious elements. The motivations of the people involved can be religious as is the organization's reason for the work, but whether that makes the practices religious is another issue. Scientology is an organization attempting to operate under the category of religion (and be thereby exempted from taxes). In some countries it qualifies as a religion, whereas in some others it is simply regarded as business.[67] In New Age, it is likewise difficult to draw any meaningful boundary between religion and business. Some features of religion have turned fluid to the extent that it can be questioned whether there is a point in trying to keep religion as a clearly demarcated category, as is often the case.[68]

It is claimed that the generic concept of religion was only formulated in the European Enlightenment. The concept points to the difference between scientific rationalism and religious superstition. Faith in science is not considered religious, although it sometimes assumes fanatical forms resembling religious fanaticism and behaviors, especially among the most committed "Free Thinkers." Today, it often seems natural to speak of the generic notion of religion, in spite of the huge differences between religions. Likewise, there seems to be a consensus regarding the communities considered religious, despite difficulties finding a common definition for the concept and establishing its boundaries.

Therefore, one can conclude that because the Christian message incarnates within numerous cultures it also incarnates in religions. In this way, the translatability of Christianity is in tandem with the syncretistic nature of Christianity. One may also add that both translatability and the syncretistic nature of Christianity are dimensions of the contextuality of Christian faith and theology. Aloysius Pieris sees this belonging to the nature of Christianity as a metacosmic religion and therefore as something not particularly Christian. For him, primal religions are cosmic religions that have an open spirituality ready to receive and accommodate metacosmic religions like Christianity, Islam or Buddhism.[69] In the following section, there will be some deliberation on the theological dimensions of the incarnational element of contextuality in Christianity.

---

67. On Scientology in the borderlands of religion, business and financial criminality see Passas and Castillo, "Scientology and Its 'Clear' Business."

68. See Taira, *Notkea uskonto*.

69. Pieris, *Asian Theology of Liberation*, 54–55, 71–74, 98–100.

Incarnation as the Basis of Contextuality and the Syncretistic Nature of Christianity

Considering the contextual dimension of the mediation of the Christ-narrative, one must ponder whether the use of the term incarnation is a matter of metaphor, analogy or, simply, the extension of the incarnational process epitomized in Jesus of Nazareth. To simplify the discussion, emphasis is laid here on the verbal communication of the gospel, because it bears the closest resemblance to one of the ways in which Trinitarian theology is expressed, namely Logos-Christology. This decision does not intend to discount the value of non-verbal ways of communicating the gospel, which have plenty of Biblical examples from the Hebrew Bible prophets to the gospel accounts of Jesus, among others. This non-verbal communication is often also more profoundly able to communicate messages that would be almost non-communicable verbally. Yet, an analysis of such communication would require methods and approaches that are not possible to carry out here.

Culture can be seen as the matter in which the gospel is transmitted, just as sound waves are transmitted in any matter. In a vacuum, there is no sound. In the Trinity, Logos is the Word of the Father, the One who is the mysterious *Arché*, the Beginning,[70] Logos as a Hellenistic philosophical term does not necessarily indicate that the word must be uttered, because logos could just as well be an unspoken word, an idea or even an organizing principle of reality. In the Trinity, Logos is to be seen as the spoken Word, though. The Father utters the Word by spirating out the Word, in and through the Holy Spirit.[71] Thus, while it is correct to say that the Holy Spirit emanates from the Father, it is also correct to say that (s)he[72] proceeds from the Father through the Son because it is in the uttering of the word that the spiration of the Spirit takes place. Simultaneously, one can quite as well say that the Word is uttered by the Father in or through the Spirit. The last version of the interpretation has the advantage of not requiring the

---

70. Here, one needs to note that in Trinitarian theologies, one usually has considered that even if the Son is born of the Father, the Father does not antedate the Son but the whole process takes place in the eternal moment. The same applies to the Holy Spirit who proceeds from the Father (through the Son, would one add today as a consensus formulation between the Eastern Orthodox and western churches).

71. I owe this way of interpreting the relations between the Trinitarian persons to Charles Nyamiti (*African Tradition*, 49). Here, I attempt to develop his ideas further in order to discuss contextuality.

72. Gendered language is problematic in discussing spiritual realities, perhaps most of all the Spirit. Hebrew Ruach is feminine, Greek *Pneuma* is neuter and Latin *Spiritus* is masculine. Even here, the most appropriate choice would be to avoid choosing between gender-specific pronouns altogether.

relegation of the Spirit to an outsider, or additional bonus to the Trinity, as is easily the case with many interpretations of the Father-Son relationship—of course, with some exceptions like Charles Nyamiti's ancestral imaginary of the Trinity.[73] So, in a way, when the Word is spelled out in the Trinitarian imaginary, the Spirit takes on the shape of the matter in which the sound of the Word is transmitted.

According to Karl Rahner, there is a two-way correspondence between the Trinity and the Incarnation.[74] Therefore, what one learns about Christ and God in the Incarnation can also apply to the Trinity, and vice versa. Thus, if one sees the metaphor of the Father's utterance of the Word in the Spirit as a fitting way of understanding the Trinity, the Incarnation can also be interpreted in the same mode. This seems fitting, as it is commonplace to believe that the Father sent the Son to work in the world in the power of the Spirit. In this way, it becomes possible to construct a chain of argumentation between contextuality and the Trinity, through the Incarnation.

Metaphor is the weakest form of analogy because the equivalent parts of the metaphor share only one common feature. Thus, if I call my wife a rose in the metaphorical sense I can refer only to her beauty or the thorns injuring me, but not both. Understanding the concept of the Incarnation in context as only a metaphor would limit the use of this comparison to a single dimension. Would that dimension be that the Word, like in the Incarnation and the Trinity, which must be communicated outside and, therefore, needs to be uttered? If so, must also the Christian message be culturally and linguistically uttered? That would be a relatively meagre outcome and, therefore, it seems worthwhile to aim higher. Before considering the possibilities provided by analogical thought, one must consider whether the contextual process and incarnation are actually just dimensions of the very same process. In that case, the question would not only be of analogy but of uniformity.

Uniformity between these processes requires for the actors and subjects of the process to be considered the same. Perhaps the most salient point of comparison is found in the Word. Is the word that is incarnated in the contextual process, the very same Word as the one in the Trinitarian process or the Word that became incarnate in Jesus of Nazareth? In religious language one often speaks about proclaiming Christ or the Word of God. There is a simultaneous reference to the idea of proclaiming about Christ and proclaiming Christ. The communicative moment is considered to not only communicate the message, but also a personal experience of

---

73. Nyamiti, *African Tradition*, 49–50.
74. Rahner, *Trinity*, 22.

and relationship to Christ. In that sense, in some theological traditions, the gospel is rather seen as an event than a message. Here, while the merits of such an approach in avoiding an ossified understanding of the gospel should be acknowledged, the negative dimension of that approach is that the conceptual or cognitive dimension of faith is heavily reduced, at the cost of a personal religious sense of an encounter with God. This is perhaps too high a price to pay for liberating oneself from rigid biblical literalism. Furthermore, in such a solution, the communication process at hand becomes almost impossible to penetrate by means of empirical research, reducing the possibilities of referring to almost minimum. Additionally, it is clear that in every case of Christian proclamation, for it to be regarded as such, is a dimension of communication of or, at least reference to, the Christ narrative about Jesus of Nazareth which is an undeniable cognitive or verbal unifying dimension between different forms of Christianity. As discussed above, the interpretations and conceived implications of that narrative can be perceived very differently.

There seems to be a continuity and unity between the word proclaimed as preaching and the Word proclaimed as the reference point of the proclamation. Despite this, it is clear that the Word that became incarnate as Jesus of Nazareth is different from the word that is proclaimed. In the best case, there is a continuum or equivalence between those words. Yet, the word as proclamation is words about the Word.[75] Therefore, because the word of God in the process is not the same but, rather, a derivative of the Word of God, one cannot consider the processes as dimensions of the same. Even if one stuck to the interpretation of Christ himself being communicated in the process,[76] the incarnation that is referred to in the contextual process is more easily understood as a reference to the words about Christ and, as such, conceptualizations of the encounter with Christ rather than Christ the person. Furthermore, the conception of contextualization here does not refer to incarnation, in the sense of becoming corporeal in the material sense but, rather, analogically about something in itself incomprehensible (in the

---

75. For Barth, it was important to formulate a three-tier view on the Word/word so that Logos/Christ is the original Word of God, and the Bible is the word about the Word whereas proclamation is words about the Word. Barth, *Die Lehre vom Wort Gottes*, 98–140. Because it was argued above that there is a continuum between the Bible and the rest of the still evolving Christian tradition, there is no need to make a clear distinction between the two latter dimensions of the word of God.

76. According to Tuomo Mannermaa, for Luther, Christ is personally present in faith, giving faith its form—as a refutation of the scholastic *fides caritate formata*-principle according to which charity, or works of charity, give faith its form. Mannermaa, *In ipsa fide Christus adest*.

sense of mysteries of faith) becoming conceptualized and in many cases also tangible and visible in action and service.

In spite of the considerations above pointing towards the differences between the two processes, it is not impossible to find dimensions that are common to these processes. Let us proceed, therefore, to consider the possibility and results of analogical imagination in relation to contextuality.

Analogy is sometimes regarded with great suspicion, even contempt, in Protestant theologies. One of the loudest voices against the use of analogies, in the sense of constructing continuity between the Creator and the created in theology, was Karl Barth. According to him, the analogy of being (*analogia entis*) on which these kinds of analogies build, is the root of lots of faulty theology because it discounts the absolute difference between the Creator and her creation and dismisses the reality of sin.[77] In our case, however, one does not necessarily need to subscribe to the idea of *analogia entis* in order to draw an analogy between the Incarnation and the contextual process in theology, due to the fact that the Incarnation as an event does not belong to the sphere of creation while Jesus' body does. The Incarnation as an event is crossing the divide between the Creator and the created. The contextual theological process can also be seen as a case of the divine crossing the abyss between the Creator and the created. This already is a case of commonality between these two processes and points to the direction that there might be a deeper resemblance between them than a single dimension as in a metaphor. Therefore, building of an analogy between these two would not be a case of *analogia entis* which should make it possible to accept even from a Barthian point of view. Thus, the following includes considerations on the possible analogical dimensions between central doctrines on incarnation and the contextual process.

In these considerations, the doctrine of reconciliation is an inherent dimension of the incarnation. This doctrine, however, should not be seen as a one-dimensional equation that explains the incarnation. Rather, the incarnation is a mystery and human attempts to grasp it in the form of doctrine and theological interpretations shed a dim light on its particular form. Therefore, no theory of reconciliation should be seen as the definitive explanation. However, some theories are more useful for contemporary theology

---

77. Barth, *Die Lehre vom Wort Gottes*, viii–ix. See Johnson, *Karl Barth and the Analogia Entis*, 84–121 on how Barth's rejection of *analogia entis* developed. One needs to note that Barth did not reject all use of analogy altogether. Additionally, there were different periods in his career where his position varied somewhat. Barth even developed his own use of *analogia entis* at a point (Johnson, *Karl Barth and the Analogia Entis*, 116–18, 120) but its contents differed completely from the Roman Catholic use of the term.

than others. Anselm of Canterbury's approach, building on the theme of Christ as the substitutionary offer, ends up emphasizing God's retributive justice and divine wrath. Thus, the more one emphasizes God's mercy one seems to be required to emphasize God's wrath, as well—which is not a very attractive position for a religion that proclaims that God is Love.

The classical theory of Christ as human as well as God being a bait for Devil to break his deal with God is also problematic. The basis of redemption is namely regarded there as Devil's claiming also the totally innocent human person and thereby breaking the pact according to which sinners belong to him. This leads Devil losing his claim on sinful humankind. This theory makes God perhaps loving but also a master trickster. One may also wonder why the omniscient and omnipotent God would have entered into such a dubious deal with the Devil—just for pastime?

Christus victor, Christ the conqueror over the powers of evil is an imaginary on reconciliation allowing divine love a properly central position in theology. This is a strong image, yet one remains confused as to why the omnipotent Creator chose such a hard way of conquering the Evil. Perhaps the display of brute force in crushing evil would have rendered God violent just as the Evil she fought?[78]

Peter Abelard's interpretation of incarnation and reconciliation allows for several collateral interpretations, but his key contribution was to emphasize the Christ's redemptory work as an example that leads to moral influence on the believer that brings about the renewal of life.[79] Here, Peter deals with the effective dimension (i.e., the change in the believer) of justification as a result of reconciliation, while Anselm's theory is forensic in nature (i.e., affects the legal status of the believer in God's court of justice).

Yet another dimension of incarnation and reconciliation, proposed in poetry by Aune Vähäkangas, is that the Word became flesh in order to bridge the abyss of communication between the Creator and the created. Without this, humankind would never have properly grasped the extent of God's goodwill towards her creation. For the poet, there exists no intelligible shortcut to communication between God and the humans. This interpretation speaks volumes to the late modern times caught up in questions of (mis)communication and (mis)understanding.[80]

---

78. Aulén, *Christus Victor*.

79. Gruchy, *Reconciliation*, 62–63.

80. Additionally, my personal reason for preferring this approach is that in my upbringing, this was one of the models through which the Atonement was interpreted. My mother formulated this theology in an artistic form in her poem "Vihervarpuset" ("The Siskins"), Aune Vähäkangas, *Jumalan lintuset*, 123–24.

The word about the Word of God is incarnated in the process of mediation of the revelation. The term incarnation is proposed to be used in an analogical sense here. In the case of the Incarnation of the divine Logos, it is a matter of the personal Word assuming human flesh in material form. In both cases, it is a matter of crossing a communicational gap which relates closely to the doctrine of reconciliation. In the case of the mediation of the gospel, the word incarnated is not personal in the same or even in an analogous sense as in the incarnation of the Logos[81], nor is it a question of literal incarnation in the sense of becoming tangible flesh. The incarnation of the Logos is a matter of the unification of two entities that are completely incompatible, namely the Creator and the created. However, in the mediation process of the gospel the word is not qualitatively divine in the sense of belonging to the Godhead. Rather, as in any process of communication, the idea or narration must be cast in a linguistic and cultural mold to be transmitted to the recipients. It is, as such, a matter of a rather ordinary process, as noted above when demonstrating that the proposed model of the contextual process could be applied to any reading of a classic. It is this very dimension of the word assuming a linguistic and cultural form that makes this process contextual because, by necessity, any communication is contextual in its cultural-linguistic limitedness. However, insofar as the process of mediation is a mediation of the message about the Logos incarnate, it is also a revelatory process and, therefore, one can see an analogous encounter of the divine revelation with the human cultural-linguistic limitedness within the process. Thus, there is a similar, albeit much less drastic, gap between the divine and the human that is crossed here. Therefore, it is justified to consider that there exists an analogical relation between these processes.

One of the central dimensions of incarnation in Pauline theology is the concept of *kenosis*, that of the Logos incarnate emptying oneself and assuming the form of a servant. It could be seen as an inevitable dimension when the Infinite takes a finite form. Human bodily and other limitedness makes the process of incarnation, in any case, a matter of *kenosis*, all the more so when the human person in question belongs to a small nation occupied by a foreign power and when that person is marginalized and eventually brutalized by the very same nation in cooperation with the occupying power.[82]

---

81. Naturally, here one needs to keep in mind that any human vocabulary concerning God is a matter of analogies, at closest—and, as seen above, some theologians reject even the possibility of analogies. Thus, the word person does not quite mean the same in the Godhead as it does in the human sphere. Analogies between God and the creation always contain more differences than similarities.

82. On incarnation as God's entrance into the human limitedness see Wingren, *Växling och kontinuitet*, 28–29.

Is there *kenosis* in the transmission of the gospel? As discussed previously, the gospel can be considered as a limit[83] reality in the sense that for a human, it is impossible to conceive of a pure gospel. By its very nature, referring to the mysteries of faith, the gospel is related to the unintelligible and unlimited. As such, however, it cannot be grasped nor can it be perceived. It is always perceived and transmitted in a limited and intelligible form. Here, one could make a distinction between the transmission of the message and the experience behind it. The experience of the mystery can be verbalized as a vision, like in traditional Catholic theology the heavenly God's revelation of self is referred to as *visio beatifica* from the human perspective. This Catholic concept of beatific vision can be interpreted as the epitome of revelation, both because it is unrestricted by time, space and corporeality and because God is fully present without dimensions of hiddenness. However, in the human state in this world, already the very moment of revelation or vision contains an element of limitation because any perception is simultaneously also interpretation. Our expectations and previous experiences, as well as our cultural limitations, direct the way in which we perceive anything. Moreover, when this perception is verbally transmitted, the very limitations of the language used and the thought patterns possible for the culture, further constrain the process. Intercultural and multilingual contexts add to the mixture, not only by narrowing the possibilities of transmission, but also by opening up avenues for creative novel interpretations, as is often case in theological processes in cultures previously not in contact with Christianity. Following the considerations above, one may maintain that there *kenosis* is inherent to the transmission of the gospel, from the very beginning to the end, from the human perception of the message, not only cultural and linguistic sense, but also due to psychological and epistemological limitedness.

One could also add that in the process of the communication of the gospel, another dimension of *kenosis* is also required. Namely, that of identification with the weak and the suffering.[84] If Christian proclamation avoids this *kenosis*, it becomes a supportive element of the *status quo*, which has often actually been the case. In such situations, however, one can maintain that a central element of the gospel has been lost. The gospel has then become the gospel of the ruling culture. It has been reduced to an affirmation and has lost its dimension of challenge to conversion or change (*metanoia*). When Christian proclamation retains this dimension, it requires the act of

---

83. Here "limit" is used in the sense of mathematics—a figure (or in this case, reality) that you can come close but never reach like the π or one third in digits.

84. On the relationship between Christology and the suffering see Phan, "Doing Theology in World Christianities," 128–29.

siding with the marginalized and a varying degree of the marginalization of the Christian community as well. While this dimension of *kenosis* is not logically inevitable, it can be seen as belonging to the central dimension of the message itself, at least in one strong tradition of interpretation in today's Christianity.[85]

In incarnation, according to the Chalcedonian creed, the two natures of Christ are in union without being mixed or separated. This is a paradoxical formulation that attempts to safeguard both the full humanity and the full divinity of Christ. As discussed before, there is no way of distilling the pure, non-cultural gospel out of its different manifestations or culturally bound interpretations. Yet, the gospel cannot be equated with any of these linguistically and culturally limited expressions (even if there often has been a tendency to do so to provide the believer a solid foundation). In such a case, one would ethnocentrically indirectly deify one's own culture and turn human-made culture into the divine. It seems that application of the Chalcedonian formula would be well suited for this case: The gospel cannot be separated from its cultural expressions, yet it cannot be conflated with any of its expressions. Each cultural expression of the gospel suffers from human limitations, just like the Logos incarnated was limited by humanness. Each valid expression of the gospel could be considered as an incarnation of the word about the Word, a moment of God's revelation of herself. In that, the analogy about the contextual process as incarnation also reveals a clear difference with incarnation in Jesus of Nazareth. The mainline Christian position is that the Incarnation took place once,[86] whereas the process analogous to incarnation takes place over and again. Furthermore, the common faith of the Christians is that Christ is like us but has no sin, whereas no incarnation of the gospel in the contextual process can be considered as free of fault. Every expression of the gospel is inevitably human, also in the sense of being erroneous in part and being entangled in human aspirations

---

85. Naturally, there are forms of Christianity that do not subscribe to the identification with the marginalized, like some *status quo* supporting theologies and theologies that place emphasis on God's love being expressed through material blessings, as is the case with some kinds of the Prosperity Gospel. The Prosperity Gospel seems to be a strongly growing trend in Christian thought today. Therefore, it deserves due theological attention, not only in terms of refutation but also of sincere encounter and dialogue. However, what goes as the Prosperity Gospel does not always conform to the worst scenarios of the theologians condemning it nor is it always a question of simple wishful theological theoretizing. See, e.g., Vähäkangas, "Prosperity Gospel."

86. There are exceptions, though, like the Kimbanguists (see Broggi, *Diversity in the Structure of Christian Reasoning*), Olumba Olumba in Nigeria (Sabar and Shragai, "Olumba Olumba in Israel") and the amaNazaretha Church in South Africa (Moodley, *Shembe, Ancestors, and Christ*).

of power and glory. Every expression of the gospel must, therefore, be approached with a degree of suspicion and with a comparative mind. This attitude is called discernment of spirits in Latin American liberation theologies, a term based on Ignatian spirituality.[87]

Above, the process of the gospel being incarnated in its cultural expressions was described as a moment of God's revelation of herself. As such, the gospel, when incarnated in such an expression, functions as a kind of a window to divine realities. Likewise, Jesus of Nazareth, according to the gospel of John (14:9), says, "The person who has seen me, has seen the Father." Jesus, the Logos incarnate, is thus the icon of God in her mysterious and hidden dimension. Here, we can see another similarity between these two processes, in that they both convey revelation opening an opportunity for seeing God the invisible.

According to Pauline ecclesiology, the Church is the body of Christ. This has been interpreted either in quite a literal way, as in the Catholic *corpus mysticum* approach to ecclesiology, or in a more metaphorical sense, as in much of Protestant theology. Irrespective of how this image of the Church is interpreted, the Church can be seen as the primary locus in which the incarnational process of the gospel takes place, in word and in action. The gospel, thus, takes its visible and recognizable form in the Christian life of the Church. Simultaneously, one must remember that much of what churches do as organizations and what Christians do, even in the name of their faith, is not at all in line with the gospel. In some cases, that is clearly visible in the actions of certain churches being in blatant opposition to what Christian *sensus communis* regards as true interpretations of the gospel. In some other cases, only historical distance endows the observer with the perspective necessary to critically appraise a certain phenomenon in the churches.

However, the presence of the Logos in the world is not limited to the Church. Logos is behind all creation. A traditional Christian interpretation of Genesis 1 finds the Trinity in God's act of uttering the creative Word where the Word is spirated out (Gen 1:3). The Spirit was also hovering over the abyss of nothingness (Gen 1:2). When one considers that the world was created through the Logos, as is expressed in the ancient Christian hymn cited by Paul (Col 1:16), it is clear that the presence of Logos does not limit itself only to the Church. This idea has had different expressions in different times. Luther needed to reject the stark separation between the spiritual and secular realms of life, seeing the totality of life as sacred. This is a concern

---

87. Galilea, *Temptation and Discernent*.

which many today's African theologians have shared.[88] This totality of life has sometimes been described as "wholeness of being" or even better in the Kiswahili term *uzima*. *Uzima wa milele* is the translation for *vitam eternam* (life eternal) in the Apostles' Creed. It denotes thus the fullness of life but can also be translated as health, adulthood, salvation and to cover many other dimensions of that fullness.[89]

As one theological tool in dealing with the undividedness of life and the cosmos, Luther used the idea of ubiquity of Christ in the whole of creation.[90] For Luther, encountering other faiths was not particularly central due to his cultural, geographical and historical location within Christendom. Furthermore, most of his energy was consumed by the conflict with the Roman Catholic Church, his mother church. Therefore, one cannot identify properly formulated ideas of the meaning of Christ's ubiquity in terms of religious pluralism in Luther.

Justin Martyr, however, was completely immersed in a situation of religious pluralism just like most Christians today. He developed an idea of *logos spermatikos*, or seeds of the Word, in all of creation. For him, it meant that Logos is present everywhere in the creation, albeit not in a clearly visible manner. However, Justin may have considered *logos spermatikos* as a distinct from Christ who is the whole Logos.[91] This patristic idea has eventually inspired a plethora of theological considerations in the context of religious plurality. Raimon Panikkar's theologizing about the cosmic Christ opens Christology to interreligious interpretations,[92] while Pierre Teilhard de Chardin's theology places the omnipresent Logos in the cosmic spectacle of creation and evolution.[93] For Kwame Bediako, Logos is found behind all cultures.[94] Through this kind of vision, a possibility appears to open up for Trinitarian panentheism.[95] God is present in all of creation as the Trinitar-

---

88. See, e.g., analysis in Pöntinen, *African Theology*.

89. For different interpretations of this fullness of being see Mbiti, *Bible and Theology*, 153; Pobee, "Life and Peace," 17; Imasogie, *Guidelines for Christian Theology*, 18; Buthelezi, "Change in the Church." For a more detailed analysis of *uzima*, see Vähäkangas, "Ukristo, Uzima na Ujamaa," 45–142.

90. See Jorgenson, "Luther on Ubiquity." On ubiquity in Luther in general see Ristau, "Ubiquity and Epiphany."

91. Edwards, "On the Platonic Schooling of Justin Martyr," 23–34.

92. Panikkar, *Unknown Christ of Hinduism*.

93. Udías, "Christogenesis."

94. Bediako, *Theology and Identity*. Bediako uses Justin Martyr as his starting point in developing the idea. For an analysis of Bediako's interpretation of Justin see Helleman, "Justin Martyr and Kwame Bediako."

95. Moltmann, *Trinity and the Kingdom*.

ian creator God. Christ is omnipresent in the Spirit, just like the Father. This presence is hidden to a greater or lesser extent, depending on the theological interpretation, varying from dialectical theological negation of the salvific and revelatory value of such presence[96] to, for example Panikkar's pluralistic vision embracing, in principle, all religions, humanity and the rest of creation.[97]

If the Logos is present in the whole of creation, could the same apply to the gospel? In other words: Does Christ's ubiquity in the creation gain such revelatory dimensions that one could maintain that there is a certain presence of the knowledge of the gospel, whichever way it may be interpreted? Several Christian theologians have expressed various affirmations of this sentiment. Karl Rahner's proposal on anonymous Christians sees the connection to Christ on an existential level in such a way that knowledge of Christ stems from a personal encounter, albeit in a non-cognitive manner.[98] There have also been attempts to show how non-Christian cultures contain even cognitive elements of Christian faith, Charles Nyamiti going even as far as claiming that "adumbrations" of the Trinity in some African traditions precede contacts with Christianity.[99] Were one to regard the contextual process in the mediation of the gospel analogical to incarnation, they would be justified in maintaining that as Logos is present in the whole of creation, the gospel is also decipherable in and behind cultures. This does not necessitate a conscious level of cognizance of the Christ-narrative but means that gospel values can be found in any culture, along with cultural dimensions that are in line with the gospel.

At the same time, however, just like one should not underestimate the element of fallenness in ecclesiastic settings leading to constant vigilance about the human tendency of materializing one's ambitions of power over others even within the realm of the faith-community, one should not be naïvely admiring of non-Christian cultures and religions. They may well contain gospel values but also remain corrupted by human hubris, egoism and will to power. Considering the human limitations of each of the incarnations of the gospel, the Christian is called to turn to non-Christian religions and cultures with a sense of curiosity and appreciation. In so doing, one does not become less Christian but more Christian by learning more about the gospel through other cultures and faiths. This neither means

---

96. Kraemer, *Christian Message*.

97. Komulainen, *Emerging Cosmotheandric Religion?*

98. Rahner, *Anonymous Christianity*. For an analysis of the concept see Schwerdtfeger, *Gnade und Welt*.

99. Nyamiti, "African Preparatory Roads for the Trinity," 3.

that other faiths are reduced to mere preparation to the gospel, *praeparatio evangelica*,[100] but that these faiths are seen to be independent entities with their own values. Yet, seen from within and through the broad Christian tradition, a Christian will sometimes be able to see and value even dimensions of the religion and culture that a believer in that tradition may be unable to see herself. The presence of God in creation and the revelatory dimensions in religions and cultures do not need to be interpreted to suggest that for every religion, there is a common ground or that all religions could or should be regarded as belonging to the same family of phenomena. Rather, each culture and each religion is a possible and specific locus of God's revelation of herself. To which extent and how this revelation takes place depends on one's theological approach to religions.

To sum up, some of the theological consequences for contextually conscious theologizing are that Christianity is a syncretistic religion because in the contextual mediation process, it is a question of incarnation in an analogical sense. The body of culture cannot be separated into realms of religion and non-religion. Rather, religion is an integral dimension of any given culture. Likewise, culture is an integral dimension of religion in the sense that any expression of faith is simultaneously a cultural expression. Contextual mediation as incarnation can be seen as a way of transcending the cultural limitedness of religion, thereby giving Christianity the opportunity to become a global or intercultural religion. The view of the mediation process as incarnational means, at the same time, that each contextual mediation process of the Gospel is limited as it does not represent the whole truth and only the truth. As an outcome, no theological system can claim the role of a yardstick of the sound doctrine, but the religious authority in Christianity must be seen as decentralized both from the empirical and theological points of view. Thus, doctrinal authority lies in the process of the formation and transformation of the Christian *sensus communis*. This means that all doctrinal formulations and drawing of demarcation lines between right and wrong teaching have to be taken as provisional and subject to change. This also means that the borders between Christian and other faiths are porous, both as seen through the empirically verifiable facts on the ground as well as from a more theological point of view.

To conclude, contextually conscious theologizing does not provide anyone the luxury of theologizing in a comfortable solitude of purely Christian imagination but, rather, that all theology must deal with the fact of the multitude of religious faiths right from the beginning. Therefore, the time of theology of religions is in a sense passé or, alternatively, all theology needs

---

100. Mbiti, *African Religions and Philosophy*, 277.

to be theology of religions in the sense that it must take on that role from the very beginning, even if it naturally covers more than that. Resulting from this, what may look like variations of the same theology of religions may well be a matter of completely different theological approaches. Because theologies of religions need to be integral parts of theologies, each and every theological approach will similarly produce different approaches to religions. This means that the conventional division of theologies of religions into exclusive-inclusive-pluralist, and possibly relativist as the fourth category, is at best a slightly misleading and superficial way of classifying theologies. Therefore, we proceed to imagine a model for approaching religious plurality that builds on some of the aforementioned principles.

7

Four Levels of Theology: Do Special Revelation and Pluralism Fit Together?

THE ARGUMENT THROUGHOUT HAS been to show how all theology is conditioned by its context and how this contextuality indicates syncretism within Christianity, unclear boundaries at the fringes of Christianity as well as theological and religious plurality, both within Christianity as well as in the world of many religions. The argument has gone that this state of contextuality, syncretism, and plurality is not a failure but, rather, the natural state of affairs in a religion building on incarnation. Thus, both religious pluralism and syncretism are not problems to be solved but conditions to be recognized as inherent dimensions of the reality in which theologizing takes place. However, this position leaves us in a somewhat uneasy tension between incarnation, which is seen as the Christian special revelation *par excellence*, and pluralism, usually considered incompatible with the special revelations of religions.

In interreligious attempts to find the common denominator in religions, there often exists a reductionist dimension that tends to overlook the specificities and irreconcilable elements in different religions.[1] These kinds of endeavors run the risk of creating yet another set of religious actors that introduce additional cleavages within religions, between the interreligionists and others. The unity sought can then become a spiritual unity between the like-minded. Many religious people would object to this due to the fear of losing their identity, as well as the fear of losing faith in the specific revelation that is considered valuable to the religious tradition in question.

While the motives and argumentation of the propagators of common human nature generally appear humane and generous there is a persistent

---

1. An example of an attempt to find such a common denominator is the United Religions Initiative Africa Office, *Golden Rule*.

tendency of lifting up one's own values and culture as the yardstick of truth and beauty, even when not attempting to do so. Thus, pluralism based on common human nature is not usually quite as pluralistic as it often claims to be. Its benevolence can also be questioned and whether pluralism is just another form of cultural imperialism is brought under scrutiny. One may question whether the greatest common ethical or even doctrinal denominator (often resulting in relatively vague denominators) leads to religious pluralism in practice. It may allow for ritual pluralism as well as a plurality of religious identities, but the values or doctrines used as the building blocks for unity, by virtue of being brought to the forefront, can lead towards a kind of religious monoculture. True pluralism starts from the acknowledgement and acceptance of difference. After this stage, there is a possibility of seeking points of contact and building bridges over the dividing lines.

Here, the attempt is to launch a discussion on religious pluralism emanating from the very specifics of Christian faith. The intention is not, and cannot be, to convince non-Christians of plausibility and desirability of religious plurality because this starting point is not mutual. However, if this kind of an approach is fruitful in any way, it may encourage people of other faiths to view their traditions by interrogating the kinds of resources available in their specific tradition that would enhance the acceptance of religious plurality.

One may also pose the question of whether there is actually a need to reconcile the acceptance of religious pluralism with the conviction that one's faith is specific. Would one not be happier with the reductionist pluralism that would unite the whole of humankind? Or, sticking to one's specific faith in an insular manner? The first alternative is culturally imperialistic because any reductionist approach to religious plurality, when it turns missionary minded, is just as imposing as any other religious view would be. The second alternative would include a practical acceptance of the existence of religious pluralism but it would not promote conviviality in the world of many religions. Accepting pluralism, starting from the specificities of one's religious faith, is the way to true religious pluralism in which differences of religion are accepted and respected. In that case, the acceptance of pluralism does not lead to isolation but cooperation and mutual learning based on a strong identity which does not feel threatened by the otherness of the other. Isolation is often a symptom of a threatened identity.

However, the very diversity of faiths as the starting point and consequently as a feature retained in the end, does require of every religious person to consider their religion as relative in the same manner—if relative at all. The minimum requirement for a true acceptance of religious pluralism is that one is willing to grant all religious groups freedom of religion, which should be a natural move for any religion because unless you grant freedom to others in the sphere of your majority religion you have no mutual moral ground to claim freedom for your fellow religionists where they are in minority. The proposed view on religious equality and openness grants each and every religion the right to propagate its doctrines and ways of life, as long as they do not violate anyone else's right of self-determination or include pressurizing or bribing or other violations of freedom of religion.[2] Missionary activity of religious groups is a natural part of an open and equal society. In a democracy, religious communities have the right to attempt to convert people, and individuals have the right to convert or not to convert, without coercion from any party. When one lauds openness and trust in interreligious encounters, but denies the possibility of conversion, neither openness nor trust really exists. One starts from fixed positions and shares one's faith in a limited manner with the expectation that the outcome can be predicted and managed. The maintenance of the religious status quo becomes more central than the pursuit of truth or, in some cases, one has already established the interreligious truth, making its pursuit a futile exercise.

One may wonder whether the kind of understanding of pluralism proposed here is worth much effort. Would it not simply suffice to tolerate people of other faiths and leave them their space in society? Such tolerance is sufficient to maintain social stability in good times, as it prevents religions from contributing to the creation of conflicts. According to Durkheim, religions function as a glue that keeps a society together—namely in the late nineteenth and the early twentieth century largely Roman Catholic France.[3] In a more pluralistic society, insular religiosity contributes only to the cohesion of separate ghettos. The pluralism proposed here, however, in spite of recognizing differences, opens up to other religions in a way that goes beyond mere tolerance. The internal theological benefit of this approach for Christian theology is the acknowledgement of historicity and contextuality of Christian faith that leads to the recognition of, on one hand, special revelation through Christ, and, on the other hand, the possibility of true revelation even beyond Christianity. This revelation may also allow Christians to learn from it without becoming less Christian, but quite the contrary. This model provides for both the continuity required for religious identity and the flexibility to cope with the challenges of the contemporary pluralistic context.

---

2. *Christian Witness in a Multi-Religious World.*
3. Bellah, "Civil Religion in America."

What follows is a Christian systematic theological attempt to approach the question of religious diversity and build a theologically based plea for pluralism. The way the argumentation is constructed attempts to leave open the theological and philosophical questions that are not necessary for the construction of the main arguments. The hope in doing so is to expand the applicability of the proposed model.

Theology Informed by Pluralism or Pluralistic Theology?

In systematic theology, the starting point has traditionally been building a consistent theological system where both matters of faith and matters of reason find their places.[4] One of the underlying assumptions has been that reality is undivided. The undivided nature of reality means that both faith and reason must find their places in the totality of the theologian's worldview. At the same time, this view of undivided reality has meant that the theologian was expected to "sell the whole package" to the hearer. For example, Thomas Aquinas's theology was not only a matter of defending the articles of faith but also a project of producing a more convincing overall picture of reality than the previous theologies and philosophies had been able to achieve. Consequently, Thomas would expect his audience to be convinced of his overall view. The starting point of this chapter is that today's reality is so pluralistic that for a theologian (or a philosopher, for that matter) to aim at converting the whole or even a substantial part of an audience to his worldview in totality is not plausible.

Following from the fact of social, religious, and cultural pluralism, it is not reasonable to expect that the whole audience will share one's plausibility patterns.[5] The creation of a universally valid philosophical or theological system seems more unrealistic than ever. Simultaneously, the time of western cultural imperial hegemony in theology had better be over. The West has tried to evangelize the rest but the outcome was not that the colonial missionary could have re-created the convert in his image and likeness but, rather, that the Christian internal pluralism has boomed through local interpretations of Christian faith.[6] This has happened within the so-called

---

4. Even in the case of young Karl Barth, although he rejected the usefulness of philosophy in theology, the question was a matter of constructing a theological system.

5. See Berger and Luckmann, *Social Construction of Reality*, 110–21.

6. This is well in line with Bhabha's idea of hybridity as the outcome of colonial encounters among which he also counts the (western) mission. See Childs and Williams, *Introduction to Post-Colonial Theory*, 133–37 referring to various passages of Bhabha, *Location of Culture*. See also Haar, *How God Became African*, in which the argument is that instead of Africa converting into western Christianity, Christianity became African on the continent.

historic churches (mostly as contextual theology) as well as in the autochthonous churches and on the border zone between Christianity and other religions.

This all-permeating pluralism places theology before an unknown terrain—albeit not necessarily completely new, as many of these challenges are similar to the early Christian context.[7] However, this situation calls for a radical reassessment of the mode and role of theology. In today's world, pluralism, as a sociological and religious fact, cannot be ignored in theology. However, using Hume's guillotine, this need not mean that pluralism should automatically be accepted as a laudable principle. The social fact of pluralism does not automatically lead to the theological correctness of pluralism. As a result, a good number of theologians are wrestling with this issue.

Fundamentalism can be seen today as another of the alternatives to religious pluralism despite it originally being a reaction to Enlightenment developments whereby the western scientific worldview was proposed as the sole interpretation of reality.[8] Today, Fundamentalism continues its fight on that front but can also be seen as a response to the challenge of pluralism. Fundamentalism was simultaneously one of the vessels whereby the Enlightenment scientific (and many would say reductionist) views of reality were planted deep into western Christian worldviews. The point is not only that there is one reality but also that the reality is viewed in a one-dimensional way, almost ruling out the possibility of different layers and modes of truth.[9] By defending the Biblical inerrancy by following the rules of the scientific Enlightenment worldview Fundamentalism essentially aligns itself with these scientific premises to a greater extent than many other theological traditions. This approach is strongly opposed to any views accommodating pluralism. In this view, religious pluralism may be a socio-religious fact, but it stems from the others' fallacies. The truth can only be one and, thereby, the other needs to be converted to believe so.

At the other end of the spectrum pluralism is taken not only as a religious fact but also as a laudable principle or, at least, an inevitable result of our uncertainty of knowledge. In its vulgar version one should not even attempt to stake religious claims in theology but, rather, describe different (preferably historical) ideas and positions. What makes many modes of this version vulgar is that proper philosophical, theological or logical grounds are not proposed. What seems to matter is political correctness.

---

7. Bediako, *Theology and Identity*.

8. See Benhabib, *Claims of Culture*, 185. Note that Benhabib talks about fundamentalisms as a generic religious concept.

9. See Wingren, *Växling och kontinuitet*, 69–70.

This approach to encountering the increasing pluralism, especially in former state church contexts, has meant that academic theology turns into a second order study of theologies. That means that in order not to appear confessional and thereby limited in the academia, theologians restrain from doing constructive theology but concentrate on the analytical task of theology, namely analyzing the existing theologies, preferably of men who have already died. This solution is based on fallacious premises. First, even if analysis in this history of ideas mode looked less confessional on the surface than constructive theology, it is far from objective and impartial. The same contextual dynamics that direct the choice of themes, methods and approaches that are functional in constructive theology can be found in analytical one. The reasons why a certain text deserves to be studied in a certain way and another text does not is not an innocently objective decision. Naïve objectivism does not make one less subjective. On the contrary it is more subjective because in that case the subconscious subjectivism is left with free reign.[10]

Secondly, such a position presumes that there exists a clear difference between construction of thoughts and the analysis thereof. This presumption is interwoven with the above idea of objective analysis. However, any analysis of an idea, a text, or a language game, and so on, is always an interpretation no matter how rigid and formalized one's methodological patterns may be. This is so because even those patterns are means of interpretation, produced by and through limited cultural and linguistic contexts. Therefore, there is no clear line of demarcation between constructive and analytical tasks of theology. No constructive theology can start from a *tabula rasa*, but is built on previous rounds of interpretation in the traditions that theology relates to. Thereby, there is always an analytical moment to constructive theology. Likewise, no analysis of a theology can be merely analytical; it will always contain elements of constructive thought. The analyst always has her approach to reality which is a result of more or less conscious and systematic constructive thought. Additionally, the process of analysis has its constructive moments, for example, in the formulation and application of methodology and the way in which the results are formulated. In interpretative humanities, like analysis of theologies, there cannot be any strictly quantifiable and standardized methodologies. Methods of analysis and interpretation adjust according to the object of study[11] and the research question.

10. See Lonergan, *Method in Theology*, 292; Lonergan, *Third Collection*, 144.

11. Another related question here is that of division between the researched object and the researching subject. As one can probably deduce from the above text, I am not in a favor of separating the two. However, for methodological purposes, one needs to

Finally, any viable intellectual tradition needs to be anchored to a community or several communities. Some academic traditions can survive only in academia, but majority are also related to professional and social realities outside of the university world. Theology that severs all contact to communities of faith saws the branch she sits on. While theology in the pluralist context may no longer be in the service of one or few *status quo* churches, it should engage in dialogue with a good number of faith traditions and people outside of faith traditions in a critical and creative manner. In this way, theology can contribute to the society by challenging faith communities' positions and, thereby, advocate for them better or transform them. Such participation in theological debate calls for taking confessional positions. Even if that position is at times fictional, for the sake of argumentation, the theologian should position herself in the debate as if she were in a given tradition.

Therefore, imagined objectivity gained through resorting to a (imagined) pure analytical approach is not a proper answer to pluralism. However, the merit of such an approach is to challenge the denominationally limited monolithic theologizing whose time really is passé. In the past, one could theologize as if only one's own denominational and cultural tradition existed and act as if this theology represented the whole of humankind. However, a theologian, like any other researcher in humanities, cannot abstain from positioning oneself and thereby this position presenting itself as objective is no proper solution.

The difference between the normative position taken for the sake of argumentation and the imagined pure analytical approach has three dimensions. First, the position taken for the sake of argumentation exists because it is the position of the community one engages in dialogue with whereas total objectivity does not exist. Secondly, by imagining oneself objective a person positions herself above the others as a higher arbiter of truth whereas in the case of entering a position for the sake of argument she proposes herself as a partner in dialogue. Thirdly, unlike the supposedly objective analyst, a theologian taking an imagined argumentative position enters the language game of the other providing the community in question the possibility of accepting or rejecting the challenge. However, such a partner in dialogue cannot do the constructive theologizing for the community even if the challenges and proposals of the marginal insider in the theological process may greatly influence the theological processes of that community.

---

distinguish between the two to be able to vary the point of view by occasionally distancing oneself from the object of study. Thereby, one can contribute to a more critical and self-critical and more comprehensive result.

This positioning within the present pluralist context should, at any rate, lead to ecumenically and interreligiously more open approaches than the former denominationalist approaches which were often also coupled with nationalism.

A not-so-vulgar version of this line of thought is George A. Lindbeck's cultural-linguistic theory of theology. Lindbeck proposes in *The Nature of Doctrine* that religious statements should be taken as paroles of a language, if translated into Saussurean terminology. This basically means that religions are separate systems like languages are. Just like one cannot ask which language is truer than another, one cannot question the truthfulness of a religion.

Lindbeck's choice of language as the analogy is somewhat unhappy. First, one can easily mix languages without needing to create a new set of rules, like when a certain language absorbs great quantities of loan words. In some cases, street slang, like that of historical Helsinki, completely follows the grammatical rules of a language (Finnish) while the vocabulary is largely foreign (Swedish and Russian). While combining languages is a natural phenomenon, taking place everywhere at all times, this is not the case with games which you can mix in a much more limited manner. Most of linguistic interchange takes place in vocabulary, but even grammatical rules or forms can cross linguistic boundaries. Second, languages are not separate systems, but overlap and interchange. Take the Scandinavian languages as examples: Where does one language begin and the other end? Only the written form of a language petrifies it to an extent that it becomes a separate entity. Third, at the latest in the process of becoming written, the language is politicized and loses its innocence as a separate game. Politics, religion and economy begin to play increasingly great roles in it.[12] Now, it becomes possible to ask which language is truer than the other in the sense of representing the elites that define the parameters of knowledge in the public. Language becomes the tool of molding the political reality. This was the case in Scania which was transferred from Denmark to Sweden in the seventeenth century, as well as with the suppression of Finnish in Västerbotten in northern Sweden during the twentieth century and eventually isolating it into a dying separate language labelled as "Meän kieli" (literally: "our language"). In both cases it is clear that Swedish was made into the truer language. Discussion around the Africanness or whiteness of Afrikaans is another example in which the nature of a language is not only a question of innocent linguistic variation but of harsh political realities. The whites' dialect was taken as the standard Afrikaans during Apartheid and the language

---

12. See Anderson, *Imagined Communities*.

was, effectively, made white or European. The famous South African author André Brink consciously borrowed colored influences from the Western Cape into his literary Afrikaans rendering it more African—an approach that is popular in some circles in contemporary South Africa.

Lindbeck's position can be taken as a preliminary theory that does not need to be systematized in the sense of further questioning its epistemological consequences. However, if one follows Lindbeck's path further, asking the kinds of consequences of seeing religions as language systems, one finds drastic results. Religious language as paroles in a linguistic system becomes thoroughly symbolical to the extent that the symbols stop signifying something outside of the religious person's existential situation. Thus, religious language becomes an expression of the believer's inner feelings in a Schleiermacherian sense and has no reference to realities outside one's psyche. Alternatively, one just refrains from staking religious claims. The outcome of this kind of an approach can be unchecked relativism. Because one cannot compare the truth-claims of languages in the epistemological sense, religions cannot be approached critically from outside, as religious systems and even criticism of expressions of faith in a foreign religion becomes difficult. A non-native speaker of a language is seldom in the position of deciding which form or expression of a language should be considered correct, yet the correctness of language and the versatility of the language user are matters of convention. Thus, while religions as languages become untouchables above all outside criticism, even religious expressions as paroles only become possible to asses from the inside.

While this kind approach might provide the religious thinkers hard pressed by secularism in the West a moment of respite, it soon shows that one has painted themselves into a corner. While one may have bought the freedom to express whatever one wants in whichever manner possible within the religious community, the language of that community does not and needs not communicate outside its boundaries. There may be limited possibilities of communication over the denominational fences when the languages/faiths resemble each other enough, but each and everyone speaks her own language and plays her own game. The result is an insular plurality. As discussed above, insular plurality is not a socially preferable outcome, and neither can it be seen as a satisfactory intellectual solution. Theologically, it can be questioned whether separation is compatible with the message of Christianity about reconciliation and, thereby, mending of connections.[13]

While the contextual limitations of our ability to communicate must be acknowledged, it does not need to lead to a situation whereby the possibility

---

13. "Confession of Belhar," §2.

of any communication is denied. While one needs to acknowledge the positionality of all knowledge, it does not have to lead to an unchecked relativism where one would not accept even provisional anchoring points. While freedom of thought should not be manacled, that freedom does not mean freedom from all limitations and preconditions of our thought. It is precisely through them that our thought is anchored in traditions that in themselves are not absolute, but historical and changing. Then the outcome is checked relativity: relativity that is in relation to changing traditions which, in turn, may be in relation to something true beyond themselves.

Seen this way, religions need not be seen only as language systems. However, there is a possibility of seeing them both as languages (if such an analogy is considered useful) consisting of the language as the system and paroles, and as carriers to reference to the truth or truths. Then paroles do not only have internal references in the language game but can also have external reference.

Especially in theology of religions, there are various pluralistic proposals that have been widely discussed. Gavin D'Costa points out that pluralist theologians of religion are not usually actually pluralists but represent a peculiar exclusivist position. Thus, the pluralists tend to propose their interpretations of reality as the new normative ones not allowing for pluralism proper.[14] In the theology of religions, one of the most interesting proposals is S. Mark Heim's idea of several parallel religious ends. It avoids the trap of being superficially pluralistic.[15] He proposes that there could be different salvations allowing for several parallel religious truths. While this proposal is fresh, it is difficult to substantiate either from within religions' traditions or from scientific sources. John Hick has proposed postponing judgments until the eschatological verification, which would certainly suit Heim's proposal.[16] While Hick's idea of postponing absolute judgments can be a plausible proposal as such, one needs to make interim decisions meanwhile in order to be able to act and react. While one might want to postpone judgment in principle, this postponement is not always possible. Extreme examples could be mortal violence propagated in the name of religion, like in the cases of violent right-wing extremist groups using Christianity, militant Hindus or Buddhists attacking religious minorities, or violent Islamists. It is hardly desirable to postpone the judgment of these phenomena until the eschaton, either within one's religion or even others. As a result, the situation hardly looks different except that one agrees about her position's

---

14. D'Costa, *Meeting of Religions and the Trinity*, 37, 45–47.
15. Heim, *Salvations*.
16. Hick, *Faith and Knowledge*, 178.

preliminary character, a position that resembles the approach on Christian doctrine on the ecclesiological basis above.

Yet another alternative is to work out new ways of perceiving religious reality. Lesslie Newbigin struggled with this for most of his late career. He made use of British-Hungarian philosopher Polanyi's thinking and tried to formulate theological-philosophical thoughts that would face the postmodern challenge and save what is valuable in both Christian and modern thought.[17] But even in Newbigin, the question of needing to accept not only his theological package but also Polanyi-influenced philosophy surfaces.

In what follows, I aim to circumnavigate the confusing question of truth by starting shamelessly from the Christian doctrine. I try to figure out how, in light of that tradition, one might construct a way of relating the realities and the religious language in a way that it would not underestimate on one hand the pluralist situation and on the other hand the Christian tradition. I hope that the result will allow for both philosophical and theological pluralism without succumbing to total relativism and surrendering to, the often so attractive, agnosticism. At any rate, today theology needs to be informed by pluralism, in the sense that the social and religious fact of all-permeating pluralism affects our theologizing from the very fundamental theological questions to practical theology. While one's theology in this context does not necessarily need to be pluralistic to be relevant, it definitely needs to take the religiously pluralistic situation as a starting point or risk irrelevance. What follows is a proposal that intends both to take pluralism as a starting point and to be pluralistic, albeit in a manner that has Christian doctrinal identity as a starting point.

Four Levels of Theology

I remember having a chat with the famous Australian cardinal Edward Cassidy who was responsible for ecumenical affairs in the Vatican when I was working on my doctoral dissertation in Rome. He asked me what the topic of my study was and when I answered, grossly simplifying, "African theology," he responded: "Isn't there only one theology?" He was referring to the celestial realities. What a contrast to the all-theology-is-contextual position I subscribed to! However, in this case "theology" meant different things for each of us. And, as in so many cases, one may consider that both parties were right in their own way.

---

17. On his use of Polanyi's philosophy as a starting point see, for example, Newbigin, *Gospel in a Pluralist Society*.

It is only later that I have come to agree, in a very limited sense, this classical proposal of universal theology. Namely, if we call the subject matter of theology "theology" as well, then there might be a possibility of subscribing to the universal theology. However, a better name for that reality would be *Theos*, God, because *logia*, words, follow only later. At any rate, this reality can be considered the most fundamental level of theology. It is the matter of the divine reality that any theology attempts to refer to. To call it theology is misleading in the sense that whenever words are used to refer to it, or whenever human mind is in any way a recipient or participant in that reality, there is perception and conceptualization. This means that it no longer is a matter of pure and simple truth or reality but it is already enmeshed in the human webs of interpretation. As a result, other levels of theology discussed below are inevitably involved in the process.

It may look daring even to propose the existence of such underlying basic universal reality in these pluralistic times. However, if the choice is between the idea of there not being any reality and only emptiness, the idea of several (possibly competing) realities resulting in cosmological chaos, or one reality, this last option is a relatively common starting point even among many ascribers to pluralistic positions. If one chooses to have Christian doctrine as a starting-point, this choice is almost obvious.

As already hinted above, choosing to subscribe to the idea of one ultimate reality does not yet settle our views on the possible plurality of the perceived reality. This is because between reality, perceived reality and interpreted reality (and reinterpreted reality) there always exist various possibilities of perceiving the basic patterns of truth and interpretation differently.

In Christian tradition, there has been a strong emphasis on God as the Mystery. This is most emphatically portrayed in *via negativa* but absent hardly anywhere. This emphasis is not only specifically Christian, though. Several religions have the same emphasis, like Islam, Judaism, philosophical Hinduism and many primal religions, including African ones. God as the Mystery is also nicely in line with Kant's division of realities into *noumena* and *phenomena*,[18] God obviously being the ultimate *noumenon*. If we cannot know *die Dinge an sich*, things as they are, it is obvious that we cannot know the reality underlying the things.

According to the overwhelming majority of interpretations of Christian faith, God is not only hidden as the mystery, but she also reveals herself. Again, this view is not only specifically Christian but can be found in other religions, too. Some notion of revelation can be seen as a prerequisite for any religion. Christians share the view common to many religions that the

---

18. Kant, *Critique of Pure Reason*, 156–67.

creation conveys some revelation of God. Additionally, again in resonance with many religions, God has spoken through her followers out of whom some have specifically clear visions of God and her will, be it prophets as in Abrahamic religions or gurus as in Hinduism or sages, shamans or diviners as in many others. Finally, Christians believe, unlike most of the other religions, that God became human and, thereby, revealed herself.[19] However, the specificity of Christianity is not in any general idea, like that of incarnation or even redemption, but in anchoring one's faith to the specific narrative on Jesus of Nazareth.

Faith in the incarnation in Jesus of Nazareth gave eventually rise to the doctrine of the Trinity. Because this doctrine is peculiar to Christianity and because it is intrinsically linked with the Incarnation, I use the Trinitarian doctrine as the example through which to elaborate the levels of theology. Through formulating the distinct, but not separated levels of theology, I wish to open Christian theologizing to increasingly plural perceptions of reality yet preserve the classical theological basis.

If God is the ultimate Mystery who reveals herself, the conclusion has often been that she is *mysterium revelatum*, and the issue is considered to be solved. However, in that case, one leaps across a wide array of epistemological and fundamental theological issues. Among others, the language philosophical developments of last century have pinpointed the fact that the road from a phenomenon through perception, interpretation and expression to receiving and reinterpretation (and rereinterpretation etc.) is long and winding.[20] Therefore, considering God as the revealed Mystery does not yet reveal much about the theological process whereby I can reach the point of communicating to you about her. Rather, it is just a matter of declaring that there is a possibility of meaningful God-talk. How that would be possible and under what kind of limiting conditions, is quite another great area of discussion.

This next level of theology could conveniently be called *mysterium revelatum*, following theological traditions, albeit a clearer expression in this conjunction would be revelation of the Mystery—*revelatio mysterii*. In most of Christian theology, God is believed to be Trinitarian even though in Unitarian, liberal and some limited Pentecostal traditions this has been contested. If that is true about God, why not simply consider these two levels

---

19. The concept of God incarnating is not only specific to Christianity. In Hinduism, there are avatars, gods taking bodily forms, and in Sonjo religion in Tanzania, Ghambageu is regarded as a god incarnate. The latter may be because of Christian influence, though. Even suffering to substitute humankind's sins is not only Christian, since this view is found also in the concept of Boddhisattvas in Mahayana Buddhism.

20. See Stiver, *Philosophy of Religious Language*.

one and view God as the Trinity? This would be tempting, especially when subscribing Karl Rahner's idea of not only the economic Trinity reflecting the immanent Trinity but also the other way around.[21] That the economic Trinity reflects the immanent one is a presupposition for seeing economic Trinity (God's Trinitarian action towards the creation) as revelation of God's inner life. That connection is, thus, generally subscribed by Trinitarian Christians. However, the idea that the economic Trinity reflects the immanent Trinity is a more complex matter. In practical terms, the question is whether the economic Trinity in its all dimensions can be considered as a window into God's inner life. Even if one subscribed to this, one does not usually purport that revelation thorough economic Trinity would fully cover the Ultimate Mystery. Especially if there is a two-way correspondence between the Trinity and the divine reality why keep them distinct?

One obvious answer is related to practical interreligious relations. The fusion of God and revelation would introduce the risk of totalizing truth claims. If (Christian understanding of) revelation is considered *the* truth, Christians would hardly be in a position to learn from others. Naturally, a modest theologian would, even in this case, feel like there is much more to learn in the special revelation than what we have understood until now. Moreover, they would see that one can still find new dimensions of the revelation through creatureliness from other religions and cultures.

However, there are also theological reasons for not fusing these two. While Christians may believe that God truly revealed herself in Jesus of Nazareth, do we have reasons to expect that that was the full revelation leaving nothing unrevealed? Is there not a risk of reducing God by fusing these levels together? Bracketing God into revelation only leads me suspect that we would seriously narrow down the ineffable and unreachable mystery. Even if the economic and immanent Trinity would be correspondent in two directions, it does not necessarily mean that one could reduce the immanent Trinity into the economic one. Additionally, even if God had revealed of herself all that there is to be revealed, one may wonder whether there would be any possibility for humans receiving such revelation—*finitum non possit capere infinitum*—the finite cannot grasp the infinite. Indeed, even in the case that the revelation would not open the whole of the Mystery, the revelation can still be too large to be conceivable in human terms.

Therefore, it seems justified to make a distinction of level between God as the ultimate Mystery and God as revealed, in this case as the Trinitarian God. The first of the levels is ineffable and intellectually impenetrable, which lies as the foundation of the following level of God the revealed.

---

21. Rahner, *Trinity*, 22.

Through revealedness God becomes, to a certain extent, intellectually and experientially possible to relate to. However, even here the matter is not yet of one even having entered the human world of ideas and language.

In terms of theology of religions, the consequence of this distinction between the Ultimate Mystery and God's revelation of herself is that there is at least the possibility of other valid revelations of which Christians have no knowledge of. These revelations may resemble Christian perceptions of revelation or they may be completely different in form and content. There may also be tensions and paradoxes between true and valid revelations, but they cannot negate each other completely. For a Christian, the starting point and reference would always be the revelation received in Jesus Christ through the Bible and the interpretations of that message in Christian communities. Any assessment of revelations is, however, always only provisional and relative to the assessor's context.

The next proposed level of theology is that of (theological) concepts, like the concept of the Trinity. What is the difference between the revelation and the theological concepts of revelation, and why are they to be kept distinct? At this point, the incarnation is perhaps an easier example to begin with, because of its greater tangibility. The Incarnation as a salvation historical event is not a concept but an event, even a tangible reality at least regarding the body of the God incarnated. Thus, it seems obvious that the thing and our concept of it are easily distinguishable here.

In terms of the Trinity one must begin by posing the question of whether it is only a theological postulation, thereby only belonging on the level of concepts and lacking reference in the two deeper levels of theology. Much of classical theological tradition would emphatically maintain that the Trinity is also a reality. Again, if starting from the more social end of argumentation, one could maintain that considering the ultimate reality triune can at the same time keep our basic understanding of the reality unified while simultaneously providing us flexibility and plurality that helps in accepting the other. In the Trinity, the Other becomes the entity whereby the I is fulfilled. Without the Son, the Father cannot be the Father. Without the Spirit, the Word cannot be uttered and is, thereby, not a word but merely the idea of the word. The persons of the Trinity are made what they are, not because of their separate or even distinct substances, or because of their isolation from the others but, rather, only through their relations. The persons have everything else in common but their specific functions in the immanent Trinity; those related to their relations to each other. The Father is the one that utters the Word in the Spirit, the Word is the one uttered in the Spirit, and the Spirit is the one spirated by the Father in the utterance of the Word.²² Naturally, there is also the basic theological argumentation which gave rise to the Trinitarian doctrine in the first place: If Jesus of Nazareth was truly God, yet witnessing God the Father, and God is one, how can these two be reconciled? This was the history of dogma backdrop of the doctrine.

But if the Trinity is a (via incarnation indirectly) revealed mystery pointing to God as she is, why should we also consider it a theological concept? Theological concepts are intellectual pictures of God. In Swedish, Lund theologian Gustaf Aulén, introduced the term *"gudsbild"* which does not mean an image of God in the sense of an idol but, rather, the conception a believer has of God.²³ This is a very useful term as we all formulate our images of how God is in dialogue with Christian (and other) traditions and other cultural ideas. My God is, thus, not a reality outside of myself but rather my internalization and (largely subconscious) formulation of the Ultimate Mystery. If we lose sight of the nature of our theological concepts, we end up overestimating our theological knowledge, thereby idolizing our dogma. Then we encounter the danger of making doctrines into objects of worship. In Credo, when confessing that we believe in one God the point is hardly that we confess our faith in the concept of one God but, rather, in the reality behind the concept. The doctrine of the Trinity is a concept that attempts to depict God's mysterious self-revelation as faithfully and deeply as possible. Yet, it would be a matter of overestimating our theological knowledge to maintain that the concept would be the same as the reality. Whatever theological concepts exist, they are like arrows shot in the direction of a target that is located too far: the arrows can fly towards the target, but they do not hit it as they fall short. Yet, they can be purported to either fly in the right or the wrong direction.

Furthermore, fusion of theological concepts and the revealed realities would suggest that the theological concept encapsulates everything there is to be found in that dimension of the revealed reality. What should make us certain that just the concept of the Trinity would fully cover what that dimension of God's self-revelation is all about? The notion of *saccidananda* as the only appropriate way of describing God or Brahman in Sri Sankara's influential interpretation of the Upanishads has been taken as the starting point of many Indian theological considerations on God.²⁴ *Saccidananda*

---

22. See Boff, *Trinity and Society*, arguing how the Trinitarian notion of God leads to the most desirable social outcome and Nyamiti, *African Tradition*, 49 arguing how the Holy Spirit fulfills the Trinity.

23. Aulén, *Kristna gudsbilden*.

24. Thus Keshub Chunder Sen and Brahmabandhab Upadhaya according to Komulainen, "Kristillistä teologiaa hindulaisella maaperällä," 32, 39–40 and Henry le Saux/

is a Sanskrit philosophical and theological term consisting of three words: *sat, cit* and *ananda*. *Sat* means being, *cit* consciousness and *ananda* bliss. Brahman is the being itself, the only true being, everything else being an illusion. *Cit* as the pure consciousness does not mean that the being is conscious but that the being is consciousness and consciousness is being—the two concepts refer to the same reality. Likewise, pure bliss, *ananda*, is perfect and immutable and not divisible from *sat* and *cit*. Therefore, an immanent unity exists in the godhead, while the notion of *saccidananda* allows for dynamism.[25] In the Hindu-Christian contexts of encounter, there are views that *saccidananda* can not only convey (great parts) of the message about the Trinitarian God in the Indian context, but that it also can contribute to a deeper understanding of the Trinitarian mystery. Could we not remain open to the possibility of wider and deeper insights in some dimensions of the revealed mystery in religious traditions other than our own? If so, we need to make a distinction between our concepts and the revelation itself. The concepts are then only derivative pictures of the revealed mystery.

At any rate, even some theological concepts maintain some of the nature of mystery. This applies for example to the concept of the Trinity. It is such a rich concept that it seems to be difficult, or even impossible to empty it through explaining. It is intellectually extremely challenging, not the least because it contains the element of cognitive dissonance—that one can be many, and many can be one at the same time. The same applies to the doctrine of Incarnation where the abyss between the infinite creator God and the finite creature is bridged against what one should expect in metaphysical speculation. The doctrines of Redemption, the Eucharist, the church and so on, also seem to have a dimension of cognitive dissonance or of a paradox. One is even tempted to consider the possibility that such paradoxical nature might be one of the benchmarks of authentic Christian theological concepts! That would, of course, be a strong statement in favor of mystical traditions and against rationalistic currents.

Finally, we reach the level of religious language or expressions. One might again be tempted to slice away this level of theology with Ockham's razor—the distinction between concepts and words may seem superfluous. However, unless we want to totalize context-bound doctrinal statements as petrified markers of true classical Christianity, we need to be careful about lumping words and concepts together. It is clear that different words and,

---

Swami Abhishiktananda according to Friedrich, "'Henri le Saux.'" For criticism of the attempts to merge the two together see Thompson, "Saccidananda and the Trinity," 127–29.

25. Thompson, "Saccidananda and the Trinity," 125–26. On *sat* see also Spivak, "Can the Subaltern Speak?" 100–1.

even equivalent words, in various languages have varying connotations. This should not lead us to the idea that each and every word should stand for a concept of its own. Were we to consider every word as related to a concept of its own, we would actually make theologizing in each language a separate language game. While it is true that each language has its advantages and limitations in theological argumentation and that some words are next to impossible to translate (often due to the fact that in that language, one has developed a new concept), yet it is obvious that theological discourse is often multilingual and that there exists meaningful exchange of ideas and construction of concepts over linguistic boundaries. Ockham's razor should then lead us to postulate a distinction between the words and the concepts—otherwise we would need to postulate an endless number of concepts for each word of every language.

At the same time, even if the theological concept signified by the words was the same, different words point to it in different ways. The difference may stem from the words being constructed to denote different dimensions of the concept, like when qualifying the Trinity either as economic or immanent. Translations of words also introduce new dimensions, even if the attempt is to convey as "original" a meaning as possible. The fact that the expression takes place in a different cultural-linguistic cosmos makes it different. Thus, the Kiswahili "*Utatu*" for the Trinity may seem like almost a perfect one-to-one translation, "*tatu*" standing for "tri" and "u" standing for "nitas." However, because the Bantu linguistic world is strongly governed by the classification of nouns—which classification actually even transcends nouns to modality and space and the like—the Trinity is immediately classified in the group of immaterial nouns of "u"-class. This immediately conveys to the *Mswahili* (a Kiswahili speaker, m-prefix referring to living creatures, ki-prefix to things) connotations that are not available for an English speaker simply because the lack of such classifications in her language.[26] At the same time, Kiswahili lack of suitable linguistic forms of adequately expressing traditional Greek metaphysical ideas limits the possibilities of grasping some of the dimensions of western Trinitarian theologizing. There is, for example, no verb denoting being in the sense of existence or subsistence. Something either is somewhere or of a certain kind or quality. Ontologically-geared Greek thought has very limited linguistic avenues in that context, whereas the very classification of nouns opens up wide vistas for theological thought. In fact, this linguistic cosmos opens a cosmology entirely different to the Hellenistic. This becomes highly visible in Aristotle's Metaphysics,

---

26. For similar considerations on untranslatability see Bhabha, *Location of Culture*, 227.

which largely builds on the structure of Greek language.[27] Thus, Aristotle is equipped in his analysis with his linguistic background which, at the same time also limits him. For a Bantu (which actually is a plural of a common word in Bantu languages, *muntu*—a human being), the Greek ontological world remains closed until she is equipped with a language that provides her access to it. Likewise, someone not familiar to a Bantu language cannot access the philosophical opportunities that this language family has to offer.[28] Each language has its specific possibilities either in terms of grammar or vocabulary and expressions that render it unique intellectual possibilities.

Thus, if we maintained, for example, that the concept of the Trinity and the word *"trinitas"* were in a direct univocal connection with each other, we would make two mistakes at once. First, we would limit the possibilities of that theological concept to Latin. Doing so, we would block the possibilities of enriching the concept through other languages and cultures. This interlinguistic and intercultural extension of theological concepts has already been in place since the very beginning, not the least in the interchange of ideas between the Aramaic/Hebrew, Greek, Latin, Coptic, Armenian, Syriac, Geez, Arabic etc. spheres. It is inconceivable what Christianity would be, or whether there even would be Christianity without the linguistic and cultural cross-pollination between Hebrew/Aramaic and Greek spheres. Second, we would absolutize a culturally specific term and practically idolize it. If the idolization of theological concepts is pitiful and dangerous, idolization of theological expressions is pathetic. Contemporary theologians should be in the position of knowing the history of Christianity well enough to understand that the Hellenistic approach to Christian doctrine, while dominant for over a millennium, is not and has never been the only one. Oriental Churches' theology has always existed as an alternative and has most often built on Semitic languages and, therefore, found its expressions in a different linguistic cosmos. Idolization of dogmatic formulations from the so-called ecumenical councils is practically tantamount to an idolization of Greek language and culture. After all, the ecumenical councils were not all that ecumenical because the attendance of bishops from outside of the Roman Empire was very limited. Considering that the Persian Empire had a bulky share of the Christian population during the first centuries of church history, this was a considerable shortcoming. Context-bound doctrinal

---

27. Aristoteles, *Metaphysica*.

28. Alexis Kagame's doctoral dissertation is a fine example of this because makes use of a Bantu language's noun classes in philosophical-theological speculation on God. Kagame, *La philosophie bantu-rwandaise de l'Être*. For a general discussion on languages as worlds of representation see Gadamer, *Wahrheit und Methode*, 415–19.

statements should be understood as what they are: pointers towards theological concepts that point towards the revealed mystery.

Four Levels of Theology and the Encountering of Pluralism

What then is the significance of these four levels of theology to encountering the religiously plural context? Will they be of help in circumnavigating the pluralist challenge?

Considering the alternatives that God's revelation of herself is totally identified with the divine reality and the idea of viewing them distinct, one can readily see a considerable difference in the outcome vis-à-vis theology of religions. Totalizing fusion of these levels easily leads to a rigid exclusivist pattern in which only my position is completely correct, and the others' positions are so only insofar as they are in line with mine. The possible variations and flexibilities refer to other levels, namely to the interpretation of the revelation. If, however, we choose the humbler path of acknowledging the possibility of revelation alongside that which is known in Christianity, a door is opened for the positive affirmation of pluralism. In that case, God that is revealed according to one religion does not need to be the one and only valid revelation, but the door is left open for other possibly valid revelations. Simultaneously, if we maintain, for example, that the revelation in Jesus of Nazareth is genuine (and according to many Christians also unsurpassable) self-revelation of God, there is no case of theological relativism in any unchecked manner. Revelation in Jesus then functions as the/a Christian norm of assessing other truth claims concerning God.

The difference from the so-called pluralist alternatives of the likes of Hick and Knitter is clear. They formulate such an understanding of the content of revelation that they imagine would be the most accommodating to other faiths—yet avoiding total relativism. They can propose, for example, that love would function as the criterion of truth for all the faiths.[29] However, that proposal rises clearly more aptly from a Christian rather than, say, a Buddhist background, which makes it only seemingly pluralist. Love is a central concept in Christianity and very much in the sense of personal attachment—between God and her chosen people as well as God and humankind. For Buddhism, love in the sense of attaching to something is the opposite of virtue and leads further away from enlightenment. To serve as a proper starting point for Buddhist thought, love would need to be

---

29. See Hick, *Interpretation of Religion*, 325–26. See also D'Costa's criticism on Hick's position in D'Costa, *Meeting of Religions and the Trinity*, 24–30.

interpreted as compassion.[30] Thus, to defend this position, one would need to interpret the concept of love in various religions such differing ways that one wonders whether it is only the word that remains shared, whereas the content is altogether different.

The distinction of the levels, in turn, facilitates the open allegiance to one's own central tenets of faith, meaning that one can be open about the particular starting point one holds. Simultaneously, there is no need to absolutize that point of departure. Yet, despite that, one cannot share this point of departure with followers of another religion. While this may sound as a negative outcome from the pluralist point of view, this is not the case because the acknowledgement of each others' difference serves as a move that liberates both parties into freely being what they are. Simultaneously, a possibility of holding a complementary and corrective truth is reserved to the partner. Even if this reservation never materialized, that move already facilitates a positive acceptance of religious plurality.

This outcome could be considered a form of inclusivism. The difference to the conventional inclusivist position is that all revelation outside of Christianity need not be viewed through revelation in Christ even if Christ serves as the criterion of assessment. This means that a Christian theologian does not need to force every truth in a Christomonic all-encompassing theological system. There may be ideas and practices that I may regard as true and valuable even if they perhaps cannot be a part of my way of seeing the reality. Yet, for the assessment of true and false, right and wrong, there needs to be a criterion. The way I see it, for a Christian theologian this criterion would be the Ultimate Reality, God, revealed in Jesus Christ, no matter how God and Christ are interpreted. The questions whether and how the other revelations relate to Christ can either be left open or there would be considerable space to maneuver Christology in relation to other faiths, for example through the patristic idea of seeds of the Word (*logos spermatikos*) or the idea of cosmic Christ.

Also, the subsequent distinction between the revelation and theological concepts allows for additional flexibility in relation to revelation in other religions. On one hand, it opens the door of acknowledging genuine and original views originating from traditions of other religions, to the dimensions of revelation usually considered as Christian. A case I point could be the aforementioned concept of *saccidananda* which could be granted a full respect as another perspective of the revealed mystery that Christians view through the concept of the Trinity. It can be accepted as a completing view and does not need to be included in the Christian Trinitarian theologizing

---

30. See McCoy, "Comparison of Buddhist Compassion to Christian Love."

to also be acceptable for us. Therefore, in viewing other than Christian religious concepts there is no need of "baptizing" them or even granting them the status of anonymous Christian doctrines. Rather, they can be considered alternative ways of viewing the same revealed mysteries that remain worthy and true without compromising Christian truth claims. This distinction also allows for a freer inclusion of religious and cultural values in contextual theological processes within Christianity. That means that while the "baptizing" of non-Christian traditions is not necessary, this distinction allows for the possibility of enriching the Christian understanding of revelation through other faiths. In this way, Christian faith would even allow for variation on the level of concepts.

The last distinction between the concepts and the level of language mainly affects encounters with the pluralism within Christianity. The idea of the language being distinct from the theological concepts allows for a very liberal approach to forms of expression. In theology, this has not always been the case. When the traditional mode of speech is considered the carrier of Christian faith, maintaining that the likes of the creeds are to be preserved word for word but the concepts behind the words may be changed, a major dimension of Christian flexibility is lost. This happens in some liberal theologies where the traditional theological language is preserved but the meaning is reinterpreted.[31] Translatability, which Lamin Sanneh considers the benchmark of Christianity,[32] is then virtually lost. Translation is a very complex matter and sticking to verbatim formulations cuts its wings. The freedom and flexibility gained on the conceptual level are of little consolation to the one who does not share the cultural-linguistic background of this reinterpreted "classical" Christianity. Currently, this means the majority of Christians outside the western cultural sphere as well as the innumerable western Christians and non-Christians to whom traditional theological language is no more understandable than Medieval Latin. And, in case someone is interested in communicating the Christian message to the majority world non-Christians, also their chances of understanding the Christian messages are severely hindered by this line of thought.

In some Evangelical thinking one may be quite flexible vis-à-vis theological expressions as long as they seem to refer to the correct concepts. This is almost the mirror image of the liberal theological position described above. The distinction proposed here would make it easier to allow for

---

31. Perhaps the most noted example is Bultmann's reinterpretation of Jesus' resurrection as the renewed consciousness of the disciples. In this case, the language remains the same whereas the content takes a considerable turn. Bultmann, *Jesus Christus und die Mythologie*, 38–43.

32. Sanneh, *Translating the Message*.

flexibility on both levels. This distinction of the levels opens the possibility to dual flexibility but does not necessarily lead to an "anything goes" type of relativism. There is still the possibility of anchoring the changed language and concepts to the revealed mysteries, and naturally, as proposed in the previous part, to the broader Christian tradition.

An alert reader will have noticed that in the above argumentation, I propose two basic criteria for Christian theology: connection to the broad Christian tradition (having the Bible as the centerpiece) and ethics. Connection to the broad Christian tradition has been discussed earlier in detail and all Christian theologies propose connection to the Bible or tradition in a wider sense as a criterion for theology. Lifting ethics as a criterion of the correctness of theology may raise eyebrows in some theological circles. I have two reasons for that move, political and theological. From the political or power structure point of view, no knowledge production is innocent but all knowledge, theology included, serves someone's interests. Therefore, a theologian's crucial question should always be: whose interests does my theology serve? And, in case the answer is not in line with one's understanding of the gospel values, there is something wrong with that theology even from a system immanent perspective. The theological argument goes as follows: if God is the summit of all good, true understanding of her cannot lead to unethical and oppressive practices. If my proclamation of God the Love leads to hatred, bigotry and conflicts, there probably is something wrong with my proclamation. At the same time one needs to acknowledge the fact that the powers that be often react violently against any challenge.[33]

Facing the Critique against Essentialism

According to Gayatri C. Spivak, essentialism perceives the relations between words and their points of reference as fixed, unchanging and essential.[34] That means that a word referring to, let us say, "person," is considered to have an unchanging meaning. Furthermore, "person" is also understood as a thing out there, a reality with an unchanging essence. That kind of understanding of language shies away from the analysis of power structures, thereby, uncritically supporting status quo. In addition to that, such a view is ahistorical and overlooks the flexible and developing nature of language.

As to religious language, there have been, and still are many theologians maintaining that Christian doctrine is in a way or another fixed and

---

33. Te Paa, "Context, Controversy, and Contradiction"; Havea, "The Cons of Contextuality," 44; Pieris, *Asian Theology of Liberation*, 40.

34. Spivak, "Can the Subaltern Speak?" 79–80, see also 91.

eternal. This is the case in some Protestant circles and becomes visible for example when there are additions to the liturgies purporting that the credo read out in the liturgy is what all Christians everywhere have always believed. Another example is the five fundamentals that were made into the credo of the fundamentalist movement in the twentieth century American Protestantism. However, in Roman Catholic thought it is agreed that the doctrine can develop. Despite this, this development is seen as refinement or progress rather than changing a position as such. One can maintain that behind the visible forms of expression there is *philosophia perennis*, and that single universal theology referred to above. This view would undoubtedly be labelled as essentialist by Spivak and other critics. Even Eastern Orthodox traditions, in spite of their seeming conservatism and air of unchanging nature, tradition is seen as a living entity and not a "storehouse of facts" as in early American Fundamentalism.

A possible solution to the critique against essentialism is to move the point of reference of religious language into the human psyche, having religious language referring to human consciousness or feelings, à la Schleiermacher.[35] In this way, anti-essentialist points are placated, while the questions of whether and how religious sentiments are linked to outside realities, if any, are left unanswered.

What is clear is that doctrinal expressions have changed at least within the Roman Catholic tradition. Additionally, the concepts behind doctrinal formulations have not only developed but also clearly changed. A case in point already discussed is the teaching about *nulla salus extra ecclesiam*. Finally, in cases where the doctrinal formulations have remained the same, the way we understand them is often significantly different from the culture and time in which they were originally crafted. So, very few if any of us will be able to grasp the exact meaning of "persona" as understood by Tertullian. It is difficult for us to overlook the developments in psychology or sociology, among other disciplines, that have greatly molded our understanding of human personality. Of course, one may programmatically ignore these developments and attempt to reconstruct the antique understanding of "persona." However, even that project would lead to a fluid situation because our understanding on Roman antiquity is also constantly developing and changing. After all, the question is also whose understanding of "person" should the correct understanding of the Christian doctrine be anchored to.

By accepting the fluid character of words and concepts one does not need to succumb to a total fluidity of reality. Distinguishing between human notions of reality and their verbalizations, on one hand, and the reality of

---

35. Schleiermacher, *Über die Religion*, 50, 53.

noumena on the other hand provide us the tools required to simultaneously completely accept the fluidity of human existence, while not needing to give up the perception of having something permanent behind. The religious concept of revelation provides a possibility for the human mind to reach out towards that permanent reality. However, because our conceptualization and speech about that reality are not indefinitely fixed, religious language need not be viewed in an essentialist way. The way religious language refers to theological concepts can be seen as changing without it risking Christian ideas about truth. Additionally, even if the thought of the malleability of the theological concepts behind the verbalized forms of faith may feel threatening to many a Christian identity, this need not be the case. The anchoring point should not be theology but the reality behind it. Anchoring faith in revelation, which is understood as an opening of the noumenal world to the conceivable world, is a way of balancing between relativism and essentialism. Especially when admitting that there remains a level of reality that we have no way of grasping, the danger implicit in the essentialism of sticking to theological and religious expressions as fixed and eternal references to the truth, is avoided. Then, even if subscribing to a non-relativist view of reality, one could still share Spivak's concern for the suffocating effects that essentialism has towards the acceptance of plurality.

Gianni Vattimo shares Spivak's concerns about essentialism violating human dignity, especially of those that do not meet the criteria of normality. Vattimo joins Heidegger in labeling this metaphysics—claiming to know Being which is at the same time the most present dimension of reality of all, and a reality that constantly hides from the observer who can never observe it as if from outside.[36] However, for him the rejection of metaphysics does need not lead to Nietzschean nihilism. While Vattimo accepts Nietzsche's analysis of metaphysics as violence, thus rendering the reformulation of metaphysics immoral and politically undesirable, he wants to construct a third alternative based on Christian tradition.[37] What Vattimo rejects is "*metafisica dell'oggettività*,"[38] "metaphysics of objectivity". This should not be read as a rejection of all search of truth beyond the perceivable but as rejection of human projections of power structures into the metaphysical sphere promoted as the objective Truth.

---

36. See, e.g., Heidegger, "Zur Seinsfrage," 243–44. Heidegger's view of Being's hiding itself from us has been called "*Seinsverborgenheit*." Philipse, *Heidegger's Philosophy of Being*, 194.

37. Vattimo, *Credere di credere*, 19–23, 43–4.

38. Vattimo, *Credere di credere*, 20–21.

Vattimo dubs his alternative "weak thought" ("*pensiero debole*")[39] and in it one abstains from building philosophical and theological certainties on the basis of metaphysics. For him, this is not only a way of thinking that is more aware of its limits than metaphysics of objectivity, thus, rejecting phantasies of universal objectivity, "but above all a theory of weakening as the constitutive character of Being in the epoch of the end of metaphysics."[40] Here, the principle of weakening draws from the Pauline concept of *kenosis* which refers to the incarnation in which God emptied godself and became human. Thus, Vattimo's understanding of the deepest reality of Being builds on Réne Girard's reading of the gospel.[41] In this interpretation, *caritas* (charity; love) becomes the hermeneutical key to the reality.[42]

One can see that Vattimo's approach does not aim at unchecked relativism, but the way in which the question of relativism is solved remains open. The proposal above is one attempt at constructing weak theological thinking that rejects traditional metaphysical certainty but does not disappear into the space of no boundaries at all. To me it seems that a compromise between nihilism and objectivistic metaphysical Fundamentalism holds the possibility of providing space to live for a faith that does not pretend to be knowledge yet abstains from reducing itself only to a private opinion.

---

39. Vattimo, *Credere di credere*, 25.

40. Vattimo, *Credere di credere*, 25–26. Translation from Vattimo, *Belief*, 35.

41. Vattimo, *Credere di credere*, 26–29; 49–51. Here, Vattimo refers to Girard who proposes a non-sacrificial reading of the gospel. Girard, *Things Hidden*, 173–214.

42. Vattimo, *Credere di credere*, 75.

8

Concluding Remarks

THE WORLD HAS BEEN undergoing changes at an unprecedented pace in terms of technology, economy and environment. When life-conditions are profoundly changing with the enormous global flow of information and people, global economic possibilities expanding and centralizing in the hands of few and the environment degrading rapidly, not least through climate change, our cultures are undergoing drastic and rapid changes as well. Religion is an undividable part of culture and no religion exists in a cultural vacuum, which means that religions are also in a process of profound metamorphosis. Christianity is undergoing several major changes simultaneously. Secularism and increased religious-cultural pluralism in the West has demolished the old fortresses', like the European state churches and American mainline churches', central social position. Meanwhile, Christianity has expanded like never before in several majority world contexts, turning the global Christian demography upside down. Majority world now holds majority within Christianity as well. Simultaneous with the expansion of majority world Christianity, charismatic forms of Christianity have spread like wildfire in the form of new churches and denominations, as well as within the existing denominations. Despite several transcultural traits in the charismatic forms of Christianity, there is huge variation in ritual, spirituality, ethics and faith between churches and groups that often are lumped together as charismatic.

All these changes make a major difference to the conditions of theologizing. During the last two centuries, academic theology has been working on adapting itself to the western Enlightenment universalistic approach to reality. The result has often been rather cerebral and rationalistic interpretations of the Christian faith that have had diverse levels of success within the western academy. Despite the usually high intellectual standards these interpretations have seldom been met with much approval in western churches while being even less convincing in the majority world. Any new universal claims from the West tend to awaken suspicion in the majority world as neo-colonialism. In the West, the gradual increase of knowledge on foreign cultures and religions, ideas about hierarchies between cultures, and the hopes of the adherents of other cultures becoming "civilized," i.e., turning into clones of Europeans, and converting to Christianity, have vanished. Cultural and religious plurality is there to stay, and it will only continue to increase in the West due to immigration and pluralization from within. Thus, it seems that the era of the grand theological narratives is over, or is it?

An easy solution vis-à-vis plurality is relativism, whereby, any truth claim is taken with a pinch of salt and granted its truthfulness in its own reality bubble. Any attempts at convincing the other are meaningless, because all truths are reduced to personal opinions. There are practical and logical objections against relativism—I would not prefer to live next door to a nuclear power plant built using relativist principles and picking up the most colorful and exotic theory on uranium—but from the point of view of Christian theology, there is additionally the question of revelation. Either God reveals herself to the humankind and this revelation has meaning beyond a limited bubble, or it is not a matter of divine revelation at all in the Christian sense. At the same time, it is clear that there is no return to the old universalistic claims. Therefore, one needs to seek another solution. This book has proposed some ideas and theories that would help formulate such theologies that navigate between relativism and universalistic claims.

The first step of acknowledging that there is no one legitimate interpretation of the gospel while not giving up the idea of the gospel as revelation is to realize that there is no simple literal reading of any text. All reading that involves any level of understanding is an interpretation of the text that builds on earlier interpretations, as well as the context and the approach of the reader. Thus, all Christian theology is contextual by default if it is an interpretation of the gospel. In this interpretation, there is a hermeneutical circle where the earlier interpretations of the gospel—which can never be pure and non-cultural because it is always expressed in and through a culture—serve as the starting-point. These earlier interpretations, or tradition, enter into a dialogue with the world-view, socio-cultural context and the methodological approach of the thinker producing a new interpretation of the gospel which feeds back into the living tradition. In this process, the gospel is incarnated or enmeshed into new contexts.

Religion cannot be separated from the rest of culture—many non-western cultures do not even have any word for religion. Therefore, every interpretation of the gospel is syncretistic by default as it includes elements of other religions. Additionally, even the Bible contains elements from other religions, making the strife towards pure non-mixed Christianity even more futile.

The syncretistic nature of Christianity goes hand in hand with its translatability or the fact that all interpretations of the gospel are inevitably contextual. Because each context is different and there is a multitude of possibilities of how the contextual process can turn out, the outcome is that there are numerous forms of Christianity that are not recognized as Christian by, at least, some other Christian churches and groups. This means that the borders of Christianity are porous. There are a number of churches that are commonly seen to belong to Christianity, whereas there are other interpretations of the gospel that are generally regarded as non-Christian by the majority of churches, as well as a grey zone where the opinions differ. These diffuse borders are a natural consequence of the syncretistic nature of Christianity and the fact that there is no one central authority to draw the definite borders. Additionally, historically speaking, Christianity is not a static entity but there is a clear movement whereby some theological or ethical positions that were avant-garde in the past are today mainstream. It is only afterwards, though, that one can say with certainty which direction the Christian *sensus communis* took.

As alluded to above, contextuality and syncretism, so feared by the universalists, are not to be afraid of. Rather, they need to be seen as natural consequences of the doctrine of Incarnation. As the Word became flesh, the gospel incarnated in various contexts, including the religious. Without this process, the gospel would either remain an abstract idea or, if only one contextual interpretation were regarded as the correct one, that culture would be idolized.

But, in this scheme, how can one navigate between relativism and an exclusive universalism? My proposal is that we perceive theology as having four levels which function as if links of a chain to the anchor that fastens our thought in the depth of the unknowable. To begin with, God is the ultimate Mystery. As such, even if we have ideas about the creator and the ground of being behind everything, we have no way of assessing whether these ideas are human fabrications or not. However, according to the Christian faith, this ultimate Mystery has revealed herself in Jesus of Nazareth. This gives humans an opening towards the Mystery allowing for other levels of faith beyond acknowledging the existence of the unknowable.

The second level is that of revelation. The ultimate Mystery revealed herself in the Incarnation above all, but also in the Creation and through the Holy Spirit. Thus, God revealed is someone humans can relate to. However, we have no guarantee that this revelation is total, in the sense that in it God would have revealed herself in totality. Therefore, I propose a distinction between the ultimate Mystery and the revealed God. In interreligious relations this means that Christians cannot claim to own the whole truth, as the possibility remains of genuine revelation even outside of Christianity.

On the basis of revelation, we formulate theological concepts which, in turn, are expressed in words. The distinction between the concepts and the words is that while a word is limited to its cultural milieu and the internal logic of the language, a concept is not. Rather, a concept can be enriched by being expressed in different words from various languages.

The outcome of postulating these levels is that each relation to the following level becomes like a hinge or an interlocking of the links in a chain which allows for flexibility. This flexibility provides the possibility of plurality within Christian theology, as well as an open approach to other religions, while still maintaining the anchoring to the gospel—in the sense of God's revelation of herself.

While none of the proposals above alone, or even all of them together, would prove to be the solution to the problems of today's academic theology, I hope that they contribute to the discussion on whether and how theology as a discipline should be renewed in the light of the new world context.

Bibliography

Adogame, Afe. "HIV/AIDS Support and African Pentecostalism: The Case of the Redeemed Christian Church of God." *Journal of Health Psychology* 12 (2007) 475–83.

Agrama, Hussein Ali. "Ethics, Tradition, Authority: Toward an Anthropology of the Fatwa." *American Ethnologist* 37 (2010) 2–18.

Ahonen, Tiina. *Transformation through Compassionate Mission: David J. Bosch's Theology of Contextualization*. Helsinki: Luther-Agricola-Society, 2003.

Alava, Henni, and Jimmy Spire Ssentongo. "Religious (de)Politicisation in Uganda's 2016 Elections." *Journal of Eastern African Studies* 4 (2017) 677–92.

Aleaz, K. P. "Indigenization." In *Dictionary of Third World Theologies*, edited by Virginia Fabella and R. S. Sugirtharajah, 106–8. Maryknoll, NY: Orbis, 2000.

Álvarez, Carmelo E. "A Future for Latin American Liberation Theology?" In *Contextual Theology for the Twenty-First Century*, edited by Stephen B. Bevans and Katalina Tahaafe-Williams, 87–96. Eugene, OR; Pickwick, 2011.

Alvesson, Mats, and Kaj Sköldberg. *Reflexive Methodology: New Vistas for Qualitative Research*. 2nd ed. London: Sage, 2009.

Anderson, Benedict. *Imagined Communities: Reflections on the Origin and Spread of Nationalism*. Rev. ed. London: Verso, 1991.

Anderson, Gerard H., et al. *Witness to World Christianity: The International Association for Mission Studies 1972–2012*. New Haven: OMSC, 2012.

Appiah, Kwame Anthony. *Cosmopolitanism: Ethics in the World of Strangers*. London: Penguin, 2007.

Aquino, Thomas ab. *Summa Theologiae prima pars*. In *S. Thomae Aquinatis Opera Omnia*, 2:184–354. Stuttgart-Bad Cannstatt: Frommann-Holzboog, 1980.

Aristoteles. *Metaphysica*. Aristoteles Latinus XXV I–Ia. Bruxelles: Desclée de Brouwer, 1970.

Asad, Talal. *Formations of the Secular: Christianity, Islam, Modernity*. Stanford: Stanford University Press, 2003.

Aulén, Gustaf. *Christus Victor: An Historical Study of the Three Main Types of the Idea of Atonement*. London: SPCK, 1970.

———. *Den kristna gudsbilden genom seklerna och i nutiden: en konturteckning*. Stockholm: Sv. kyrkans diakonistyrelsens, 1927.

Awam, Imran. "Cyber-Extremism: Isis and the Power of Social Media." *Society* 54 (2017) 138–49.
Balcomb, Anthony. "Faith or Suspicion? Theological Dialogue North and South of the Limpopo with Special Reference to the Theologies of Kwame Bediako and Andrew Walls." *Journal of Theology for Southern Africa* 100 (1998) 3–19.
Barney, G. Linwood. "The Supracultural and the Cultural: Implications for Frontier Missions." In *The Gospel and Frontier Peoples*, edited by R. P. Beaver, 48–57. Pasadena: William Carey Library, 1973.
Barrett, David B., et al. *World Christian Encyclopedia*. Vol. 1. Oxford: Oxford University Press, 2001.
Barth, Karl. *Learning Jesus Christ through the Heidelberg Catechism*. Grand Rapids: Eerdmans, 1964.
———. *Die Lehre vom Wort Gottes: Prolegomena zur kirchlichen Dogmatik*. Die kirchliche Dogmatik I/1. 2nd ed. Munich: Kaiser, 1935.
Bateson, Nora. "#Metoo is Complex." *Explorations in Media Ecology* 17 (2018): 71–76.
Bauer, Walter. *Orthodoxy and Heresy in Earliest Christianity*. Philadelphia: Fortress, 1971.
Bediako, Kwame. *Theology and Identity: The Impact of Culture upon Christian Thought in the Second Century and Modern Africa*. Oxford: Regnum, 1992.
"Being Christian in Western Europe." Pew Research Center, 2018. https://www.pewforum.org/2018/05/29/being-christian-in-western-europe/.
Bellah, Robert N. "Civil Religion in America." *Daedalus* 96 (1967) 1–21.
Bendroth, Margaret. "Time, History, and Tradition in the Fundamentalist Imagination." *Church History* 85 (2016) 328–42.
Benhabib, Seyla. *The Claims of Culture: Equality and Diversity in the Global Era*. Princeton, NJ: Princeton University Press, 2002.
Berger, Peter L. *The Heretical Imperative: Contemporary Possibilities of Religious Affirmation*. Garden City, NY: Anchor, 1980.
———. *The Sacred Canopy: Elements of a Sociological Theory of Religion*. New York: Anchor, 1990.
Berger, Peter L., and Thomas Luckmann. *The Social Construction of Reality: A Treatise in the Sociology of Knowledge*. London: Penguin, 1991.
Bergmann, Sigurd. *Gud i funktion: En orientering i den kontextuella teologin*. Stockholm: Verbum, 1997.
Bevans, Stephen B. "Migration and Mission: Pastoral Challenges, Theological Insights." In *Reforming Theology, Migrating Church, Transforming Society: A Compendium for Ecumenical Education*, edited by Uta Andrée et al., 178–91. Hamburg: Missionshilfe, 2017.
———. "Models of Contextual Theologizing in World Christianity." Kerr lecture at Trinity College, Glasgow University, 1st February 2018.
———. *Models of Contextual Theology*. Revised and expanded ed. Maryknoll, NY: Orbis, 2002.
———. "What Has Contextual Theology to Offer the Church of the Twenty-First Century?" In *Contextual Theology for the Twenty-First Century*, edited by Stephen B. Bevans and Katalina Tahaafe-Williams, 3–17. Eugene, OR; Pickwick, 2011.
Bevans, Stephen B., and Roger Schroeder. *Constants in Context: A Theology of Mission for Today*. Maryknoll, NY: Orbis, 2004.
Beyer, Peter. *Religions in Global Society*. Abingdon: Routledge, 2006.

Bhabha, Homi K. *The Location of Culture*. London: Routledge, 1994.
Bialecki, Jon, et al. "The Anthropology of Christianity." *The Religion Compass* 2 (2008), 1139–58.
Boff, Clodovis. *Theologie und Praxis: Die erkenntnistheoretischen Grundlagen der Theologie der Befreiung*. Munich: Kaiser, 1983.
Boff, Leonardo. *Church, Charism & Power: Liberation Theology and the Institutional Church*. New York: Crossroad, 1992.
———. *Trinity and Society*. Maryknoll, NY: Orbis, 1988.
Boff, Leonardo, and Clodovis Boff. *Introducing Liberation Theology*. Kent: Burns & Oates, 1987.
Bosch, David J. "The Roots and Fruits of Afrikaner Civil Religion." In *New Faces of Africa: Essays in Honour of Ben (Barend Jacobus) Marais*, edited by J. W. Hofmeyr and W. S. Vorster, 14–35. Pretoria: University of South Africa, 1984.
———. *Transforming Mission: Paradigm Shifts in Theology of Mission*. Maryknoll, NY: Orbis, 1991.
Broggi, Joshua D. *Diversity in the Structure of Christian Reasoning: Interpretation, Disagreement, and World Christianity*. Leiden: Brill, 2015.
Buckley, James J. "Revisionists and Liberals." In *The Modern Theologians: An Introduction to Christian Theology since 1918*, edited by David E. Ford, 213–28. Oxford: Blackwell, 2005.
Budden, Chris. "The Necessity of a Second Peoples' Theology in Australia." In *Contextual Theology for the Twenty-First Century*, edited by Stephen B. Bevans and Katalina Tahaafe-Williams, 55–68. Eugene, OR; Pickwick, 2011.
Budnitsky, Stanislav, and Lianrui Jia. "Branding Internet Sovereignty: Digital Media and the Chinese-Russian Cyberalliance." *European Journal of Cultural Studies* 21 (2018) 594–613.
Bultmann, Rudolf. *Jesus Christus und die Mythologie: Das Neue Testament in Licht der Bibelkritik*. Hamburg: Furche, 1964.
Buqa, Wonke. "Storying *Ubuntu* as a Rainbow Nation." *Verbum et ecclesia* 36 (2015) 1–8.
Buthelezi, Manas. "Change in the Church." In *Mission Trends no. 1: Crucial Issues in Mission Today*, edited by Gerald H. Anderson and Thomas F. Stransky, 195–204. New York: Paulist, 1978.
Cahoone, Lawrence. "Introduction." In *From Modernism to Postmodernism: An Anthology*, 1–13. Oxford: Blackwell, 2003.
Capra, Fritjof. *The Tao of Physics: An Exploration of the Parallels between Modern Physics and Eastern Mysticism*. Boulder, CO: Shambhala, 1975.
Carrión, María M. "Scent of a Mystic Woman: Teresa de Jesús and the *Interior Castle*." *Medieval Encounters* 15 (2009) 130–56.
Césaire, Aimé. *Discours sur le colonialisme*. Paris: Présence Africaine, 1955.
Chabal, Patrick, and Jean-Pascal Daloz. *Africa Works: Disorder as a Political Instrument*. Bloomington: Indiana University Press, 1999.
Childs, Peter, and Patrick Williams. *An Introduction to Post-Colonial Theory*. Harlow, Essex: Prentice Hall, 1997.
Christian Witness in a Multi-Religious World. 2011. https://www.oikoumene.org/en/resources/documents/wcc-programmes/interreligious-dialogue-and-cooperation/christian-identity-in-pluralistic-societies/christian-witness-in-a-multi-religious-world.

The Church in Africa and Her Evangelising Mission Towards the Year 2000: "You Shall Be My Witnesses" (Acts 1:8) Instrumentum Laboris. Synod of Bishops Special Assembly for Africa. Nairobi: St. Paul Publications Africa, ca. 1993.

Clooney, Francis X. *Comparative Theology: Deep Learning across Religious Borders.* Chichester: Wiley-Blackwell, 2010.

Coleman, Simon. *The Globalisation of Charismatic Christianity: Spreading the Gospel of Prosperity.* Cambridge: Cambridge University Press, 2000.

Collins, Patricia Hill, and Sirma Bilge. *Intersectionality.* Cambridge: Polity, 2016.

Comstock, Gary. "Truth or Meaning: Ricoeur versus Frei on Biblical Narrative." *Journal of Religion* 66 (1986) 117–40.

"Confession of Belhar." 1986. https://www.pcusa.org/site_media/media/uploads/theologyandworship/pdfs/belhar.pdf.

Conradie, Ernst M. *Redeeming Sin? Social Diagnostic amid Ecological Destruction.* Lanham, MD: Lexington, 2017.

Davie, Grace. "Is Europe an Exceptional Case?" *Hedgehog Review* 8 (2006), 23–34.

Dawkins, Richard. *The God Delusion.* London: Bantam, 2006.

D'Costa, Gavin. *The Meeting of Religions and the Trinity.* Maryknoll, NY: Orbis, 2000.

Dickson, Kwesi A. *Uncompleted Mission: Christianity and Exclusivism.* Christian Theology in African Scholarship. Nairobi: Acton, 2000.

Documento de Medellín: La Iglesia en la actual transformacion de America Latina a la luz del concilio. Segunda Conferencia General del Episcopado Latinoamericano, 1968. https://www.scribd.com/document/401034908/CELAM-Documento-Conclusivo-de-Medellin.

Donovan, Vincent. *The Missionary Letters of Vincent Donovan 1957–1973.* Eugene, OR: Pickwick, 2011.

Dulles, Avery. *Models of Revelation.* Maryknoll, NY: Orbis, 1983.

———. *The Survival of Dogma.* Garden City, NY: Doubleday, 1971.

Dupuis, Jacques. *Toward a Christian Theology of Religious Pluralism.* Maryknoll, NY: Orbis, 1997.

Eboussi Boulaga, Fabien. *Christianisme sans fétiche: Révélation et domination.* Paris: Présence Africaine, 1981.

Edwards, Mark J. "On the Platonic Schooling of Justin Martyr." *Journal of Theological Studies* 42 (1991), 17–34.

Eliade, Mircea. *The Myth of the Eternal Return.* Bollingen series 46. New York: Pantheon, 1954.

"La evangelización en el presente y en el futuro de América Latina." In *Documento de Puebla III Conferencia General del Episcopado Latinoamericano*, CELAM, 1979, 20–180. http://www.celam.org/doc_conferencias/Documento_Conclusivo_Puebla.pdf.

Fabella, Virginia. "Contextualization." In *Dictionary of Third World Theologies*, 58–59. Maryknoll, NY: Orbis, 2000.

Ferrer, Jorge N., and Jacob H. Sherman. "Introduction." In *The Participatory Turn: Spirituality, Mysticism, Religious Studies*, 1–80. Albany, NY: SUNY, 2008.

Fisher, Ali. "Swarmcast: How Jihadist Networks Maintain a Persistent Online Presence." *Perspectives on Terrorism* 9 (2015) 3–20.

Fitzgerald, Timothy. *Religion and the Secular: Historical and Colonial Formations.* London: Routledge, 2014.

Ford, David, and Rachel Muers, eds. *The Modern Theologians: An Introduction to Christian Theology Since 1918.* 1st ed., 1989; 2nd ed., 1997; 3rd ed., 2005. Oxford: Blackwell, 1989, 1997, 2005.

Fosu, Augustin Kwasi. "Growth, Inequality, and Poverty Reduction in Developing Countries: Recent Global Evidence." *Research in Economics* 71 (2017) 306–36.

Fotiou, Evgenia. "'We are the Indians of Greece': Indigeneity and Religious Revitalization in Modern Greece." *CrossCurrents* 64 (2014) 219–35.

Foucault, Michel. *Discipline and Punish: The Birth of the Prison.* Harmondsworth: Penguin, 1979.

———. "Nietzsche, Genealogy, History." In *From Modernism to Postmodernism: An Anthology,* edited by Lawrence Cahoone, 241–52. Oxford: Blackwell, 2003.

Frankopan, Peter. *The Silk Roads: A New History of the World.* London: Bloomsbury, 2015.

Frederiks, Martha. "Whither Theology in World Christianity?" Paper presented in the conference of the Institute for Contextual Theology Sweden in Lund, 24th November 2017.

Fridlund, Patrik, and Mika Vähäkangas, eds. *Theological and Philosophical Responses to Syncretism: Beyond the Mirage of Pure Religion.* Leiden: Brill, 2018.

Friedman, Milton. *Capitalism and Freedom.* Chicago: University of Chicago Press, 1962.

Friedrich, Thomas. "'Henri le Saux' Gott der Saccidananda-Trinität: Eine hindu-christliche Integration." *Zeitschrift für Missionswissenschaft und Religionswissenschaft* 87 (2003) 181–99.

Frostin, Per. *Liberation Theology in Tanzania and South Africa: A First World Interpretation.* Lund: Lund University Press, 1988.

Fukuyama, Francis. *The End of History and the Last Man.* New York: Free, 1992.

Fulkerson, Mary McClintock. *Places of Redemption: Theology for a Worldly Church.* Oxford: Oxford University Press, 2007.

Gadamer, Hans-Georg. *Wahrheit und Methode: Grundzüge einer philosophischen Hermeneutik.* 2nd ed. Tübingen: J.C.B. Mohr, 1967.

Galilea, Segundo. *Temptation and Discernment.* Washington, DC: Institute of Carmelite Studies, 1996.

Gaudium et spes. 1965. http://www.vatican.va/archive/hist_councils/ii_vatican_council/documents/vat-ii_cons_19651207_gaudium-et-spes_en.html.

Geertz, Clifford. *The Interpretation of Cultures.* New York: Basic, 1973.

Girard, René. *Things Hidden Since the Foundation of the World.* London: Bloomsbury Academic, 2016.

Glendon, Mary Ann. "A Source of Human Rights." *Wilson Quarterly* 26 (2002) 97.

Grosfoguel, Ramon. "Decolonizing Post-Colonial Studies and Paradigms of Political-Economy: Transmodernity, Decolonial Thinking, and Global Coloniality." *Transmodernity* 1 (2011). http://dialogoglobal.com/texts/grosfoguel/Grosfoguel-Decolonizing-Pol-Econ-and-Postcolonial.pdf.

Gruchy, John W. de. *Reconciliation: Restoring Justice.* London: SCM, 2002.

Haar, Gerrie ter. *How God Became African: African Spirituality and Western Secular Thought.* Philadelphia: University of Pennsylvania Press, 2009.

Hanciles, Jehu. *Beyond Christendom: Globalization, African Migration, and the Transformation of the West.* Maryknoll, NY: Orbis, 2008.

Harjula, Raimo. *God and the Sun in Meru Thought*. Helsinki: Finnish Society for Missiology and Ecumenics, 1969.

———. "Towards a Theologia Africana," *Svensk Missionstidskrift* 58 (1970) 88–102.

Harnack, Adolf von. *Das Wesen des Christentums*. Gütersloh: Gerd Mohn, 1977.

Havea, Jione. "The Cons of Contextuality . . . Kontextuality." In *Contextual Theology for the Twenty-First Century*, edited by Stephen B. Bevans and Katalina Tahaafe-Williams, 38–52. Eugene, OR: Pickwick, 2011.

Haynes, Naomi. "Pentecostalism and the Morality of Money: Prosperity, Inequality, and Religious Sociality on the Zambian Copperbelt." *Journal of the Royal Anthropological Institute* 18 (2012) 123–39.

Heidegger, Martin. *Zur Seinsfrage (1955)*. Gesamtausgabe Bd. 9, Wegmarken, 385–426. Frankfurt: Klostermann, 1976.

Heim, S. Mark. *Salvations: Truth and Difference in Religion*. Maryknoll, NY: Orbis, 1995.

Helleman, Wendy E. "Justin Martyr and Kwame Bediako: Reflections on the Cultural Context of Christianity." *Africa Journal of Evangelical Theology* 24 (2005) 3–18.

Hick, John. *Faith and Knowledge*. 2nd ed. London: Macmillan, 1967.

———. *An Interpretation of Religion: Human Responses to the Transcendent*. Basingstoke: Macmillan, 1989.

Hiebert, Paul G. "Critical Contextualization." *Missiology* 12 (1984) 287–96.

Hornborg, Anne-Christine. "Mindfulness: An Enrichment of Christian Lifestyle?" Forthcoming.

Hu, Enyi. "Spreading the Intellectual Gospel: A Study of the American Educational Missionaries in Yenching University." MA thesis, University of Hong Kong.

Hungary 2017 International Religious Freedom Report. 2017. https://www.state.gov/wp-content/uploads/2019/01/Hungary-2.pdf.

Imasogie, Osadolor. *Guidelines for Christian Theology in Africa*. Achimota, Ghana: Africa Christian, 1983.

Irvin, Dale T., and Scott W. Sundquist. *Modern Christianity from 1454–1800*. History of the World Christian Movement 2. Maryknoll, NY: Orbis, 2012.

Jackson, Michael. *At Home in the World*. Durham: Duke University Press, 1995.

Jaeschke, Ernst. *Bruno Gutmann: His Life, his Thoughts, and his Work; An Early Attempt at a Theology in an African Context*. Erlangen: Verlag der ev. luth. Mission, 1985.

Janssen, Bram. "'Day Zero': What Cape Town's Water Crisis Says about Inequality." *USA Today*, 2018. https://www.usatoday.com/story/news/world/2018/02/03/day-zero-what-cape-towns-water-crisis-inequality-south-africa/303542002/.

Jenkins, Philip. *The Lost History of Christianity: The Thousand-year Golden Age of the Church in the Middle East, Africa, and Asia—and How It Died*. New York: HarperOne, 2008.

———. *The New Faces of Christianity: Believing the Bible in the Global South*. Oxford: Oxford University Press, 2006.

Jenson, Robert W. *Systematic Theology*. Vol. 1, *The Triune God*. Oxford: Oxford University Press, 1997.

John Paul, Pope, II. *Post-Synodal Apostolic Exhortation Ecclesia in Africa*. Vatican City: Vatican, 1995.

———. *Redemptoris missio*. Vatican City: Typographia Polyglotta Vaticana, 1991.

Johnson, Keith L. *Karl Barth and the Analogia entis*. London: T&T Clark, 2010.

Jørgensen, Jonas Adelin. *Jesus Imandars and Christ Bhaktas: Two Case Studies of Interreligious Hermeneutics and Identity in Global Christianity.* Frankfurt: Peter Lang, 2008.
Jorgenson, Allen G. "Luther on Ubiquity and a Theology of the Public." *International Journal of Systematic Theology* 6 (2004) 351–68.
Kagame, Alexis. *La philosophie bantu-rwandaise de l'Être: Excerpta ex dissertatione ad Lauream in Facultate Philosophica Pontificiae Universitatis Gregorianae.* Classe des Sciences morales et politiques, Nouv. Série, Tome VI, fasc. 1. Bruxelles: Académie royale des Sciences coloniales, 1955.
Kähler, Martin. *Schriften zur Christologie und Mission.* München: Kaiser, 1971.
Kant, Immanuel. *Critique of Pure Reason.* Rev. ed. New York: Willey, 1943.
Kaunda, Chammah. "From Fools for Christ to Fools for Politicians." *International Bulletin of Mission Research* 41 (2017) 296–311.
Kerr, Fergus. "Yves Congar and Henri de Lubac." In *The Modern Theologians: An Introduction to Christian Theology in the Twentieth Century*, edited by David F. Ford, 105–17. Cambridge, MA: Blackwell, 1997.
Klein, Naomi. *The Shock Doctrine: The Rise of Disaster Capitalism.* London: Penguin, 2007.
Knitter, Paul. "Comparative Theology is not 'Business-as-Usual Theology': Personal Witness from a Buddhist Christian." *Buddhist-Christian Studies* 35 (2015) 181–92.
———. *No Other Name? A Critical Survey of Christian Attitudes Toward the World Religions.* Maryknoll, NY: Orbis, 1985.
Komulainen, Jyri. *An Emerging Cosmotheandric Religion? Raimon Panikkar's Pluralistic Theology of Religions.* Leiden: Brill, 2005.
———. "Kristillistä teologiaa hindulaisella maaperällä." In *Teologian ilmansuuntia: Näkökulmia uskontulkintoihin Aasiassa, Afrikassa ja Latinalaisessa Amerikassa*, edited by Tiina Ahonen and Jyri Komulainen, 21–79. Helsinki: Gaudeamus, 2004.
Kongo Dumbi, Donatien. *La doctrine du Saint Esprit et sa problematique dans l'Eglise Kimbanguiste: Ce que l'on peut aujourd'hui savoir de Simon Kimbangu.* Kinshasa: Editions Kimbanguistes, 2006.
Kraemer, Hendrik. *The Christian Message in a Non-Christian World.* 3rd ed. Grand Rapids: Kregel, 1969.
Krems, Burkhardt. "'Bürokratie' bei Max Weber: Zusammenfassung und Textauszüge." 2013. http://www.olev.de/b/max-weber-buerokratie.pdf.
Kurth, James. "Religion and Globalization." *Review of Faith & International Affairs* 7 (2009) 15–21.
Küster, Volker. *Theologie im Kontext: Zugleich ein Versuch über die Minjung-Theologie.* Studia Instituti Missiologici Societas Verbi Divini 62. Nettetal: Steyler, 1995.
Laukkanen, Pauli. *Rough Road to Dynamism: Bible Translating in Northern Namibia 1952–1987; Kwanyama, Kwangali and Ndonga.* Helsinki: Luther-Agricola-Society, 2002.
Lauterbach, Karen. "Fakery and Wealth in African Charismatic Christianity: Moving Beyond the Prosperity Gospel as Script." In *Faith in African Lived Christianity: Bridging Anthropological and Theological Perspectives*, edited by Karen Lauterbach, and Mika Vähäkangas. Leiden: Brill, 2020.
Leirvik, Oddbjørn. "Islamic University Theology." *Studia Theologica* 70 (2016) 127–44.
Lindbeck, George A. *The Nature of Doctrine: Religion and Theology in a Postliberal Age.* London: SPCK, 1984.

Lonergan, Bernard. *Method in Theology*. Toronto: University of Toronto Press, 1979.
———. *A Third Collection: Papers by Bernard J.F. Lonergan, S.J.* New York: Paulist, 1985.
Lubac, Henri de. *Catholicism: Christ and the Common Destiny of Man*. San Francisco: Ignatius, 1988.
Lundström, Klas. *Gospel and Culture in the World Council of Churches and the Lausanne Movement*. Uppsala: Swedish Institute for Mission Research, 2006.
Luther, Martin. *Martin Luthers Werke: Kritische Gesamtausgabe*. Weimar Ausgabe. 59 vols. Weimar: Herman Böhlaus Nachfolger, 1883–1983.
Lyotard, Jean-François. *The Postmodern Condition: A Report on Knowledge*. Minneapolis: University of Minnesota Press, 1984.
MacKenzie, Debora. "The Arab Spring Runs Dry." *New Scientist* 214 (2012) 32–33.
Mannermaa, Tuomo. *In ipsa fide Christus adest: Luterilaisen ja ortodoksisen kristinuskonkäsityksen leikkauspiste*. Helsinki: Missiologian ja ekumeniikan seura, 1979.
Maroney, Eric. *Religious Syncretism*. London: SCM, 2006.
Martey, Emmanuel. *African Theology: Inculturation and Liberation*. Maryknoll, NY: Orbis, 1993.
Martin, Marie-Louise. *Kirche ohne Weisse: Simon Kimbangu und seine Millionenkirche in Kongo*. Basel: Reinhardt, 1971.
Matheny, Paul Duane. *Contextual Theology: The Drama of Our Times*. Eugene, OR: Pickwick, 2011.
Matisonn, John. *God, Spies and Lies: Finding South Africa's Future through Its Past*. Vlaeberg, South Africa: Missing Ink, 2015.
Mbembe, Achille. *On the Postcolony*. Berkeley: University of California Press, 2001.
Mbiti, John S. *African Religions and Philosophy*. Nairobi: Heinemann, 1969.
———. *Bible and Theology in African Christianity*. Nairobi: Oxford University Press, 1986.
McClure, John A. "Post-Secular Culture: The Return of Religion in Contemporary Theory and Literature." *CrossCurrents* 47 (1997) 332–47.
McCoy, Daniel J. "A Comparison of Buddhist Compassion to Christian Love." Diss. Northwest University, Potchefstroom, South Africa, 2015.
McGrath, Alister E. *Christian Theology: An Introduction*. 2nd edition. Oxford: Blackwell, 1997.
Middleton, John. *Lugbara Religion: Ritual and Authority among an East African People*. London: Oxford University Press, 1960.
Miroshnikova, Elena. "The Evolution of the Byzantine Legacy in Modern Church-State Relations in the West and in Russia." *European Journal for Church and State Research* 11 (2004) 125–37.
Moltmann, Jürgen. *Der gekreuzigte Gott: Das Kreuz Christi als Grund und Kritik christlicher Theologie*. Gütersloh: Kaiser, 1972.
———. *Gott im Projekt der modernen Welt: Beiträge zur öffentlichen Relevanz der Theologie*. Gütersloh: Kaiser, 1997.
———. *The Trinity and the Kingdom: the Doctrine of God*. Minneapolis: Fortress, 1993.
Montagu, Ashley. *Man's Most Dangerous Myth: The Fallacy of Race*. Walnut Creek: AltaMira, 1997.
Montesquieu, Charles de Secondat. *The Spirit of the Laws*. Cambridge: Cambridge University Press, 1989.

Moodley, Edley J. *Shembe, Ancestors, and Christ: A Christological Inquiry with Missiological Implications*. Eugene, OR: Pickwick, 2008.
Mugambi, Jesse N. K. "Evangelistic and Charismatic Initiatives in Post-Colonial Africa." In *Charismatic Renewal in Africa: A Challenge for African Christianity*, edited by Mika Vähäkangas and Andrew A. Kyomo, 111–44. Nairobi: Acton, 2003.
———. *From Liberation to Reconstruction: African Christian Theology after the Cold War*. Nairobi: East African Educational, 1995.
Nassar, Jamal R. "Sectarian Political Cultures: The Case of Lebanon." *The Muslim World* 85 (1995) 246–65.
Neuberger, Eszter. "The Hungarian Lutheran Church Opens Its Doors to Refugees." *New Eastern Europe*, 2017. http://neweasterneurope.eu/2017/10/15/hungarian-lutheran-churches-open-door-refugees/.
Newbigin, Lesslie. *Foolishness to the Greeks: The Gospel and the Western Culture*. Grand Rapids: Eerdmans, 1986.
———. *The Gospel in a Pluralist Society*. London: SPCK, 1989.
Niebuhr, H. Richard. *Christ and Culture*. New York: Harper & Brothers, 1951.
Nieminen, Tarja, et al. *Ulkomaista syntyperää olevien työ ja hyvinvointi Suomessa 2014*. Tilastokeskus: Helsinki, 2015.
Niwagila, Wilson. *From the Catacomb to a Self-Governing Church: A Case Study of the African Initiative and the Participation of the Foreign Missions in the Mission History of the North-Western Diocese of the Evangelical Lutheran Church in Tanzania, 1890–1965*. Perspektiven der Weltmission, Wissenschaftliche Beiträge Bd. 6. Hamburg: Verlag an der Lottbeck Peter Jensen, 1988.
Nkéramihigo, Theoneste. "Inculturation and the Specificity of Christian Faith." In *What is so New about Inculturation?* edited by Arij A. Roest Crollius and Theoneste Nkéramihigo, 19–29. Rome: Editrice Pontificia Università Gregoriana, 1991.
Nyamiti, Charles. "African Preparatory Roads for the Trinity." Essays on African Theology 9. Unpublished manuscript, available in the archives of MUCo, 1981.
———. *African Tradition and the Christian God*. Eldoret, Kenya: Gaba, 1977.
Oduyoye, Mercy Amba. *Daughters of Anowa: African Women and Patriarchy*. Maryknoll, NY: Orbis, 1995.
Oliveira, Rosenilton Silva de. "Orixás, a manifestação cultural de Deus: uma análise das liturgias cathólicas inculturadas." Master's thesis, faculty of philosophy, University of São Paulo, 2011.
Ott, Ludwig. *Fundamentals of Catholic Dogma*. 4th ed. Rockford, IL: Tan, 1960.
Pace, Enzo. "The Socio-Cultural and Socio-Religious Origins of Human Rights." In *Oxford Handbook of the Sociology of Religion*, edited by Peter B. Clarke, 432–48. Oxford: Oxford University Press, 2011.
Palm, Anders. "Att tolka texten." In *Litteraturvetenskap: en inledning*, edited by Staffan Bergsten, 189–204. Lund: Studentlitteratur, 2002.
Panikkar, Raimundo. *The Unknown Christ of Hinduism*. London: Darton, Longman & Todd, 1964.
Pannenberg, Wolfhart. *Grundfragen systematischer Theologie: Gesammelte Aufsätze*. Göttingen: Vandenhoeck & Ruprecht, 1967.
———. *Systematic Theology*. Vol. 1. Grand Rapids: Eerdmans, 1991.
Passas, Nikos, and Manuel Escamilla Castillo. "Scientology and Its 'Clear' Business." *Behavioral Sciences & the Law* 10 (1992) 103–16.

Peterson, V. Spike. *A Critical Rewriting of Global Political Economy: Integrating Reproductive, Productive, and Virtual Economies.* London: Routledge, 2003.

Phan, Peter. "An Asian Christian? Or a Christian Asian? Or an Asian-Christian? A Roman Catholic Experiment on Christian Identity." *Studies in World Christianity and Interreligious Relations* 47 (2011) 57–74.

———. "Doing Theology in World Christianities: Old Tasks, New Ways." In *Relocating World Christianity: Interdisciplinary Studies in Universal and Local Expressions of the Christian Faith*, edited by Joel Cabrita et al., 115–42. Leiden: Brill, 2017.

Philipse, Herman. *Heidegger's Philosophy of Being: A Critical Interpretation.* Princeton, NJ: Princeton University Press, 2001.

Phillimore, Jenny, and Lisa Goodson. "Problem or Opportunity? Asylum Seekers, Refugees, Employment and Social Exclusion in Deprived Urban Areas." *Urban Studies* 43 (2006) 1715–36.

Pieris, Aloysius. *An Asian Theology of Liberation.* Edinburgh: T&T Clark, 1988.

Pieterse, Jan Nederveen. "Globalization as Hybridization." In *Global Modernities*, edited by Mike Featherstone et al., 45–68. London: Sage, 1995.

Piketty, Thomas. *Capital in the Twenty-First Century.* Cambridge, MA: Belknap, 2014.

Pobee, John S. "Life and Peace: An African Perspective." In *Variations in Christian Theology in Africa*, edited by Carl Hallencreutz and John S. Pobee, 14–31. Nairobi: Uzima, 1986.

Pöntinen, Mari-Anna. *African Theology as Liberating Wisdom: Celebrating Life and Harmony in the Evangelical Lutheran Church in Botswana.* Leiden: Brill, 2013.

Poole, Steven. "Lies, Damned Lies and Alternative Facts." *New Statesman* 146 (2017) 42–43.

Potkanski, Tomasz. "The Sonjo Community in Face of Change." *Hemispheres* 4 (1987) 191–222.

Price, R. M. "'Hellenization' and Logos Doctrine in Justin Martyr." *Vigiliae Christianae* 42 (1988) 18–23.

Queen, Christopher S., and Sallie B. King, eds. *Engaged Buddhism: Buddhist Liberation Movements in Asia.* Albany, NY: State University of New York Press, 1996.

Rahner, Karl. *Anonymous Christianity and the Missionary Task of the Church.* Theological Investigations 12. London: Darton, Longman & Todd, 1974.

———. *Foundations of Christian Faith: An Introduction to the Idea of Christianity.* New York: Crossroad, 1995.

———. *Observations on the Problem of Anonymous Christians.* Theological Investigations 14. London: Darton, Longman & Todd, 1976.

———. *The Trinity.* Kent: Burns & Oates, 1970.

Räisänen, Heikki. *Marcion, Muhammad and the Mahatma: Exegetical Perspectives on the Encounter of Cultures and Faiths.* London: SCM, 1997.

———. *The Rise of Christian Beliefs: The Thought World of Early Christians.* Minneapolis: Fortress, 2010.

Rauch, Jennifer. "Are There Still Alternatives? Relationships Between Alternative Media and Mainstream Media in a Converged Environment." *Sociology Compass* 10 (2016) 756–67.

Ricoeur, Paul. *Soi-même comme un autre.* Paris: Seuil, 1990.

———. *Time and Narrative.* Vol. 1. Chicago: University of Chicago, 1984.

———. "Toward a Hermeneutic of the Idea of Revelation." *Harvard Theological Review* 70 (1977) 1–37.

Ristau, Harold. "Ubiquity and Epiphany: Luther's Doctrine of the Lord's Presence in Space and Time." *Logia* 22 (2013) 25–31.
Robbins, Joel. *Becoming Sinners: Christianity and Moral Torment in a Papua New Guinea Society*. Berkeley: University of California Press, 2004.
———. "The Globalization of Pentecostal and Charismatic Christianity." *Annual Review of Anthropology* 33 (2004) 117–43.
———. "World Christianity and the Reorganization of Disciplines: On the Emerging Dialogue between Anthropology and Theology." Inaugural lecture as honorary doctor at Lund University, 26th May 2016.
Robertson, Roland. *Globalization: Social Theory and Global Culture*. London: Sage, 1992.
———. "Glocalization: Time-Space and Homogeneity-Heterogeneity." *Global Modernities*, edited by Mike Featherstone et al., 25–44. London: Sage, 1995.
Robins, Kevin. "Interrupting Identities: Turkey/Europe." In *Questions of Cultural Identity*, edited by Stuart Hall and Paul Du Gay, 61–82. London: Sage, 1996.
Roca, Roger Sansi. "Catholic Saints, African Gods, Black Masks and White Heads: Tracing the History of Some Religious Festivals in Bahia." *Portuguese Studies* 21 (2005) 182–200.
Roest Crollius, Arij A. *Teologia dell'inculturazione*. Roma: Pontificia Università Gregoriana, 1996.
———. "What is So New about Inculturation?" In *What is so New about Inculturation?* written by Arij A. Roest Crollius and Theoneste Nkéramihigo, 1–18. Rome: Editrice Pontificia Università Gregoriana, 1991.
Rupprecht, Tobias "Orthodox Internationalism: State and Church in Modern Russia and Ethiopia." *Comparative Studies in Society and History* 60 (2018) 212–35.
Sabar, Galia, and Atalia Shragai. "Olumba Olumba in Israel: Struggling on All Fronts." *African Identities* 6 (2008) 201–25.
Saeed, Abdullah. *The Qur'an: An Introduction*. London: Routledge, 2008.
Sahlberg, Carl-Erik. *From Krapf to Rugambwa: A Church History of Tanzania*. 2nd ed. Nairobi: Evangel, 1986.
Sahlins, Marshall. *Islands of History*. Chicago: University of Chicago Press, 1989.
Sanneh, Lamin. *Translating the Message: The Missionary Impact on Culture*. American Society of Missiology Series 13. Maryknoll, NY: Orbis, 1989.
Schineller, Peter. *A Handbook on Inculturation*. New York: Paulist, 1990.
Schleiermacher, Johann Friedrich. *Über die Religion: Reden an die Gebildeten unter ihren Verächtern*. Göttingen: Vandenhoeck & Ruprecht, 1913.
Schreiter, Robert. *Constructing Local Theologies*. Maryknoll, NY: Orbis, 1985.
———. *The New Catholicity: Theology between the Global and the Local*. Maryknoll NY: Orbis, 1997.
Schüssler Fiorenza, Elisabeth. *In Memory of Her: A Feminist Theological Reconstruction of Christian Origins*. New York: Crossroad, 1992.
Schwerdtfeger, Nikolaus. *Gnade und Welt: Grundgefüge von Karl Rahners Theorie der "anonymen Christen."* Freiburg: Herder, 1982.
Shorter, Aylward. *African Christian Theology: Adaptation or Incarnation?* London: Chapman, 1975.
———. *Toward a Theology of Inculturation*. Maryknoll, NY: Orbis, 1988.

Skolverket. "Skol- och förskoleverksamhet i kyrkan eller annan religiös lokal." 2012. https://docplayer.se/4790376-Skol-och-forskoleverksamhet-i-kyrkan-eller-annan-religios-lokal.html.

Søgaard, Viggo. *Media in Church and Mission: Communicating the Gospel*. Pasadena, CA: William Carey Library, 1993.

Spivak, Gayatri Chakravorty. "Can the Subaltern Speak?" In *Colonial Discourse and Post-Colonial Theory: A Reader*, edited by Patrick Williams and Laura Chrisman, 66–111. New York: Columbia University Press, 1994.

Stackhouse, Max L. "Social Graces: Christianity and Globalization." *Review of Faith & International Affairs* 5 (2007) 41–49.

Stark, Rodney. *The Rise of Christianity: A Sociologist Reconsiders History*. Princeton, NJ: Princeton University Press, 1996.

Stearns, Jason. "Causality and Conflict: Tracing the Origins of Armed Groups in the Eastern Congo." *Peacebuilding* 2 (2014) 157–71.

Stiver, Dan R. *The Philosophy of Religious Language*. Cambridge, MA: Blackwell, 1996.

Strenski, Ivan. "The Religion in Globalization." *Journal of the American Academy of Religion* 72 (2004) 631–52.

Syse, Aslak. "Breivik—The Norwegian Terrorist Case." *Behavioural Sciences and the Law* 32 (2014) 389–407.

Taira, Teemu. *Notkea uskonto*. Turku: Eetos, 2006.

Tcherkézoff, Serge. "Black and White Dual Classification: Hierarchy and Ritual Logic in Nyamwezi Ideology." In *Contexts and Levels: Anthropological Essays on Hierarchy*, edited by R. H. Barnes et al., 54–67. JASO Occasional Papers 4. Oxford: JASO, 1985.

Te Paa, Jenny. "Context, Controversy, and Contradiction in Contemporary Theological Education: Who Bene 'Fits' and Who Simply Doesn't Fit?" In *Contextual Theology for the Twenty-First Century*, edited by Stephen B. Bevans and Katalina Tahaafe-Williams, 69–86. Eugene, OR: Pickwick, 2011.

Terreblanche, Sampie. "The American Empire and the Entrenchment of Global Inequality." In *Globalisation: The Politics of Empire, Justice and the Life of Faith*, edited by Allan Boesak and Len Hansen, 31–47. Stellenbosch, South Africa: SUN, 2009.

Tétreault, Mary Ann. "Contending Fundamentalisms: Religious Revivalism and the Modern World." In *Gods, Guns, and Globalization: Religious Radicalism and International Political Economy*, edited by Mary Ann Tétreault and Robert A. Denemark, 1–30. Boulder, CO: Lynne Rienner, 2004.

Thompson, Sam. "Saccidananda and the Trinity: Hindu-Christian Conversations on the Supreme Reality." *Lutheran Mission Matters* 25 (2017) 123–32.

Tolo, Arne. *Sidama and Ethiopian: The Emergence of the Mekane Yesus Church in Sidama*. Uppsala: Acta Universitatis Upsaliensis, 1998.

Topolski, Anya. "Spinoza's True Religion: The Modern Origins of the Contemporary Floating Signifier." *Society and Politics/Societate și Politică* 8 (2014) 41–59.

Tracy, David. "Theology: Comparative Theology." In *Encyclopedia of Religion* 14:446–55. New York: Macmillan, 1987.

Tshibangu, Tharcisse Tshishiku. *La théologie africaine: Manifeste et programme pour le développement des activités théologiques en Afrique*. Kinshasa: Éditions Saint Paul Afrique, 1987.

Turner, Harold W. "A Typology for African Religious Movements." *Journal of Religion in Africa* 1 (1967) 1–34.
Udías, Agustín. "Christogenesis: The Development of Teilhard's Cosmic Christology." *Teilhard Studies* 59 (2009) 1–22.
Ukpong, Justin S. *African Theologies Now: A Profile.* Spearhead 80. Eldoret: Gaba, 1984.
United Religions Initiative Africa Office. *The Golden Rule.* Addis Ababa, n.d.
The Uppsala Report: Official Report of the Fourth Assembly of the World Council of Churches, Uppsala July 4–20, 1968. Edited by Norman Goodall. Geneva: World Council of Churches, 1968.
Vähäkangas, Auli. *Christian Couples Coping with Childlessness: Narratives from Machame, Kilimanjaro.* American Society of Missiology Monograph Series 4. Eugene, OR: Pickwick, 2009.
———. "Conformity and Resistance in Personalized Same-Sex Prayer Rituals in Finland." In *Theology & Sexuality*, 25 (2019) 81-97.
Vähäkangas, Aune. *Jumalan lintuset.* Helsinki: SLEY-kirjat, 1985.
Vähäkangas, Mika. *Between Ghambageu and Jesus: The Encounter between the Sonjo Traditional Leaders and Missionary Christianity.* Helsinki: Luther-Agricola-Society, 2008.
———. "Can the Study of Mission become Postcolonial? On Mission Studies in Today's World." *Ortodoksia* 56 (2016) 39–64.
———. "Doctrinal Relationship between Protestantism and Charismatic Renewal." In *Charismatic Renewal in Africa: A Challenge for African Christianity*, edited by Mika Vähäkangas and Andrew A. Kyomo, 66–90. African Christianity Series. Nairobi: Acton, 2003.
———. "Gender, Narratives and Religious Competition among the Sonjo of Tanzania." *Missionalia* 41 (2013) 66–89.
———. "Ghambageu Encounters Jesus in Sonjo Mythology: Syncretism as African Rational Action." *Journal of American Academy of Religion* 76 (2008) 111–37.
———. "How to Respect the Religious Quasi-Other? Methodological Considerations on Studying the Kimbanguist Doctrine of Incarnation." In *Faith in African Lived Christianity: Bridging Anthropological and Theological Perspectives*, edited by Karen Lauterbach and Mika Vähäkangas. Leiden: Brill, 2020.
———. *In Search of Foundations for African Catholicism: Charles Nyamiti's Theological Methodology.* Studies in Christian Mission 23. Leiden: Brill, 1999.
———. "Modelling Contextualization in Theology." *Swedish Missiological Themes* 98 (2010) 279–306.
———. "Om mig, den andre och mig i den andre: Med Weber och Lévy-Bruhl på besök hos en tanzanisk helare." In *Årsbok 2014*, edited by Henrik Rahm, 158–73. Lund: Vetenskapssocieteten i Lund, 2014.
———. "The Prosperity Gospel in the African Diaspora: Unethical Theology or Gospel in Context?" *Exchange* 44 (2015) 353–80.
———. "Theo-logical Positions vis-à-vis Syncretism." In *Theological and Philosophical Responses to Syncretism: Beyond the Mirage of Pure Religion*, edited by Patrik Fridlund and Mika Vähäkangas, 68–87. Leiden: Brill, 2018.
———. "Ukristo, Uzima na Ujamaa: The Theology of the Evangelical Lutheran Church in Tanzania in Relation to Tanzanian Socialism." MTh thesis. University of Helsinki, 1992.

Vansina, Jan. *Oral Tradition as History*. Madison, WI: University of Wisconsin Press, 1985.

Vattimo, Gianni. *Belief.* Oxford: Polity, 1999.

———. *Credere di credere: È possibile essere cristiani nonostante la Chiesa?* 2nd edition. Milan: Garzanti, 1999.

Vellem, Vuyani S. "Ecumenicity and a Black Theology of Liberation." In *South African Perspectives on Notions and Forms of Ecumenicity*, edited by Ernst Conradie, 173–80. Stellenbosch: SUN, 2013.

Vessey, David. "Gadamer and the Fusion of Horizons." *International Journal of Philosophical Studies* 17 (2009) 525–36.

Vokes, Richard. *Ghosts of Kanungu: Fertility, Secrecy & Exchange in the Great Lakes of East Africa*. Woodbridge, Suffolk: James Currey, 2009.

Vosloo, Robert. "The Bible and Justification of Apartheid in Reformed Circles in the 1940's in South Africa: Some Historical, Hermeneutical and Theological Remarks." *Stellenbosch Theological Journal* 1 (2015) 195–215.

Waardenburg, Jacques. "Official and Popular Religion in Islam." *Social Compass* 25 (1978) 315–41.

Wahl, Peter. "International Financial Markets, Crisis and Development." In *Globalisation: The Politics of Empire, Justice and the Life of Faith*, edited by Allan Boesak, and Len Hansen, 17–29. Stellenbosch, South Africa: SUN, 2009.

Wallerstein, Immanuel. "The West, Capitalism, and the Modern World-System." *Review* 15 (1992) 561–619.

Warren, Max A. C. "General Introduction." In *Primal Vision: Christian Presence amid African Religion*, written by John V. Taylor, 5–12. London: SCM, 1963.

Wight, Jonathan B. "The Treatment of Smith's Invisible Hand." *The Journal of Economic Education* 38 (2007) 341–58.

Wijsen, Frans J. S. *There is only One God: A Social-Scientific and Theological Study of Popular Religion and Evangelization in Sukumaland, Northwest Tanzania*. Kampen: Kok, 1993.

Wild-Wood, Emma. "Afterword: Relocating Unity and Theology in the Study of World Christianity." In *Relocating World Christianity: Interdisciplinary Studies in Universal and Local Expressions of the Christian Faith*, edited by Joel Cabrita et al., 324–42. Leiden: Brill, 2017.

Wingren, Gustav. *Växling och kontinuitet: Teologiska kriterier*. Lund: Gleerup, 1972.

Wittfogel, Karl A. *Oriental Despotism: A Comparative Study of Total Power*. New Haven: Yale University Press, 1973.

Working Together: Skills and Labour Market Integration of Immigrants and their Children in Finland. Paris: OECD, 2018.

World Values Survey. *WV5_Results, Finland, technical record*. 2005. http://www.worldvaluessurvey.org/WVSDocumentationWV5.jsp

Wynter, Sylvia. "'Genital Mutilation' or 'Symbolic Birth'? Female Circumcision, Lost Origins, and the Aculturalism of Feminist/Western Thought." *Case Western Reserve Law Review* 47 (1997) 501–53.

Index

Africa/African, x, 4, 5, 9–10, 14, 15, 16–17, 19, 20, 27, 30, 38, 41, 48, 53, 59, 65–75, 78, 81, 82–85, 91, 98, 100, 102, 103, 106–8, 112, 116, 117, 128, 132, 136, 144, 146, 147, 154–55, 156, 157, 159, 162, 169, 170, 174
Anderson, Benedict, 46, 166
Anthropology (cultural/social, physical), ix, 49, 51–53, 71, 84–85, 106
Appiah, Kwame Anthony, 3, 27
Aquinas, Thomas. *See* Thomas Aquinas
Aristotle, 70, 83, 99, 137, 176–77
Asad, Talal, 59
Aulén, Gustaf, 5, 150, 174

Barth, Karl, 41–42, 111, 138, 148, 149, 162
Bediako, Kwame, 1, 100, 155, 163
Bergmann, Sigurd, 49, 77, 134
Bevans, Stephen, x, 11, 46, 50, 74, 79, 80, 81, 83, 86–89, 95, 99, 100, 102, 103, 107, 111, 112
Beyer, Peter, 11, 12
Bhabha, Homi, 124, 162, 176
Bible, ix, 38, 63, 73, 75–77, 82–83, 87, 89, 91–93, 101–2, 104, 109, 110, 113–15, 120, 121, 123, 125, 128, 131, 133–35, 139–40, 146, 148, 155, 163, 173, 181, 186
Boff, Clodovis, 70, 90

Boff, Leonardo, 70, 120, 133, 143–44, 174
Bosch, David, 46, 107

Capitalism, 10, 13–19, 25–28, 38, 40, 44, 126–27
Catholic/Roman Catholic, 4, 5, 11, 27, 33–34, 44, 55, 63, 70, 75–81, 84–86, 100, 108–9, 115, 122–23, 128, 130, 133, 137, 143, 149, 152, 154–55, 161, 182
Césaire, Aimé, 2, 10
China, 10, 11, 13, 14, 17, 24, 37, 40, 53, 71, 84, 102
Christendom, 1, 11, 13, 29, 35, 37, 50, 101, 122, 155
Coleman, Simon, 11, 12
Colonialism, 2–3, 9–10, 14–16, 45, 47–48, 69, 70–71, 75, 103, 186
Confessionality, 5, 39–46, 50, 53, 56–60, 81, 128, 164–65

D'Costa, Gavin, 56, 137, 138, 168, 178
Dulles, Avery, 74, 77, 78, 79, 137

Ecumenism, 4, 56, 100, 108, 120, 128, 166, 177
Enlightenment. *See* modernity
Ethiopia, 11, 40, 105–6, 122
Eurocentrism, 39–52, 57
Europe/European, 1, 4–11, 16, 17, 19, 22, 24–27, 29–44, 48, 54–55,

59–60, 63–76, 82, 83, 92, 101, 110, 117, 121, 122, 128, 131, 134, 145, 167, 185, 186
Evangelicalism, 11, 35, 38, 39, 70, 81, 109–10, 128, 180
Extra ecclesiam nulla salus est, 78, 137, 182

Fascism, 24–25, 29, 30, 33, 44
Finland, ix, 13, 18, 26, 39, 136
Foucault, Michel, 75, 121
Friedman, Milton, 17, 28, 126
Frostin, Per, 49, 51, 72, 106
Fundamentalism, 12, 13, 35, 43, 133, 163, 182, 184

Gadamer, Hans-Georg, 75, 93, 94, 177
Geertz, Clifford, 93, 101
Globalisation, 3, 6, 7, 9–29, 38, 45, 57
Greek, 31, 40, 74, 91–92, 101, 104, 114, 122, 123, 133, 138, 146, 176–77
Grosfoguel, Ramon, 2, 10, 40, 51, 61

Hanciles, Jehu, 11, 13, 29
Heidegger, Martin, 183
Heim, S. Mark, 131, 135, 136, 138, 168
Hellenic. *See* Greek
Hick, John, 56, 141, 168, 178

Islam, 21, 24–25, 30–31, 34, 40, 54, 55, 56, 58, 59, 62, 63, 77, 88, 104, 114, 120, 130, 132–34, 137, 145, 168, 170

Kagame, Alexis, 83, 177
Kant, Immanuel 71, 87, 111, 170, 182–83
Kenosis, 138, 151–53, 184
Kimbanguism, ix, 129–31, 140, 153
Klein, Naomi, 13, 16, 126, 127
Knitter, Paul, 56, 75, 178
Küster, Volker, 79, 81, 82, 83, 84, 85, 86, 90, 96
Latin, 40, 84–85, 146, 177, 180
Latin America, 14, 16, 29, 33, 42, 44, 48, 70, 109, 154

Lindbeck, George A., 166–68
Lonergan, Bernard, 87–88, 164
Lubac, Henri de, 79
Luther, Martin, 97, 98, 107, 108, 123, 138, 148, 154–55
Lutheranism, 5, 26, 33, 34, 77, 97, 107–8, 109, 115, 121, 123, 128, 130

Martey, Emmanuel, 84, 85
Mbembe, Achille, 105
Mbiti, John S., 155, 157
Mission, 2–3, 11, 13, 14, 21, 25, 26, 35, 37–38, 45–50, 67–71, 74, 82–84, 105–6, 117, 144, 160–62
Mission studies, 4–5, 41, 47–50, 57–58
Modernity, 5–7, 32, 35–36, 39, 43, 48, 55, 57, 58–60, 63, 75–76, 91, 108, 121, 124, 135, 145, 163, 178, 185
Moltmann, Jürgen, 42, 55, 155
Mugamabi, Jesse, 69, 70, 97
Muslim. *See* Islam

Nationalism, 1–3, 330–36, 38, 42, 44–46, 68, 166
Nazi, 31, 34
Newbigin, Lesslie, 44, 89, 169
Niebuhr, H. Richard, 95–104, 112
Nkéramihigo, Theoneste, 82, 85, 93
Nyamiti, Charles, ix, 86, 143, 146, 147, 156, 174

Oduyoye, Mercy Amba, 103
Orthodoxy (Eastern), 6, 10, 31–33, 40, 44, 77, 122, 146, 182
Orthodoxy (doctrinal), 6, 55, 87, 131, 137–41

Panikkar, Raimon, 155–56
Pannenberg, Wolfhart, 119, 120, 144
Pentecostals, 12, 26, 34–35, 77, 89, 97, 108, 114, 130, 136, 171
Phan, Peter, 54, 76, 138–39, 152
Piketty, Thomas, 17
Prosperity Gospel, 25–26, 54, 153

Rahner, Karl, 42, 65, 87, 147, 156, 172

INDEX

Räisänen, Heikki, 73, 77, 120, 125
Ricoeur, Paul, 23, 59, 72, 114, 116
Robbins, Joel, 12, 26
Russia, 16, 24, 32–33, 45, 166

Sanneh, Lamin, 74, 82, 101, 132–33, 180
Schleiermacher, Friedrich, 167, 182
Schreiter, Robert, 13, 73, 81–84, 90
Secularization, 2, 4, 5, 25, 26, 29–36, 50, 52, 54, 55, 58–63, 67, 88, 127, 144, 154, 167, 185
Sensus communis, 139–41, 154, 157, 187
Shorter, Aylward, 84, 86
South Africa (Apartheid), 18, 22, 65, 124, 153, 106–7, 166–67
Soviet Union. *See* Russia
Spivak, Gayatri C., 175, 181, 182, 183
Sweden, 5, 34, 59–60, 144–45, 166

Thomas Aquinas, 94, 99–100, 137, 162
Tradition, 4, 6, 7, 14, 27, 30, 34–35, 39–40, 48, 50, 52, 54–56, 58, 59–60, 64, 65–69, 70, 72, 75–81, 86, 89–93, 99, 101, 103–4, 106, 109, 112–16, 120–21, 125, 126, 128, 130–31, 133, 134, 136, 137–41, 143, 146–48, 152–53, 156–57, 159, 160, 163–86
Trinity 173–75, 179–80

Ukpong, Justin, 81, 83, 144
USA, 10, 12, 16, 21, 22, 35, 78, 110

Vattimo, Gianni, 138, 183, 184

Wallerstein, Immanuel, 10, 13, 40
Weber, Max, 60
Wingren, Gustav, 80, 101, 102, 119, 120, 125, 128, 131, 133, 134, 151, 163
World Christianity, 26, 29, 37, 38, 40, 48–58, 64, 130, 185
World Council of Churches (WCC), 38, 81, 129–30
World-systems theory, 10, 130

www.ingramcontent.com/pod-product-compliance
Lightning Source LLC
Chambersburg PA
CBHW070325230426
43663CB00011B/2221